LET THE TIGER TURN TAIL

LET THE TIGER TURN TAIL

TURN TAIL

SPURR'S WAR

RUSSELL SPURR

MAINSTREAM
PUBLISHING

Copyright © Russell Spurr 1992

All rights reserved

The moral right of the author has been asserted

First published in Great Britain in 1992 by
MAINSTREAM PUBLISHING COMPANY (EDINBURGH) LTD
7 Albany Street
Edinburgh EH1 3UG

ISBN 1 85158 479 X

A catalogue record for this book is available from the British Library

Typeset in Stempel Garamond by Saxon Printing Ltd, Derby

Printed and bound in Great Britain by
Butler & Tanner Ltd, Frome and London

To Frank Worth

my fellow rascal and lifelong friend

Let the robber retreat – let the tiger turn tail
In the name of the Empress, the Overland Mail!

Kipling, *The Overland Mail*

ACKNOWLEDGMENT

I would like to thank the *South China Morning Post*, Hong Kong for kind permission to reprint some of the material published in this book.

CONTENTS

PART ONE

The train was puffing out of Aberdeen before I realised my mistake. It hit me the moment the women spoke. The compartment was filled with motherly Scottish housewives who seemed moved to befriend the forlorn young Englishman curled up by the window, struggling to decipher the poems of Robert Burns. Presumably it was reassurance they offered as I looked up from the book, staring in disbelief at the snow-flecked hills. Snow in April? Spring had already refurbished southern England. But that, it occurred to me, was not the worst of it. There was something else, something equally odd – the truth dawning with sudden horror – for try as I might, it was impossible to understand a single word these Scotswomen said.

I smiled blankly back at them, the lunacy of my adolescent fantasies growing alarmingly apparent. No doubt about it: I was blundering blindly into alien territory. Grimsby, my most recent home, had been unfamiliar enough to a much-coddled youth from the north London suburbs, but this … this Celtic hinterland, was the back of bloody beyond. It constituted the ultimate sentence of exile. The place where the map ran out, where civilisation dribbled away into the heather.

This time there could be no turning back. I had pocketed the King's shilling, enlisted in the Argyll and Sutherland Highlanders, received a surprise present from the recruiting officer's daughter and survived a nasty air-raid only to land myself in darkest, north-eastern Scotland. It was the first irrevocable predicament of my life. Nobody, not even Mother, could get me out of this one.

'Banff!' shouted the guard, and added something I failed to understand. I might as well have reached Zagreb. Timorously, I climbed on to the platform clutching my cheap fibre suitcase.

It was early in 1941; the days when Britain stood alone. The French had collapsed, to everyone's surprise, while the flower of the British army had barely escaped (next exit: Dunkirk) by the skin of its élitist teeth. The Russians still hung back, chuckling on the sidelines, and the Americans dispatched Bundles to Britain – but swore their boys would be the one bundle Britain wouldn't get.

'We're not going over,' Walter Winchell had told his radio audience, 'until it's all over, over there!'

No word of this got past the British censors, of course. The impression conveyed by our slender newspapers was that Uncle Sam couldn't wait to wring Hitler's scrawny neck. In fact, the Americans had opted for strict neutrality, piously pocketing the wealth amassed by our Victorian forefathers in cash payments for US arms. By now the money was running out. Churchill was badgering Roosevelt for 'the tools to finish the job'. But his rhetoric did not sound particularly convincing. Most of us youngsters were cynical enough to grasp the truth: the chestnuts would have to be pulled out of the fire by the British Empire and eventually, it was hoped, by the US of A.

The Dunkirk evacuation was at its height when I joined a Northcliffe newspaper in Grimsby. The east-coast fishing port was a far cry, socially, from our modest family seat in stockbroking suburbia. Professionally, though, the *Grimsby Evening Telegraph* was a leap ahead of the weekly I had worked on in Essex.

The move north had inflicted its degree of culture shock. Grimsby was little more than five hours by train from London. But to me, it might have been a continent away. The food was different – the meat pies were a revelation at the Monkey, Pig and Pie Shop – and attitudes were different, too. There was none of the surly reticence that bedevils social intercourse down south. There was, on the other hand, a peculiar conformity. Every house wore an aspidistra in its front window. There must have been thousands of them, brass-potted and uniformly displayed, excluding the light from a front-room nobody used, complete with a piano nobody played.

People looked greyer and older. Most of the over-twenties displayed flashing false teeth, and their main diversion was singing oratorios. A couple of hours spent belting out *The Messiah* left everyone aesthetically, as well as spiritually, fulfilled. More profane entertainment centred around the radio though – I chiefly remember an egalitarian rag-and-bone man handing out hosts of soothing platitudes – and, less respectably, a vaudeville theatre where comedians told smutty jokes about the female dancers who posed, very still and naked to the waist, beneath coloured spotlights. Cavorting on the stage in any state of undress was strictly forbidden. The slightest unclothed movement attracted the attentions of the police. And youngsters like me crowded into the sixpenny seats in the gods waiting hopefully for an unclad dancer to sneeze.

The women were more tangible at the nightly *thé dansant* in the Cleethorpes pier pavilion. Municipal authorities in the nearby seaside town were anxious to provide healthy recreation for the servicemen and women surging into the area. Plenty of young wives, bereft of their husbands, gravitated to the dancefloor seeking relief from unaccustomed chastity. Together with their teenage pubescent sisters, they made a beeline for the youthful officers who came searching for companionship in their becoming uniforms. Callow civilians like myself could only glower hungrily from the sidelines. Pilots from the surrounding airfields always seemed to walk off with the best-looking birds. It hurt to watch them. More than anything in the world I wanted a girl of my own. A fresh, cuddly teenager of awakening appetites was the premier status symbol of my peer group, ranking close to smoking a pipe and drinking Pimms Number One. The best way to get my hands on such a girl, I hastily decided, was to change into uniform. Something Scottish would surely do the trick.

The Scottish thing was my grandfather's fault. The old chap came from Thornhill, a grim stone village on the Kirkcudbrightshire border. During his last years, he stuffed me full of Walter Scott and Robert Louis Stevenson – 'a great literary stylist if ever there was one' – and threw in his own tales of the Covenanters and Moss Troopers who once enlivened life in Galloway. South-west Scotland must have been a wild old place a couple of hundred years ago. It was the birthplace of 'that traitor John Paul Jones' – grandfather Sloane never forgave the founder of the US Navy for fighting on 'the rebel side'. But he waxed lyrical about Bonnie Prince Charlie and the great rebellion of 1745. It was visions of the claymore-wielding warriors who hacked a trail halfway down England that inspired me to join the Argyll and Sutherland Highlanders.

The Sloane family happened to have enjoyed a long-standing connection with the Argylls; officially the 92nd Regiment of Foot, Princess Louise's Own. Two uncles had died with the regiment on the Somme. Other more distant relatives had served in the Crimea and India. Inspired by Kipling and some of the lesser Victorian writers, it was India I finally planned to reach. The army in India was being hastily expanded to confront the Italians in Ethiopia, Eritrea and the Middle East. I saw the Argylls as a stepping-stone to an heroic career with the Bengal Lancers, wearing dress turbans on mess nights, galloping triumphantly through the Khyber Pass ...

It was, of course, pure dream-stuff direct from Hollywood. I couldn't even ride a horse (and can't today). Some time would pass before I would learn that cavalry was not deployed in the Khyber. But at seventeen I was immersed in make-believe. There was only one snag: I was too young to join the regular army – you had to be eighteen. The alternative was one of the 'young soldiers' battalions' for boys above the age of sixteen. These were designated 70th battalions, to distinguish them from genuine field force units; real soldiers could hardly be expected to serve in anything so militarily down-market.

My immediate problem was the ticket collector at Banff station. The man needed sub-titles. His dialect came across like a sing-song machine-gun. Slowly and deliberately I said: 'Can ... you ... please ... direct ... me ... to the headquarters of the Argylls.'

The poor fellow recoiled shocked. Slowly and deliberately he replied: 'Ye're ... no ... joining ... that mucking shower, is ye?'

The recruiting officer back in Grimsby had described the battalion in glowing terms. His daughter had egged me on. She actually promised me a present the day I signed on the dotted line. The girl bewitched me. She was tall, dark-haired and a little older than myself, with a body that beckoned when she walked. Thus far she seemed to prefer smart young officers to unkempt junior journalists. A present? I couldn't for the life of me imagine what this unattainable creature had in mind but was all innocent eagerness the day I took the oath.

The pair of us went out that night to celebrate. The air-raid sirens sounded as I escorted her home. Searchlights flicked on around the blacked-out city. The girl invited me in to await the all-clear. There was also that present she had promised me. We slipped unnoticed into the front-room. Standing there, silhouetted against the open fire, she demurely slipped off her dress.

Aircraft grumbled overhead. The guns opened up. Bombs burst nearby raining plaster on the hearthrug. The earth moved, but it wasn't the Luftwaffe. The raid roared over us unnoticed. There on the rug we were completely absorbed. Not until I started off home did it dawn on me that something dreadful had been happening. There were deep craters in the surrounding streets. My parents had rented a terraced house about a mile away. Father was a sea captain, temporarily between ships, and he had wanted to see me during the last weeks of my civilian life. The area where we lived had taken a lot of punishment. Fire engines and ambulances blocked our street. An officious air-raid warden tried to prevent me from reaching my house.

'Number 56 has been hit,' he said. 'Everyone's dead.'

I brushed past him and ran. The street was full of debris. The next-door house had taken a direct hit and rescue teams were ferreting through the rubble. Our house was untouched. I burst through the front door and dashed upstairs. My parents were asleep in bed. They swore they hadn't heard a thing.

A few hours later I caught the train for Scotland. I was brimming with confidence. The way things were going, our family was on to a winning streak. A quick commission in the Argylls would speed my transfer to India. Nothing to it. A piece of cake.

Then the let-down at journey's end ... The Banff ticket collector regarded me with genuine compassion. 'The Argyll and Suffering Highlanders!' he sighed. 'A nice wee lad like you? Ye'll find those bastards in Duff House. Or what's left of it. The bloody place has been bombed. And so it should be. Whoremongers, the lot of 'em!'

Duff House had undoubtedly seen better days. The one-time seat of the Earls of Fife had been conceived as a handsome Georgian mansion, massively assembled from reddish-grey sandstone, with marble steps leading into a spacious pillared portico which was crowned, somewhat incongruously, by a stained-glass dome. Most of the glass was now shattered, as was the entire south wing. Part of the roof had gone, and the walls were blackened by fire. The previous summer a marauder from one of the Luftwaffe bases in Norway had whipped out of the clouds and dropped a stick of bombs. Two of them struck the south wing, setting the roof ablaze. The pilot must have spotted the high barbed-wire and watch-towers around the place and assumed it had military significance: ironically, the place was being used to house German prisoners of war. Several were killed. The house was so obviously vulnerable that its inmates were promptly moved out. But with billets at a premium throughout Britain, new occupants were easily found. Who else but the young hooligans of the Argyll and Sutherland Highlanders? The battalion had made itself so unpopular in Stonehaven, south of Aberdeen, that the War Office was desperate to find some less sensitive location. Enraged residents of the port were pressuring the authorities to 'remove this scum'. Their petitions threatened to reach Westminster. Someone in Scottish Command took the easy way out, and transfer of the battalion was considered such a victory for law and order that, when the Argylls finally marched out, the townsfolk lined the streets to cheer them on their way. 'Fer Gawd's sake don't come back agen!' they are said to have chanted in parody of the Jacobite song.

The extreme isolation of Banff, on the Moray Firth, had obvious attractions; there were far fewer wealthy burghers to antagonise. Banff was Scotch whisky country – the region was dotted with distilleries – and it was something of a political maverick. The headquarters company of the young soldiers' battalion was moved into the ruins of Duff House while other companies took up residence in surrounding factories – one ended up in a bonded whisky warehouse. The Argylls had already made their mark on Banff, though I did not realise this the day I arrived. For the life of me, I couldn't think why people stared with such hostility as I made my way through the town. 'Here comes another one,' folk seemed to be saying. I might have cottoned on faster if I had understood the dialect. It took me ages just to find my way. A postman finally directed me by sign language into a vast deer park, down the long, winding drive to the great house where Prince Bertie (later King Edward VII) once weekended with sundry mistresses.

A soldier in a flat khaki bonnet bearing the oversized Argyll badge stopped me at the entrance gate. He was a small, sallow youth with beady eyes and a narrow, cruel mouth.

'Whaurdyehinkyergaun?' he demanded, in broadest Glaswegian.

Oh well, welcome to the Zagreb Hussars. 'I've come to join this regiment,' I explained politely.

The youth looked me up and down with growing incredulity. 'You?' he piped, convulsed with laughter. He called out fellow members of the picket to join in the general mirth, 'Come to join this regiment?' the youth mimicked my southern accent. 'Look at this, fellas: we got ourselves *anaither* English poof!'

A thin, craggy figure popped up out of nowhere. It was a redfaced man in his late thirties. The sour set of his hawk-like features proclaimed anger and disappointment.

'What the muck's going on?' The accent was English enough this time. The guard snapped to attention. Nobody spoke. The redfaced man flicked through my papers.

'Where you from?' he snarled.

'Brentwood in Essex,' I said conversationally. It was a relief to find someone speaking a known language. 'Though actually I came – '

A shriek cut me short.

'When you speak to me you say *sir*, see?' The man gestured at the crowns on his uniform sleeve. 'What you think these are? Vaccination marks? I'm your company sergeant-major. See? The name's Hoskins. CSM Hoskins. I'm God around here and don't you muckin' well forget it.'

He stepped back a pace to examine me derisively. 'I know your type,' he growled. 'I know Brentwood. I'm from Essex myself. You went to that bleeding grammar school?'

I nodded dumbly.

'You think you're coming here to get a quick commission, eh? Put a pip on your shoulder and scoop up the girls?' It was so unerringly accurate that I wondered if he also happened to be psychic. The CSM leered at me sadistically. The bile fairly dripped from his fat, wet lips. 'Well I got news for you, sonny. This is a *reformatory* battalion. No one but no one ever got a commission out of this mucking shower. You're here for the duration. And you'd better bloody well accept it.'

Sergeant-Major Hoskins marched me into Duff House. A bespectacled clerk entered my name in his ledgers.

'Don't mind the sar'nt-major, darling,' he told me quietly. 'The bastard hates being here. All the regulars hate it. You can't blame 'em.' The clerk spoke fluent Cockney with a decided lisp. 'Anyone who does anything around here is English, darling. The officers are English. Most of the NCOs as well. Have to be. The Jocks are jailbirds. Savages. Glaswegian gangsters. A rough lot. You won't know what hit you.'

A short square man with a pug face appeared in the doorway. 'Where's the English poof?' he demanded angrily. The accent was more Edinburgh than Glasgow and vaguely understandable.

'Meaning me?' the clerk inquired. 'Sergeant Maguire,' he whispered in my ear. 'In charge of the training company. A great big beastly old thing. Watch it: he'll eat you for breakfast.'

'Not you!' the sergeant shouted at the clerk. 'The new one wot arrived this morning.' He subjected me to another contemptuous examination. 'Make a soldier out of you?' he groaned in mock horror. 'Thank Gawd we got a navy!'

He hustled me up four floors to a small room near the roof. It was bitterly cold. The window was broken. The floor was stone. There was no furniture. Nothing.

'Where's the bed?' I asked. Under mother's capacious wing I had led a sheltered life. My wife and children still remind me that I never faced the rigours of boarding-school.

'Ye're no' in yer mammy's arms noo.' Sergeant Maguire thrust an unfriendly face close to mine. His breath smelt like a blacked-out bar shortly before closing time. 'Ye'll sleep there' – he indicated the uninviting flagstones – 'after ye've drawn a couple of blankets frae the store. Now let's check out yer belongings.'

He emptied my suitcase on to the floor and stirred the contents with a well-polished boot. A pair of new pyjamas. The collected poems of Robert Burns. A paperback *Teach Yourself Gaelic*. One hefty history of Scotland.

'No teddy bear?' the sergeant crowed. He sniffed my aftershave as if it contained mustard gas. 'Ugh, such muck!' he bawled. 'Now pack all this junk back in the case and we'll send it back to yer mammy wi' yer civvy clothes. From noo on ye're going tae be a soldier.' He kicked the hallowed Burns volume across the room. 'Get this intae yer heid! Soldiers don't read or write. They don't even think! They do as they're *mucking well told!*'

The noise attracted a fellow recruit from a neighbouring room. He was a small, dark youth wearing a new, ill-fitting uniform and a thoughtful, dreamy expression. Urquhart came from western Scotland – the only true Highlander in the battalion – and he spoke a soft, crooning English even I could understand. His mother tongue was Gaelic.

'I know how you feel,' the dark youth sympathised when Sergeant Maguire had stormed off. I stood in the centre of that icy, stone-floored room surrounded by my scattered possessions ... Robbie Burns crumpled to hell, new blue pyjamas already smeared with dirt. The enormity of it brought me close to tears.

'Now don't you worry, friend,' Urquhart advised. 'Everything will work out fine. You'll see.' He took me down to the store to draw blankets, uniform and equipment. We then stopped in the canteen to buy blanco, boot and metal polish.

'There's an awful lot of polishing to be done,' Urquhart told me. 'You know the motto of this outfit? "Bullshit Baffles Brains".' It was the first thing I'd heard that made the slightest sense. It's been my motto ever since.

A group of young Argylls propped up the NAAFI bar. One of them swaggered over to me.

'Huvyegotenytabby?' he inquired. I shrugged helplessly, back in Zagreb.

'He wants to know if you've got any tabbies, any spare cigarette butts,' Urquhart translated. Not cigarettes, notice, but cigarette butts. They were ready to smoke the ends you threw away. I did not smoke cigarettes. The Jock retreated grumbling.

'Watch him,' Urquhart warned. 'One of the Billy Boys.'

'The *what*?' I asked.

Urquhart shook his head sadly. My ignorance verged on the dangerous. 'One of the Glasgow gangsters,' he whispered. 'Watch those laddies. They fight with razors.'

The bugle woke me at dawn. The thin, mournful notes seeped up the central staircase to the stone-floored room where I had spent my first fitful night, one blanket beneath me, as a North Sea storm drove icy rain through the broken windows. 'Get out of bed … get out of bed … you lazy bastards!' Half a century later I can still recall the words we hummed to that bugle call.

Painfully, I dragged myself off the floor, cramped and numb, and fought my way to a wash-basin. It was already surrounded by milling recruits. Why, I demanded to know, was there no hot water? My fellow soldiers broke into mocking laughter. They shouted incomprehensible things at me in their Glaswegian patois, or 'patter' as they called it; the French influence on Scottish dialects was strikingly apparent. Sergeant Maguire appeared, spotlessly turned out, with knife-edge pleats sewn into his battledress trousers.

'Inspection in five minutes,' he roared. 'And youze better look good.'

I reckoned I had done my best. I'd spent my first evening with the battalion furbishing my brand-new kit. I was especially proud of my boots. Mother usually did the shoe-cleaning in our family (my, my, how times have changed!) but this once I had gone to town with brushes and polish.

The training company paraded in the gravelled driveway. The rain had lifted, though a keen wind cut through our inadequate clothing. The sergeant made his way slowly down our ranks grunting critical remarks. Opposite me he stopped, looking as if something had crawled out of the nearest sewer.

'Wot was ye doin' last nicht?' he boomed. 'Wankin'?' Sorrowfully, he shook his head. 'Ye know what ye are' – the little bloodshot eyes glittered dangerously ' – yeer a bloody scarecrow.'

Boots were not merely meant to be cleaned, I now discovered; the toecaps had to be made mirror-like with unending applications of polish and spittle. The mixture was massaged in with the handle of a toothbrush, an operation known as 'boning'. Besides the boots, there was webbing to be coated and recoated with layers of blanco until it became a uniform pale green. Brass buttons and belt buckles were then worked on, isolated from the material to which they were attached by an instrument called a button stick. The metal had to gleam like gold. It was a job that would obviously take weeks.

Company Sergeant-Major Hoskins got into the act. He raged up and down our ranks finding fault with everyone. Confronting me, he let out his customary shriek: 'Jesus Christ!' he cried. 'Who the hell we got here? Mister Rip Van mucking Winkle!'

I hadn't shaved. At seventeen only the lightest down shadowed my top lip. One shave a week was generally enough. 'But I don't need to shave... sir!' I indignantly protested.

The sergeant-major smiled maliciously. He plainly hated my guts. His face thrust into mine, eyeball to eyeball. Most military dialogue was apparently conducted at the closest possible range.

'Just in case you hadn't noticed, Mister Grammar School Boy, this is the mucking army!' he shouted. The noise set the rooks cawing in the nearby trees. 'The mucking army says you shave every mucking day whether you need to or not. Understand?'

'Yes, sir!' I quavered.

The sergeant-major turned to Maguire. 'Put this poof on lavatory duty tonight.' He laughed. Maguire laughed. My fellow squaddies laughed. Their hilarity crushed and deflated me.

'Everyone hates me,' I complained afterwards to Urquhart as we went in for breakfast.

'You're a foreigner,' the gentle Highlander reassured me. 'It wasn't your fault you got sent to the Argylls.'

'I volunteered,' I told him. Useless to explain the family connection, my mad suburban romanticism, Bonnie Prince Charlie and all that jazz. Urquhart gazed at me sadly and shook his head. Anyone crazy as me deserved everything he got.

Breakfast was unspeakable. There was plenty of food but the cooks had wrought a special kind of havoc. They had burned the porridge, barely fried the bacon and reconstituted powdered eggs into glassy, glutinous mounds that might have been congealed vomit. An officer came from table to table asking if there were any complaints. It was one of those rituals laid down by King's Regulations. The corporal at our table snapped automatically to attention.

'No complaints, sir!' he declared.

I jumped to my feet gesturing at the mess tins heaped with inedible food. 'You can't expect me to eat this,' I complained.

The officer looked genuinely shocked. He was a little man with a fruity English accent. A bookie's runner in civilian life, if ever there was one; I could imagine him in brown suede shoes and a loud check suit.

'I've never heard a complaint –' he began to mumble when an enormous man loomed over his shoulder. It was the sergeant cook, still wearing his dirty apron, a look of outrage on his stubbly neolithic face.

'Wozayurgonersey?' the cook growled menacingly. Urquhart planted both hands on my shoulders and seated me with a thud.

'No complaints, sir,' Urquhart declared. And when cook and officer had departed he whispered, 'Keep your stupid mouth shut. The sergeant cook's a maniac. He'll beat you to a pulp if he catches you later.'

I sat transfixed, staring in disgust at my mess of potage. The youth on my left leaned over and grabbed it.

'Dinnaeyawannaeeatit?' he asked. I shrugged. I didn't understand a word he said. I didn't care. I watched aghast as the youth wolfed down the dreadful stuff. Given a week or two, I would be doing the same.

Things brightened up when we returned to the parade ground. My boots hurt, my body was stiff and the renewed rain soaked us all right through. But I had served in the cadet corps at my grammar school, and, for a short time, in the Home Guard. Sergeant Maguire was pleasantly surprised to find I knew my drill. Not up to his standards perhaps, but way ahead of the other recruits. Some did not know left from right and kept turning in the wrong direction. It was perfectly apparent why someone like the sergeant, a peacetime regular, resented his posting to this rag-tag outfit.

During the lunch break one of my squad, a burly youth called Gillespie, took me aside and, speaking slowly and distinctly, inquired whether I was truly a journalist. If so, would I write a letter for him to his girlfriend? I was only too glad to oblige. The squad gathered round while I composed a flowery love letter.

'She won't mind it being in my writing?' I asked.

'The wee hen knows I cannae write, so what's the matter?' Gillespie replied. He wrote 'NORWICH' across the back of the envelope. It was the acronym, I later learned, for 'Nickers Off, Ready When I Come Home'. I had always thought the word 'knickers' was spelt with a 'k', but Gillespie didn't seem to care. He brandished the letter proudly under his fellows' noses.

'At least there's saime use fur the English poof!' he told them.

'What do you do in civilian life?' I inquired.

Gillespie expanded his chest like a belligerent gorilla.

'Do? Wottcher mean "do"?' he laughed. 'Listen Mac, I'm a fly boy! I'm frae Aeroplane Street!'

An airman? Well no, Urquhart afterwards explained. 'He means he's smart. He doesn't have to work.' The Highlander stayed at my elbow quietly translating. 'I think Gillespie's got the street wrong, though. He's another one from Hoy Street.'

'Aye, one of the boys,' Gillespie boasted. He whipped off his flat balmoral cap and swished it through the air. Everyone winced.

'See this,' he confided, revealing razor blades sewn into the brim. 'And this –' he plucked a cut-throat razor from inside his battledress blouse and made an imaginary slash at the nearest face. 'That's frae the Hoy Street Boys,' he said, as if it explained everything.

I had yet to learn about the two main juvenile gangs that stalked the slums of Glasgow back in those bad old days. The Billy Boys were

Protestants. The Hoy Street Boys were 'Romans', 'Papists' or, in our vernacular, Catholics. The rival gangs fought like tomcats for sections of territory and when they weren't fighting each other they worked off their aggressions on the police. Most of the members of my training company had tales to tell of bloody encounters with 'the polis' which earned them sentences in the reformatory. Joining the 70th Argylls had bailed them out from behind bars.

A military policeman singled me out at the end of the day. I'd almost forgotten that my hirsute condition had earned me defaulter's punishment. Feeling fit to drop, I changed into fatigues and followed the man into the downstairs lavatories. The smell was unbelievable. All toilet bowls were blocked and overflowing. I looked frantically around for a plunger.

'You use yer hands,' the MP grunted. 'And get the place spotless. I'll be back in half an hour.'

It was the nearest I ever came to desertion. Dreams of kilts, glinting bayonets and the Bengal Lancers died out among the pools of poo. My civilian clothes had not yet been shipped off. I could sneak them out of the store, catch the first train south and make my way to Ireland. Maybe even to America. Any place but this hell-hole.

'Why sure it's mucky,' said a voice behind me. 'But we'll get it done in no time.'

It was Gillespie with a couple of his mates.

'Yer write the letters,' he said, 'we'll clear the crap.'

I retreated into a corner, blowing my nose loudly. I might have been the world's biggest wimp but I didn't want these goodhearted lads to see me crying.

The first month was torture. Recruits were traditionally subjected to an exhausting round of square-bashing, physical exercise, fatigues and, footsore and weary at the close of day, an hour or two of spitting, polishing and laying on with the blanco brush until sleep erased their miseries. All this within the confines of Duff House and its capacious park; new boys like me weren't yet considered fit to loose upon the nearby town. The closest we came to a whiff of civilian life was when the townsfolk of Banff strolled past on Sunday evenings, regarding us with unfriendly curiosity through the high barbed-wire. It was the first but by no means the last time I felt like a monkey in the zoo. Occasionally, girls came past, smiled and said things I couldn't catch and was far too tired to care. Celibacy was fast becoming the normal way of life.

The odd thing was that despite my soft, southern upbringing, my problems with the language and an aversion to my fellow-squaddies' peculiar delights – sneaking and quaffing a tin of brass polish was their way of getting high – I found myself being gradually accepted as one of the boys. A shared feeling of anger and injustice seemed to endear me to these tough young Glaswegians. The feeling was directed exclusively against the officers. The sergeant cook could serve the most awful slops – and threaten to beat up any consumer who demurred – the platoon sergeants could shriek their obscenities, reducing each fumbling recruit to conspicuous paralysis, but the Jocks took it in their stride. It was the officers, idle, privileged, with their effete, fluting voices, who became the focus of our teenage frustrations. God knows where they came from. The 70th Battalion, the Argyll and Suffering Highlanders, must have been way down the list when it came to postings. It was the kind of outfit a hard-pressed commander remembered whenever he wanted to rid himself of some newly-commissioned nitwit of monstrous inability.

Our own platoon commander, Lieutenant Horatio Coot, was a mustachioed mutant who concealed total ineffectuality beneath a nervous, jocular manner. His braying laugh was a gift to the many cruel mimics in the ranks. The man in charge of headquarters company, a certain Major Crawford, was treated with little more respect. The major had been a schoolmaster in civilian life. A great animal lover, he was often seen furtively feeding the deer with cookhouse slops in the surrounding park. Otherwise, he kept to himself, shy to the point of embarrassment, refusing to look you in the eye, while turning an even blinder one to the lax and lazy practices of his subordinates. Ordered out on a route march, for instance, those of us in the ranks paraded in full kit, steel helmets, the lot; everyone from corporals upwards appeared in unencumbered battledress carrying swagger sticks. They might have been strolling off to the village dance.

However, I had been less than two weeks with the battalion, growing accustomed to the outlandish food and language, when the bugler began blowing unfamiliar, alarming blasts. Officers and NCOs snapped out of their customary lethargy, emerging from the woodwork, running and shouting. An air-raid? Something almost as serious: the colonel commanding the battalion was coming to inspect the new recruits.

Everyone went off into a frenzy of pants-pressing and polishing. Like the Grenadier Guards, we were all set to die, with our boots uncommonly clean. The training squad had just been issued rifles. Equipment was desperately short in the wake of Dunkirk. The standard British Lee Enfield was rare enough to be a collector's item and was carried only by sergeants and above. The rank and file had to put up with P-14s, a version of the American army Springfield, produced during a fraught moment of the First World War to take British calibre ammunition. With less than a hour to go before the colonel's arrival, our flustered platoon sergeant tried hopelessly to teach the training squad to present arms; thanks to my cadet corps training, I was the only one who could do it. Sergeant Maguire appointed me section leader on the spot. It was a purely honorary position but it set me off, in its tiny way, on the road to India.

A shambolic honour guard greeted Lieutenant-Colonel Lord Rowallan DSO, MC. Several rifles flew from unskilled hands when the backsight on the wretched P-14s snagged our respirators as we raggedly ordered arms. Maguire groaned. 'Get er hold on the muckin' things!' he hissed. His Lordship graciously ignored our ineptitude. He was a cut above his fellow officers: a huge man with immense whiskers and the Etonian accent affected by members of the Scottish nobility. He had served with distinction in the Highland Brigade during the retreat to Dunkirk.

After a perfunctory inspection, he spent the next hour boring us to death with tales of gung-ho derring-do. It was immediately apparent that the dear man was still fighting the Battle of Waterloo. The incredible feats of the German Panzer columns slicing through France, sweeping the British into the sea, were, in his opinion, a strategic fluke permitted by flabby opposition ('those spineless Frogs') and backed by hordes of spies and saboteurs. Never a suggestion that the Germans might have found a new way of waging war. The colonel's minuscule store of military knowledge was rooted firmly in the past. He had served on the Somme in the First World War and had come to believe that the kilted Highlanders – 'the Ladies from Hell' – had struck terror into German hearts with their savage use of the bayonet, according this unpleasant weapon the same mystical qualities as Excalibur.

'Imagine it, pitch dark,' he droned. 'Huns on every side.' It was during the 1940 fiasco in Belgium when his battalion had managed to capture a real, live German. Trying to creep past some enemy tanks the prisoner yelled for help.

'The fellow was right in front of me. He'd been told to keep mum,' Colonel Rowallan declared. He spoke in short simple sentences that the mentally retarded could easily understand. 'When the blighter yelled, I bayoneted him in the back and pitch-forked him over my shoulder!'

It was entirely believable. Lord Rowallan was straight out of the Imperial War Museum. Or was it the *Boy's Own* paper? When it came to fighting, tanks and dive bombers, the techniques of *blitzkrieg* were little more than a vulgar intrusion.

'Cold steel, that's all the Hun understands.' Milord peered at us short-sightedly. He was an imposing, magisterial figure who later channelled his experience with young soldiers into the office of Chief Scout. This particular morning he rambled on and on. Several recruits fainted. Standing that long on the same spot was an unpleasant experience; giddiness overcame me as my feet and legs went numb.

'Watch it!' Maguire spat in my ear. 'The next man to fall goes on a charge.'

The colonel appeared not to notice. 'Got to smarten things up,' I heard him saying. 'Learn to be a lot tougher.'

The officers responded with cringing smiles. Lieutenant Coot let out an appreciative bray of laughter. There was obsequious applause on the announcement that a new second-in-command was arriving the following day. Less enthusiasm would probably have been expressed had our betters known what was coming. It wasn't just an officer who arrived; it was a revolution.

Captain Matthew Craig had served with the Scots Guards. He carried himself stiffly erect, face dark, unsmiling and immobile, speaking with a purring Lowland accent that rose to an absurd falsetto when shouting orders. The orders sounded ridiculous, so piercingly delivered, but nobody laughed. The man had a look about him, a look of purpose – one almost might say of dedication – which sounded internal alarms every time he told anyone what to do. When he said 'Jump!', to coin a worn, old phrase, we just asked 'How high?'

Minutes after his arrival, the new second-in-command called for a route march to be held the following day. Shortly after breakfast our four platoons formed up before the battered façade of Duff House: all of us Jocks weighted down as usual with back-packs, rifles, gas-masks, ammunition pouches and all the regulation clobber; the officers and NCOs lounging among us, innocent of so much as a water-bottle.

Captain Craig emerged from the portico and stared disbelievingly down the entrance steps. He was in full marching order, steel helmet, back-pack, you name it, carrying an oiled and polished rifle. It was in faltering tones that Sergeant-Major Hoskins reported us ready and correct. The captain's face was terrible to behold.

'Is this some kind of joke?' he snarled. Officers and NCOs fled pell-mell to re-emerge, panting, in all the requisite gear. The captain looked about him with ominous satisfaction. 'Now,' he gritted, 'we shall march!'

And march we did until our feet were blistered and raw. After every mile the captain broke into a run and dragged us after him, gasping and stumbling, down the rain-drenched Scottish roads. Every hour we halted briefly and tried to relieve the pain by changing socks from one foot to the other. It didn't help. During one halt I overheard Lieutenant Coot trying to suck up to our new tormentor.

'Suppose we dumped these men way out in the country with a map,' he trilled. 'Do you reckon any of them would find their way home?'

Captain Craig shot him a cool, unfriendly glare.

'I doubt whether even the officers would, Mr ... what's the name?'

'Coot,' replied our platoon commander, turning very red indeed.

'Well, Mr Coot, you'll take a squad out yourself next Saturday night and see how you get on. I'll select the squad myself.'

It was a squad selected with the utmost malice. Lieutenant Coot, Sergeant-Major Hoskins and, of all people, the dreaded sergeant cook spent the night, hopelessly lost, on mountainous moorland twenty miles from Banff.

'Something went wrong with the compass,' burbled the mud-spattered platoon commander. This time he didn't laugh. Nor did the others. They came back vowing to murder the captain at the first opportunity.

'Just wait 'til we get into action,' the sergeant-major muttered darkly. It was the first time I had ever heard him express a desire to face the foe. 'A bullet in the back. That's all that's needed.'

Captain Craig had served in France but, unlike the colonel, had no lurid tales to tell. He had come through the ordeal impressed with the urgent need to drag the British Army into the twentieth century. It was essential, he told our sergeant, to get away from outmoded peacetime concepts. Mobile warfare required men to *think*.

Sergeant Maguire had never heard such heresy. It was positively subversive. Like most of the senior NCOs, he was an old-time regular, schooled to unquestioning obedience, full-dress parades and immaculate drill. Much of his peacetime service had been spent in India and he still saluted with right hand high above the hair line as if avoiding the brim of a tropical topee.

'That man should have had a taste of the [North-west] Frontier,' Maguire muttered darkly. 'Then he'd know what muckin' fightin' was all aboot.'

But the captain had really been to war. 'We were taught a bitter lesson in Belgium,' he told us at his first lecture. 'The Germans call it *blitzkrieg* and they're right. It's warfare at its most mobile. Everyone is in it. Any moment you could be on your own, taking your own initiatives. You'll have to be using your *brains*.'

The regulars looked blank. Yet the new second-in-command wrought wonders. He had been sent to make soldiers of the 70th Argylls, rumour had it, following complaints of our ill-discipline from folk in the surrounding countryside. The captain hauled us out on to field exercises, where we operated in smallish units, devising weird ways of defeating German paratroops. The gruelling pace had us dropping in our tracks. One consolation was seeing non-combatant staff, especially the sergeant cook and his mates, stomping across the springtime meadows with the rest of us. Invasion still seemed a possibility a year after the Battle of Britain; rumours were mounting of a planned German invasion of Russia. But the Russkies would be finished off in a matter of weeks, most of us assumed, and then the Nazis would be back at our throats. My squad specialised in infiltration and had the satisfaction of capturing the 'enemy' commander, Sergeant-Major Hoskins, snatching an unguarded pee in a cabbage field. The captain thoroughly approved, the sergeant-major did not. I should have been warned. It was time to watch my step.

Company Sergeant-Major Hoskins had never liked me. Capturing him (by trickery, he claimed) proved me too clever for my own good. From that day onwards he descended upon me so often that even my platoon sergeant, Maguire, and Captain Craig were forced delicately to intervene.

'Don't worry, I'll get you,' the CSM snarled in my ear after one particularly fruitless bout of harassment. 'You'll never get a commission, you grammar-school poof!'

His chance came the night I was given charge of the picket. This was the unarmed guard responsible for checking the main gate through the barbed-wire fencing surrounding Duff House. The handsome if battered mansion still looked remarkably like a prisoner-of-war camp. A night on picket duty was nobody's idea of fun because the man in charge had to stay awake after a hard day's work and face the whole of the next day's duties without sleep. At 5 a.m. sharp the picket commander was responsible for awakening the cooks, the bugler and the orderly officer. Failure to comply invited massive retaliation.

The oddest duty, I soon found, was checking the appearance of the men who were going to Banff on leave passes. Since my picket was mounted on a Friday, most of those no longer classed as recruits were heading for the bars and the town hall dance. Some wore kilts, borrowed or bought, and I was faced with the embarrassing task of lifting the hem-lines with a bayonet scabbard to see if the wearer wore anything underneath. Anyone who did was put immediately on a charge.

Now, I know there's always been jocular controversy over the question of kilts. Do Scotsmen wear anything underneath them? It is still a subject on which I cannot generalise. But back in 1941 any member of the 70th Battalion of the Argyll and Sutherland Highlanders who ventured, kilted, abroad was not expected – nay, not permitted – to gird his loins with so much as a jock-strap.

'Ye're the Ladies from Hell, remember?' Sergeant Maguire hectored us. 'So what's a wee bit of draught up yer muckin' bums?'

My picket included the notorious urchin 'Wee' McCloskie. He was the vicious midget who had jeered the day I joined the regiment. As a former member of one of the toughest street gangs in the Glasgow Gorbals, he was treated with a wary respect even by the senior NCOs. It was like consorting with someone intimately connected with the Mafia. There was no sense in upsetting him unduly. You never knew whether one of his relations might come after you at some later date, demanding vengeance.

'Of course ye wear naethin' beneath the kilt!' McCloskie snorted scornfully. 'All ye have ter do when ye gets to the toon hall hop is ...'

The instructions were crudely explicit. The drill was to approach a woman and perform an act of gross indecency (I still feel 'flashing' isn't the adequate term) at the same time inviting her – how does one put it? – to try it on for size. Whatever happened to the romance of courtship?

'Works like a muckin' dream,' McCloskie gloated.

The sergeant cook ambled up to the gate. Imagine a gorilla in a kilt and you've got the picture precisely. Nobody but Sigourney Weaver could possibly have gone for him. To me, the man looked as terrifying as ever and I hesitated to give him the bayonet scabbard treatment.

'Shy, are we?' the gorilla chuckled, flicking up the front of his kilt. The revelation was breathtaking.

'The wee hens will scream at that lot,' McCloskie sighed enviously in my ear. Scream? The type of girls I knew in the soft English south would most likely faint on the spot.

The potential of the kilt as an instrument of sexual stimulation, a male seventh veil, was nonetheless intriguing; once the drunks and skirt-chasers had been re-admitted to camp I slipped off into lewd reverie. It took no great stretch of the imagination to gauge the reaction of the recruiting officer's daughter back in Grimsby when I returned kilt-clad and, beneath it, naked. I dreamed of revelation before her fireside, giving *her* a present as the ground heaved again and ... someone was shaking me. It was Wee McCloskie.

'Christ, man, ye're in trouble,' he wailed. 'Ye've been asleep. So have we. It's nearly six o'clock.'

Members of the picket were allowed to sleep between turns at the gate. After three in the morning they were all stood down, though the picket commander remaining wakeful throughout the watches of the night. And now there would be hell to pay. The cooks weren't wakened, the duty officer slept blissfully on, the bugler ...

Sergeant-Major Hoskins was ablaze with delighted rage. 'You're on every kind of charge, Spurr!' he howled triumphantly. 'With *that* on your record you'll *never* get a commission.'

He might have been exaggerating but it sounded to me like a sentence to eternal torment. A commission was my release from purgatory. The prospect of continued service in this penal battalion scared me half to death.

'The sar'nt-major's enjoying this,' Wee McCloskie coolly observed. He saw the frantic look on my face. 'Dinnae worry. Just deny everything and call me as witness.'

Each morning at ten o'clock sharp, defaulters were doubled in hatless – that is, trotted out on the double before the company commander 'wi'oot yer bunnet', as my fellow Argylls put it. That day I was the star criminal. The CSM read off a list of transgressions as long as your arm. The wording I've long forgotten but the implication was clear. Directly the company commander found me guilty I would be passed on for judgment by Colonel Rowallan, stripped of my acting rank of section leader and condemned to a spell of grievous punishment. I had seen men being forced to double around a sand-pit in full marching order until they collapsed exhausted. The military police took sadistic pleasure in breaking you physically and mentally. But it would not end there. My service record would receive a very black mark indeed; sleeping on duty was unlikely to endear me to an officer selection board.

Major Crawford sat behind his desk refusing, as usual, to look anyone in the eye.

'What have you got to say?' he asked, staring hard at his blotting-pad. This particular case was going to hurt him, I felt, nearly as much as it hurt me.

'There was a reason, sir,' I blethered desperately, though I couldn't for the life of me imagine what it would be. 'Perhaps you would be so good as to call Private McCloskie.'

The sergeant-major threw me a venomous stare. He obviously smelt collusion. 'But, sir – ' he protested.

'Let's hear what McCloskie has to say,' the major interposed wearily. As a former schoolmaster he plainly disliked caning his underlings.

'Well, yer see, sir,' said Wee McCloskie. 'Aboot five o'clock we heerd this noise way doon on the boundary fence. The picket commander took me off to see what was happening. A wee deer was caught in the barbed-wire and it took us uncou time ter release the poor thingy. We wuz late calling the cooks, sir, as a result.'

Major Crawford glanced at me questioningly. The depth and breadth of the lie had left me dumbstruck.

'Is this true?' the major inquired.

'Yes, sir,' I gulped. May heaven forgive me.

'We must all be kind to animals,' the major mumbled mildly. I remembered him out in the park feeding the deer. He was a notorious nature-lover, what we would nowadays call an environmentalist. Thoughtfully, he tapped his teeth with his pencil. 'Of course, we must not allow this to interfere with our duties,' he went on. 'Still, the circumstances are so unusual, and the initiatives shown so admirable, that I feel the charge should be dismissed.'

'But, sir – ' the sergeant-major howled as the prize fish slipped off his hook.

'Dismissed,' Major Crawford repeated with unexpected finality. He looked me shyly in the face and smiled. It was a conspiratorial smile. The major had not believed a word he had heard.

'You think you're mucking clever,' CSM Hoskins snarled outside the orderly room. 'Well, I haven't finished with you. Not by a long chalk.'

That night in the canteen I bought Wee McCloskie all the beer he could drink. How else could I thank him?

''Twas naethin',' McCloskie drawled. 'We cannae let that Hoskins do yer. Ye're one o' the boys. Basic Training is up this week. Come oot wi' us and we'll show yer the toon.'

He downed another pint of strong Scottish ale.

'And while ye're aboot it, we'll find ye a kilt tae wear.'

It felt strange being one of the gang. Mastering the Glasgow dialect seemed to have helped; I no longer looked blank when fellow recruits addressed me and it was possible to answer them back in a fair approximation of 'the patter':

'Hey, Jock, ye're muckin' manky, so ye are.'

'Och awa' wi' ye, ye muckin' wee turd!'

And such-like comradely endearments. Impossible as it might seem, I was pretty well inured to the inedible food, the punishing drills and exercises, the mindless and meaningless rituals so dear to the military heart – to the impositions, in fact, of spartan army life. There was a promise of release. Minimal parade ground skills and an unusual level of literacy had marked me down as a Potential Officer. The chances of getting before a Selection Board were maddeningly remote but hope of blessed relief carried me through those first doleful weeks.

Britain was eighteen months into the war. The army was at last expanding. The all-conquering Wehrmacht was by this time deep into Russia, slashing the Red Army to ribbons; it wouldn't be long – a couple of months, we reckoned – before the Russkies caved in and the Lunatic of Berchtesgaden turned west again to settle accounts with a determined, if indefensible, Britain. There would have to be a vast scraping of the manpower barrel – or we would be suffering the most appalling casualties – before officers were sought from the ranks of our young soldiers' battalion. The quick fix could only be found in the Commonwealth. The Dominions were once again being asked to bail out the mother country. Canadians were flooding into England – doomed to later decimation at Dieppe – while in Tobruk the Aussies were giving the Italians the beating they deserved. Indian troops were overrunning the rest of Mussolini's empire in Ethiopia and Somaliland. The Indians were doing so well, according to the propaganda press, that dozens of new regiments were being raised throughout the Raj. This was my opportunity. A notice appeared on the company order board in mid-July requesting applications for Indian commissions. Those who applied would get a hearing, the notice advised, with the utmost dispatch.

Captain Craig looked disappointed when I rushed in panting, to put my name down. 'You want out, Spurr?' he inquired in his purring Lowlands accent.

'No, sir,' I lied, truthfully adding, 'I want adventure.'

The second-in-command looked doubtful.

'You're not ready for a commission yet,' he declared. But seeing the disappointment on my face he went on: 'Still, if it's adventure you want, I'll recommend you anyway.'

It was nearly a month before I could go out and celebrate. My duties seemed endless. But by now the quarantined period of training was well and truly over and I was permitted the occasional trip into Banff and celebrate I would, with a pint or two of my favourite Pimms No. One. Good as Banff Scotch was reputed to be, I preferred to drink something sweet. The habits of a liquor-filled lifetime had yet to mature.

'Yev no forgotten us, huv ye?'

The speaker was Wee McCloskie, my saviour from slumber on the picket guard.

'We're all goin' oot the nicht,' he grinned. 'We're goin' tae Aberdeen.'

The north-east fishing port was about an hour from Banff by train. There were spasmodic connections, especially on weekends. The place catered for the migrant habits of males from all over the region who converged for one uproarious night in the only swinging city north of Edinburgh.

'It should be quite a nicht.' McCloskie smiled his demonic smile. 'And see here. We've borrowed a kilt fur ye.'

I cannot to this day understand why he bothered to be so friendly. My letter-writing had apparently impressed these streetwise children ('in the country of the blind the one-eyed man is king'), but there was little else to recommend me. My personality wasn't exactly magnetic. I was scarcely the macho type, at least not by their bare-knuckle standards. To put it frankly, I was an oddity, tolerated like a small, lost dog.

This was no time, though, to look gift horses in the mouth. The kilt my comrades produced suited me to perfection. I was young, lean and quite good-looking in a soft, southern way. The swing and sway of this unlikely garment was bound to beckon *beaucoup* girls.

The Argyll and Sutherland kilt is a dark-blue and green affair, its tartan identical to that of the Black Watch. The difference is in the pleating and detectable only by the *aficionado*. Like most tartans, it's an historic fiction, cooked up, in this case, by the government – it is known to this day as 'government issue'.

The only trouble with kilts, I found, was the draught inside. I'd never realised before why women wear knickers. There was an unwonted coolth around the crotch that induced an extraordinary feeling of nakedness. The gate picket made sure – with many a nasty jibe – that I was innocent of underwear. Still, I had grown accustomed to the exceptional ventilation by the time we settled noisily into the train. A well-dressed woman occupied the seat opposite. She was old by my standards – thirty, if she was a day – and married, I learned, to a Gordon Highlander serving in North Africa. The Gordons were the principal regiment raised in that part of Scotland. Their headquarters depot was in Aberdeen. I sat back chattering, delighted to indulge in civilised conversation and trying for the while to distance myself from my ebullient comrades. The woman's eyes strayed down to my kilt. She blushed charmingly.

'Would you be doing anything tonight?' she asked. I hastily crossed my legs.

'He's wi' us,' McCloskie interposed rudely. In a stage whisper audible as far as the engine he added, 'And we'll get ye much be'er than that!'

Aberdonians speak with defensive pride of their 'silver city by the sea'. Sure enough, when we left the train, the rows of weathered stone houses gleamed sterling-bright in the evening sunshine. I'm told the place has grown rich on North Sea oil these days, but back in 1941 its main business was fish. The smell reminded me of Grimsby.

My companions homed in on a bar which featured a large reproduction of *The Thin Red Line*. The once-famous Victorian painting immortalises a crucial moment in the Crimean war following the Light Brigade's misadventure at Balaclava, when the then-Sutherland Highlanders in their red jackets and government-issue kilts formed line abreast, shoulder to shoulder, and beat off attempts by Russian cavalry to overrun the British positions. The painting made Mac's Bar the assembly zone for the heirs to the Red Line tradition. The Sutherlands, the 93rd Foot, were known as *An Reisimeid Chataich* (Gaelic for 'The Regiment of the Cat') and, before their amalgamation with the Argylls in 1881, were considered the most Highland of all the Highland Corps. The fact that my companions were not Gaelic-speaking Highlanders but razor-boys from the Glasgow slums did not strike us then as particularly strange. The descendants of the real Highlanders, forced from their lands by the Scottish aristocracy, had long migrated to Canada and the Antipodes. They were a tough, hard-drinking lot, by all accounts. The teenage soldiers who'd taken their place maintained the same traditions. They'd certainly learned to drink as hard as anyone in Bonnie Prince Charlie's First Eleven.

'Hauf an' a hauf all round,' McCloskie ordered. Eight small whiskies and eight halves of ale slid towards us over the bar. They went down before you could blink. I spluttered a bit but humbly followed suit. There was something about the mixture that was more satisfying than my habitual Pimms. Soon we were on to 'a glass and a glass' (double Scotch and a pint) and the little pinched faces of my wiry companions began glowing like beetroots.

'Now we'll pick up some skirt,' Wee McCloskie boasted. 'This toon is fu' o' it. Just stick wi' us and get ready to show 'em –'

He broke off, glaring across my shoulder. We all stopped talking. A group of Gordon Highlanders had entered the bar. Their kilts were different from ours, striped with yellow. They were not looking for trouble, of that I'm sure, but their intrusion presented some primordial challenge.

'Who shot the cheese?' Wee McCloskie called out. The Gordons were leaning on the far end of the bar ordering their drinks. The six of them stiffened. They had been offered an arcane insult (the Gordons were supposed to have panicked in some long-forgotten campaign and mown down one of their ration parties).

'Who've got a yellow streak in their kilts that goes right up into their guts?' yelled a young Argyll named Mackie, a vociferous midget who acted as McCloskie's wing-man. Slowly and deliberately he turned his empty beer glass upside down on the bar. It reminded me of a show-down in a wild Western saloon. Everyone reached, figuratively, for his gun. The symbolic, upturned glass polarised Argylls and Gordons into contending camps, leaving me sitting there stupidly at the bar way out in no-man's-land. Foolishly, I felt myself uninvolved. Regimental pride might be a wonderful thing but what quarrel did I have with these strangers?

The Gordons were not young soldiers, but quite elderly men: probably in their late twenties. They were broad-shouldered and burly, like men used to manual labour. There seemed nothing to stop them making mincemeat of our bunch of scrawny teenagers. One of their group smashed a glass on the bar and dived for McCloskie's face. The little Glaswegian ducked, grabbed the man by the collar and tore open his jacket, pinning his arms to his sides. Then he smashed him in the face with his forehead – a technique known in local parlance as 'geein' the heid'. It can be fearfully effective.

The Gordon reeled back nursing a broken nose. Blood streamed down his face. The others closed in cursing while I sat there, drunk and bemused, playing the uncommitted observer. But there was no room for voyeurs once battle was joined. The Gordons charged in, arms flailing. Something hit me on the back of the head and I went out like a light …

I came round to sharp slaps on my face. It was Wee McCloskie, with a great welt on his right cheek and his battledress jacket torn. He and the others had dragged me into the street.

'Quick!' he was shouting. 'On yer feet! The muckin' polis is comin'.'

He helped me up. My ribs hurt so much I could hardly walk.

'Those bastards wur kickin' you tae death,' Mackie advised as the gang half-carried me, chortling to each other, in the direction of the station. They doubted whether I could handle the woman they had hoped to find for me that night.

'A grand evening,' McCloskie proclaimed as they eased me into the train. 'We might a' been back in Glasgow!'

I thought fleetingly of the soldier's wife and nursed my wounds in silence. I made painful passage back to Duff House to find my platoon sergeant waiting up for me.

'What the hell have you been doing?' Sergeant Maguire gasped. I was still bleeding from a gash on the back of my head. My body ached all over. 'You've not been fighting have yer?'

I nodded.

'Not wi' the bloody Gordons?'

Another nod.

'Then ye're in muckin' trouble,' the sergeant declared. 'I've been waitin' up to tell ye. It's Aberdeen for you Monday. Officer Selection Board in Brig O' Don.'

Brig O' Don was the Gordons' depot. I asked whether they would have heard about the encounter in Mac's Bar. The sergeant examined my cut head, clucking with sympathy.

'Those bastards will have heard about it all right,' he declared. 'And you're going to be right in among 'em. You'll be lucky if ye ever reach that muckin' board.'

I entered the Gordons' headquarters feeling close to panic. Trust my luck to land there in such threatening circumstances. There was no way out of it. Brig O' Don barracks in Aberdeen was the regional site for the Officer Selection Board; it was here I would face the crucial and, I'd been warned, gruelling interview which would transmute me from a downtrodden private in the Argyll and Suffering Highlanders to Spurr Sahib, glamour-boy of the Bengal Lancers. There would be no second chances. Everything hung on this one interview. It would hopefully transport me from a world of pain and humiliation to the gentlemanly, girl-grabbing life of the Imperial Indian Army. Flavoured as these fantasies were by the unrealities of Hollywood, I remained convinced they offered the easy-option escape route I had long been seeking.

There were two inescapable obstacles, and one was bluffing the Selection Board into believing I would make a suitable officer. It wouldn't be easy, if rumour had it right. The Board set out deliberately to test a candidate's nerve and reliability. Given my gift of the gab, I reckoned on muddling through. The second obstacle, however, was more immediate – and more serious. I had to survive the twenty-four hours before the Board convened in a potentially hostile environment. Brig O' Don was the headquarters of our mortal enemies. The big silver badge on my balmoral proclaimed me a member of the Argylls. The two regiments were traditionally at odds. Tensions could only have been enhanced by the bar-room brawl that ended, for me, so painfully. By now reports of the punch-up would be all around the barracks where an unfriendly reception would await me – of this I was certain – even if I was lucky enough to pass unrecognised. Recognition could have near-lethal consequences.

Things looked bad the moment I limped through the gate. My body still ached from the kicking I'd received. My chest was heavily bandaged – at least one cracked rib was suspected. The sergeant of the guard glared at my cap badge with chilling animosity.

'One o' the muckin' Boys Brigade?' he sneered. 'Can't think how one of your shower could set foot among real soldiers.'

He gazed disbelievingly at my papers.

'Officer selection? Jesus! What's the world coming to? They'll be taking 'em in nappies next!'

A surly orderly conducted me to a barrack-room. It had real beds. Seated on one was a boy of about my own age, busily polishing his boots. He wore the flashes of the Black Watch.

'Havershum-Crumley,' the boy solemnly announced, shaking my hand. 'Robert Havershum-Crumley. You can call me HC.' He spoke with the accents of Eton ('Harrow actually'); his handsome, refined features, his obvious self-assurance, spelt money and privilege. The Gordons orderly lingered in the room. He was eyeing me suspiciously.

'You wouldnae ha' been in Mac's Bar last Saturday?' he growled.

Havershum-Crumley cut the man down with a withering stare.

'Are you suggesting this gentleman haunts bars and such-like?' he shrilled. The Gordon scowled and shrank away.

'In a spot of trouble?' HC inquired.

I gave him the unvarnished truth. I had to tell someone. Havershum-Crumley nodded understandingly.

'Stick with me,' he said. 'Take refuge in the class system.'

HC proclaimed himself an enemy of class. He claimed, in fact, to be a communist. His family were wealthy rural landowners (the shootin' and fishin' set I both loathed and envied) and he had joined the young soldiers' battalion of the Black Watch when Hitler invaded Russia.

'Had to support the socialist motherland,' he told me confidently. 'Socialism's the hope of the world.' He lit himself an Egyptian cigarette. 'Daddy has these fags made specially in Cairo.' He went back to boning his boots. 'The beloved parents hate my politics. Think I've gone communist to twit them. Real high Tories, the lot of them. They wanted to wangle me a direct commission in the Lifeguards. But I needed to serve in the ranks.'

'Whatever for?' I asked. 'You must be a glutton for punishment.'

HC rubbed thoughtfully at his boot-cap. 'This may sound odd, but I felt it was about time I met the working class. Interesting experience. Between you and me, they're not all they're cracked up to be. I don't mind campaigning for them, politically and all that sort of thing, but mingling with them can become tiresome.'

He said it so innocently and inoffensively I couldn't help laughing.

'So now I'm applying for the Indian Army,' he went on. 'Got to overthrow imperialism. Great Grandpa founded So and So's Horse' – a fashionable Indian cavalry regiment – 'no problem getting in. Not with my polo.'

'I rather fancied the Bengal Lancers,' I told him. He looked me over dubiously.

'Bit beyond you I'd think,' he said with crushing honesty. 'Ever ride to hounds?'

'Never sat on a horse,' I said.

'Opt for something easier,' he advised. 'The Madras Sappers and Miners might suit you better.'

It was the least fashionable outfit, I later learned, in the entire Indian Army.

The pair of us went out for dinner – 'My treat,' he told me – at a fashionable hotel. I had never been anywhere quite so grand.

'Officers only,' said the *maître d*' the moment we entered the dining-room. HC transfixed him with a haughty stare.

'I beg your pardon?' he drawled. The *maître d'* wilted visibly. 'We may not be commissioned yet, my man, but the pair of us are Potential Officers.'

The flunkies grovelled. We ate magnificently. My new-found friend preached communism throughout the meal – 'the trick is to get the workers to unite. Lead 'em but don't join 'em' – and to my relief stuck by his promise to pick up the tab.

Back at Brig O' Don we returned to our pressing and polishing. Appearances carried considerable weight, we'd been warned. Other candidates had arrived, most of them English, and were similarly at work. The one Scot had been to a top public school in Edinburgh. He spoke almost exactly like my friend from Harrow.

'Accents count for everything in this feudal society,' HC remarked. 'And it won't be that much different under the dictatorship of the proletariat.' I wondered how my accent would sound. It was neither expensive nor polished; a mixture of lower-middle-class English and the nasal dialect of Essex.

Disaster struck at breakfast. Potential Officers were ushered into a corner of the mess-hall. Every one of us sparkled diamond-like in immaculate uniforms and gleaming boots. The Gordons regarded us jealously. One of them near our table sported a black eye. He nudged his mates and pointed when I sat down. They followed me when I lined up for food. The eye-blacked one bumped deliberately into me as I walked away with a mess-tin full of porridge.

'Sorry,' he said out loud. Under his breath he snarled, 'Take that for Mac's Bar!'

My beautiful battledress was ruined. Fellow candidates helped sponge me down but the damage was done. There was no time to change and nothing to change into; I would be forced to face a hypercritical Selection Board in unpresentable condition.

HC went in first. He came out perspiring and flustered.

'I think the bastards failed me!' he muttered. 'Talk about the bloody Inquisition! They went mad when I told them the Russians would defeat Hitler. Thought I was some kind of a Bolshie!'

Heart in my boots, I stumped into the interview room and stiffly saluted.

'Aha!' cried the colonel in charge. 'Spilt your breakfast down your trousers?'

It was a ploy guaranteed to unnerve the bravest. The interview board was supposed to be divided between good and bad guys in an effort to throw you off balance. The problem was there did not appear to be any good guys. The faces of the other three officers registered nothing but enmity.

'Had an accident in the mess-hall, sir!' I spluttered feebly.

The major on the colonel's left sniggered out loud. 'What school are you?' he demanded. A lieutenant-colonel who never spoke throughout the interview sat back assessing me coldly. Another major was thumbing lazily through my records.

'Sir Anthony Browne's School, Brentwood, sir!' I replied. It used to be a grammar school but was upgraded to minor public-school status somewhere in the mid-1930s. The new name was supposed to make it sound more up-market.

The major looked at me as though I'd done something dirty on the floor.

'Brent-what?' he inquired. The syllables dripped distastefully from his lips.

'It was the best my parents could afford, sir!' I snapped back. The anger rose in me. My accent began to slip.

'Sounds like a grammar school,' said the colonel in charge. He seemed supremely unimpressed. 'Did you serve in the school cadet corps?'

'Oh yes,' I said, 'Sir, I mean …' moving thankfully to safer ground.

'But you left school quite early,' interposed the cynical major.

'Well yes, sir,' I gabbled. 'I wanted to get into journalism.'

'Into what?' gasped the colonel. Better to have confessed to being an illegal abortionist.

'A gentleman of the press,' sneered the major. 'Do you consider that a suitable background for an officer in the Indian Army?'

Something snapped inside me. A murderous rage brought suicidal protests spluttering to my lips. So much hateful servitude and now this unconcealed snobbery … it was more than I could bear.

'Let me tell you – ' I started to say, teetering on the brink of aborting my Indian Army career, but the other major cut me short. He passed my records to the colonel. They both laughed.

'You *captured* your sergeant-major?' the colonel chuckled. 'You must be extraordinarily brave or extraordinarily foolish.'

'A bit of both, sir,' I answered, swallowing my rage.

'You appear to have caught him in an, er, unguarded moment,' smiled the colonel, passing the papers around the table. It was a detailed report from our second-in-command, Captain Craig.

' … "An original mind, shows unusual initiative … ",' the colonel read from the report. Oh blessed, blessed Craig!

'You remember Craig: that's the chap from the Scots Guards,' said one of the majors. 'Capital fellow. Thinks the world of you, young man. Don't play polo by any chance?'

'No, sir, cricket,' I lied. I hated cricket. I used to sneak off the field when we were supposed to be fielding and read lurid romances.

'Ah, cricket,' said the colonel, screwing a monocle into his eye. 'Sounds eminently suitable for the Indian Army. You'll soon learn of our decision.'

I sprang into a crashing salute.

'One thing more,' the colonel added, as I turned towards the door. 'An officer is more careful with his breakfast.'

Overnight I was an object of wonderment and envy in the 70th Argylls. No one had been accepted for a commission from the young soldiers' battalion since the unit was formed in early 1940. It was understandable with such a raffish cross-section of humanity fleshing out its disreputable ranks. The fact that I had been snapped up in a moment of administrative desperation by the Indian army, eager to take anyone, but anyone, to lead its expanding legions, was overlooked in the welter of self-congratulation. The battalion commander, Lieutenant-Colonel Lord Rowallan, summoned me to his intimidating presence and rambled on about honour and the regiment. The monologue was shot through with references to Kipling and the 'white man's burden'. Service to the King Emperor required me to exude Christian virtues, play the game, maintain a stiff upper-lip and avoid familiarity with the natives.

'India is an easy place to go off the rails,' his Lordship warned. He lapsed into unexpected intimacy. 'A man has to get a grip on himself. When mixing with Asiatics my maxim has always been – keep the bowels open and the mouth shut.' This good, if crude, advice sounded strange from those aristocratic lips. I bade Milord farewell with a quivering salute.

Captain Matthew Craig, the real mastermind of my heaven-sent promotion, smiled grimly and said: 'I hope I did the right thing. You'll never be worth a damn until you take this war seriously. But you will. Indeed you will.' He was right, though it took longer than even he suspected. The Second World War was nothing more than a mighty lark, as far as I was concerned. It would stay that way until I faced my moment of truth, typhoon-hit, in the Bay of Bengal.

My bitterest enemy, Company Sergeant-Major Hoskins, cackled his disbelief. '*You* a muckin' officer?' he shrieked. One octave higher his voice would be audible only to dogs. The other senior NCOs trundled to his support. 'Salute *you*?' sneered the fearsome cook sergeant. 'That'll be the muckin' day!'

Wisely I followed the colonel's advice and kept my mouth shut tight. The overwhelming urge to get in the last word, no matter how fatuous, has always been my most damaging weakness. Bearing in mind the many slips yet lying between cup and lip I bit back the witty ripostes that leaped angrily to mind. Manfully, I cleaned lavatories and scrubbed floors or whatever fatigues the envious might pile upon me, confident that the call to India would eventually come through. The joyous day the movement order reached the company office I squandered most of my remaining cash buying beers all round. 'We'll miss ye,' was Wee McCloskie's verdict. And I was inclined to believe him. He listened, totally engrossed, to my description of the hurried exit from Brig O' Don barracks after my ordeal before the Officer Selection Board.

'Yer mean the bastards hadnae forgotten our wee duffy?' McCloskie noted gleefully.

'So they tried to do ye?' laughed one of McCloskie's side-kicks.

'They did enough,' I said, remembering the porridge spilt disastrously over my uniform.

'But it didnae stop ye!' crowed McCloskie.

Not quite, I admitted.

The Indian Army must have been hard up in the extreme. But why? It was not at all clear. India was relegated to a secondary role in the struggle with Germany, sending troops to help eliminate Italian resistance in the Western Desert, Ethiopia and Somaliland. The possibility of some other enemy looming over the horizon never occurred to me. The Indian Army was the lynch-pin of British power in the Middle East, performing garrison duties in dozens of places with exotic names. Little fighting was involved, as far as I could make out; indeed, I seemed certain to avoid all conflict, leaving the Nazis to wipe out the Bolsheviks. The United States would then come to our rescue. The New World would be forced, in Canning's words, 'to redress the balance of the old'.

I joined a draft of Indian Army cadets one chilly November day in camp at Aldershot. It was and, as far as I know, still is the largest military centre in southern England. There were guardsmen whose drill sessions were almost a ballet in boots. There were commandos training on the assault courses for raids on the French coast. French Canadians of the 22nd Regiment ('The Van Dooze') sang *Alouette* loudly in the pubs in their distinctive Norman patois. Some 500 of us, temporary sahibs in waiting, checked into Blenheim Lines; together we comprised an incredible mishmash of manpower from every unit in the British Army. Many were quite young, like me, though the majority were conscripts in their mid-twenties. Most proved to be exceptional individuals, born to command. But there appeared to be a leavening of con-men. Plenty of commanders seemed to have leaped at the chance to thrust their second-raters into the King Emperor's lap.

No sooner had we reported to the Movements Officer than passes were handed out for embarkation leave. It was time to go home to Essex to show off my uniform – regrettably, without a kilt – and gulp the beers friends bought me as if I were already a man. I was, in fact, too young to be served alcoholic drinks but nobody seemed to care. My grandmother was the only member of the family to betray unease. She had seen brothers, uncles and cousins vanish into the meat grinder in Flanders.

'So many went,' she wept. 'So many never returned.'

Mother said nothing, but I guessed what she was thinking. The slaughter of what we then called the Great War had been the dominant topic when I was small. A shadow would flit across gossip-filled drawing-rooms, while the women's talk tailed off in thoughtful silence. You knew what they had on their minds. It was the illustrious dead. Some of them claimed to see visions, spectral visitations from sons and husbands who had marched cheerfully away and never came back. My great-grandmother was said to have sat up suddenly on her death-bed crying, 'I'm coming, Bill!' She thought she could see the son who had died in the bloodbath of the Somme.

Mother kept off the subject of war. She was an exceptional woman: strong, self-willed, original. We chatted inconsequently about my childhood. We had always been very close. Father had never figured in the family relationship. My brother and sister perhaps, but not the stranger who barged in briefly two or three times a year and upset the entire household. Mother and I declined to speculate about the future. But I'd be home, I reckoned, in no more than a couple of years. When we said goodbye at Liverpool Street station, Mother gave me one crushing hug and slipped off in the crowd. It was typical of her: calm and unsentimental to the last.

All I felt was a sense of glorious release and a mounting excitement at the promise of adventures beckoning ahead. No morbid thoughts for me – I believed, as all young folk believe, that calamity was destined solely for others – and it was years before I faced the fear of death that comes with age and biting, bitter experience. Excitement buoyed me through the uncomfortable train journey to Glasgow where Draft Number 116, Officers' Training School, Bangalore, was poured aboard a darkened troopship. We were assigned to three-tier bunks in F-deck, well below the waterline, condemned to drown like rats if ever the ship went down. But that was the last thought any of us had on our minds. The mounting U-boat threat was generally glossed-over in the press.

Icy rain splattered the camouflaged upperworks the night we crept down the Clyde. The ship, the port and the surrounding city were effectively blacked out. Nothing existed beyond blodgy shapes against the overcast sky. Sirens sounded and we struggled into clumsy kapok life-jackets and made our way to emergency stations on the deck. The groping fingers of a dozen searchlights scuttled across the lowering cloud. Bursting flak winked above our heads. I sheltered from the keen, wet wind, dreaming I was leading the Bengal Lancers, pennants flying, swords gleaming, in some harmless ceremonial parade far from bleak, beleaguered Scotland. Bonnie Prince Charlie was welcome to the lot of it – pipes, tartans, kilts and all. I would request the next dance of the colonel's daughter at some colonial levee. There would be punch-bowls full of potent drinks, superb ball-gowns and dashing dress uniforms. The lovely girl in my arms might even want to know what Scotsmen wear beneath their kilts ...

Still immersed in fantasy, I returned below to strip off my soaking uniform. Almost unnoticed, the loudspeaker system was squawking out strange news. Something about the Japanese. The funny little men with protruding teeth and pebble spectacles (as they were commonly regarded in those days) had attacked some place in Hawaii. A naval base. Somewhere I'd never heard of that belonged to the Americans. It was called Pearl Harbor.

PART TWO

The Japanese entry into the war thrust me into a completely new ball-game. The bulletins screeching from the troop-deck speakers made it chillingly clear, the first day out of Glasgow, that the Japanese were not merely lambasting the Americans, launching them unwittingly into war, but that they'd had the temerity to take on the British Empire. One superbly executed raid on the American naval facilities in the Hawaiian Islands had caused grievous damage. The communiqués made no bones about that. It was also becoming evident that the surprise blow – what President Roosevelt angrily called 'the Day of Infamy' – had secured the Japanese flank for a deep southward thrust to the Philippines, Malaya and the Dutch East Indies. The object was seizure of natural resources, chiefly oil and rubber, denied Japan by a recent US embargo. It was this sharp expression of American displeasure, we know now with hindsight, that provided the war faction in Tokyo the excuse to launch hostilities.

Japanese ambitions would obviously out-run their abilities, we told ourselves; one puny island chain could scarcely sustain a far-flung campaign against major world powers. They lacked the know-how. Our new-found enemies had built a reputation as imitators during the 1930s but were considered quite incapable of evolving anything themselves. My father was a skipper in the P&O line who regularly visited Japan – he even did a gentle spot of spying, I later learned, drawing aspects of the Japanese docks and coastline – and he was full of stories about Japanese warships that capsized because their designers had misjudged the centre of gravity. Indeed, pictures I'd seen of Japanese warships reinforced this dangerously mistaken impression. The bigger ships in the Imperial Navy featured what we called 'pagoda' upperworks which sprouted crazily from the warships' hulls. It was a matter of record that a new Japanese cruiser *had* capsized in an unusually vicious typhoon. And one of the wiseacres on our troop-deck had worked in Japan. He talked as though the whole nation suffered from myopia.

'Their eyesight is so bad they can't fly fighter planes,' he confided. 'That's assuming the little bastards could even build them.'

Silly as it may sound today, this was a widely-held view. The imperial powers had been pushing Asians around for close on two hundred years.

Arrogant Westerners were now due for a frightful shock. Japanese invasion forces were soon making the most amazing progress in the Philippines against Douglas MacArthur, the much-vaunted American commander, and were widening an easily-established beach-head in north-east Malaya. The way the communiqués spelled it out, the isolated Anglo-Canadian garrison in Hong Kong was already in dead trouble. Soon we would learn that the Japanese were fielding an incredibly manoeuvrable fighter plane, the Mitsubishi Zero, that put our best to shame. Japanese carrier forces, fresh from their Hawaiian triumph, were backing the thrust into south-east Asia with fearful efficiency. Warships that looked absurdly top-heavy were literally blowing our best ships out of the water. But it was their squat, cycle-riding soldiery who were about to puncture the last myths of white invincibility.

I was more than a little concerned. Romantic dreams of mess nights in the Bengal Lancers were rapidly fading. There could be no question, I told myself, of the Japanese capturing Singapore – the fleet there had lately been reinforced by the battleships *Prince of Wales* and *Repulse* – and the jungles of Burma spread an impenetrable buffer between India and the war zone. But it was also becoming apparent that the army I was going to join would now face tougher opponents than the Italians or a few rebellious Arabs. I might eventually find myself (God forbid!) facing Hirohito's legions in some patch of Malayan jungle. The 1st Battalion of my old regiment, the Argylls, was doing so at this very moment. And it was perfectly clear, despite the persistent optimism of the communiqués – even a day or two into the Pacific war – that the Jocks had a fight on their hands.

Daylight found us joining an enormous convoy in an assembly zone north of Ireland. Troop and supply ships rode out a mounting gale, stretching as far as the eye could see. The angry grey ocean seemed filled with ships. There was a formidable naval escort led by the elderly battleship *Warspite* and the carrier *Ark Royal*. Presence of a seasoned fleet carrier indicated the importance of our convoy, we were told; only occasionally could one be spared for escort duties. There was also a host of cruisers and destroyers, among them the elegant county-class cruiser *Dorsetshire*, soon doomed to destruction by the Japanese.

The *Dorsetshire* was sunk by Japanese bombers in an Easter Sunday dawn attack in the waters of Ceylon – now Sri Lanka. I was not to know, watching the fated ship slicing cleanly through those heavy seas, that its final end would be filmed by someone I was yet to meet and who would slake some, at least, of my thirst for wartime adventure. He was Frank Worth, a naval combat cameraman, and if it was danger I sought, teaming up with this inspired tearaway was to provide it in abundance. But more of that later …

Our cadet draft was packed aboard one of the newest P&O luxury liners, the 23,000-ton *Strathallan*, completed just before the war began. Six

Straths had been planned on the eve of the Great Depression for the so-called Australia run. My father had sailed the route many times. The *Straths* – *Strathnaver, Stratheden, Strathallan* and so on – were considered a daring design for their day because they had only one funnel. Liners were thought unsafe and undistinguished at that time unless they had at least three.

The *Strathallan*, in her role as troop-ship, still contained some choice accommodation. This was given over to the large draft of junior officers bound, like us, for the Indian army. Below decks it was a different story. Goodness knows how many thousand men were crammed into crudely converted troop-decks which reached way down into the bilges. With every possible porthole firmly sealed to avoid light-leak at night, the smoke and the sweat ('the fug', as we called it) sent me topside periodically gasping for air.

But not for long: a circuitous northern route had been selected to outwit the Wolfpacks. Synchronised attacks by groups of German submarines were taking a heavy toll in what was being dubbed the Battle of the Atlantic, though it seemed unlikely that any U-boat commander would be able to glimpse, let alone line up, a target in the kind of weather we were experiencing. The tiny escort ships scuttling around us were bursting their way, literally, through mountainous seas. Great icy waves exploded on to our upper decks, frosting rails and rigging, as we surged head-on into the eye of a winter storm. German dive-bombers had long since severed the shorter, more salubrious sea route to India through the Mediterranean and the Suez Canal.

The convoy must have been heading towards Iceland when I was sent up on anti-aircraft watch. You'd have thought air attack posed only the remotest danger this far into the North Atlantic. The explanation given at our infrequent briefings was that a danger-spot still existed within range of the four-engined German Condor bombers but beyond reach of our land-based fighters.

It was four o'clock in the morning of our third day out and blowing an almighty gale, stiff with stinging sleet, when I climbed up the slippery steel ladder to my anti-aircraft position above the boat deck. The open steel tub contained twin Lewis guns. The possibility of an air attack on such a night seemed as unlikely to me as my chances of beating attackers off with this antique weaponry. But watch was ordered: watch was kept. The cadet I relieved had been sheltering from the wind behind the gun shield. So much for maintaining lookout. As he numbly remarked, there was nothing to see anyway. The night was black as the tomb. Funnel stays and assorted rigging creaked unseen in the bitter wind. At this height, the ship's roll took on a new and perilous dimension. Dawn broke and I watched fascinated as the sea came boiling up towards me, threatening to engulf my freezing perch.

The convoy was struggling along at reduced speed. Out on our starboard beam the bulbous black shape of the *Warspite* blundered into awesome seas. Plunging through the wind-whipped waves she looked solid, steady and invulnerable. Torrents of green water sluiced over her ice-glazed forward turrets; the few sailors in oilskins working the forecastle were strung together with lifelines. The saying was that if anyone went overboard the best the crew could do was line the rail and wave goodbye. There could be no stopping to pick anybody up. The safety of the convoy overrode everything.

Several of the attendant troopships, briefly seen through the storm-wrack, were daubed with 'dazzle' camouflage. Brilliant blocks of colour broke up their outlines in the hope that, come the moment of truth, the U-boat commanders would be put off their aim. But the newfangled radar apparatus was making optical trickery irrelevant. The once-white hull and orange upperworks of the *Strathallan*, lately repainted in Canada, were now a uniform grey. Our ship might be the last word in luxury for the privileged few but she was no place for mere troops. Live sheep are shipped more comfortably (and more carefully) these days to Saudi Arabia. Down on F-deck the atmosphere was unspeakable. Everybody was being sick. Everybody, that is, except myself. The rocking and rolling did not affect me – I kept thinking how Father would have sneered had I succumbed – and after thawing out at the end of my watch I went alone to the mess-hall and consumed an enormous brunch. The *Strathallan* had lately revictualled in Halifax, Nova Scotia. The cooks were serving real steak and onions, neither of which were obtainable at that time in Britain, and the first bananas I had seen for nearly two years.

I was enjoying a musical interlude on my upper bunk when the next burst of shocking news came through. The one luxury I had managed to stuff into my kitbag was a wind-up portable gramophone with two old 78 shellac records. One featured the aria *Pourquoi me reveiller?* and something from *The Pearl Fishers*; the other thundered out the overture to *The Meistersingers*. After a few days everyone was growing heartily sick of my limited, oft-repeated repertoire. Hoots and groans greeted the Wagnerian *ta tumpty ta!* as an urgent announcement came over the speakers.

'Attention ship's company! Attention ship's company! The Admiralty announces with regret that His Majesty's battleships *Prince of Wales* and *Repulse* have been lost in action against Japanese forces off the east Malayan coast.'

It did not seem possible. We were not to know that the admiral-in-charge, pint-sized Tom Phillips, who had to stand on a box to see over his own bridge combing, had sailed confidently north from Singapore without air cover. He was essentially a battleship admiral with little understanding, even at this stage of the war, of the efficacy of air power. His faith in battleships proved fatal. Two of the finest ships in the Royal Navy, helpless without fighter escort, were sent to the bottom by Japanese torpedo bombers in little over an hour.

The set-back aroused worries for my adventurous future. I wandered up on deck, expectation tempered by fear, to see the *Warspite* wearing her ensign at half-mast. The elderly battleship no longer looked invulnerable. No battleship would ever look that way again. The key to sea power lay with carriers like the *Ark Royal*, hull down on the horizon beneath a darkening sky.

The convoy was even bigger than I'd imagined. The weather cleared when we turned south, revealing two vast columns of stately shipping. The big, converted passenger liners, packed with troops, formed double lines which stretched far beyond the horizon.

One morning on anti-aircraft watch, perspiring for the first time in my now sun-scorched gun position, I watched the great, grey bulk of the *Queen Elizabeth* pull close abeam, decks swarming with pale-faced soldiers toasting gratefully in unfamiliar sunshine. It was comforting to sail in such distinguished company. The *QE* had only recently been completed and drafted straight to trooping. No one was going to allow this magnificent vessel, pride of the British merchant marine, to fall victim to the U-boats. Right now, sedately riding a diminishing sea, she was screened by her own private destroyer escort. The *Warspite* also kept protective station close at hand, along with a milling mob of cruisers and minor vessels. Signal bunting billowed from a dozen halliards as the escorts raced among us like worried sheepdogs. The submarine threat had grown more serious now that the German skippers were refining their tactics. Come the crunch, many of us aboard the *Strathallan* would stand little chance. Boat drill confirmed my earliest fears. It took our cadet draft a good twenty minutes to reach lifeboat stations from our overcrowded quarters in the bowels of the ship. Given a palpable hit by several well-aimed torpedoes, we would never have time to scramble up six decks through never-ending ladders and companionways.

One good thing: the threat of air attack appeared to have eased. The aircraft-carrier *Ark Royal* was no longer with us. This could only mean we had steamed beyond the mid-Atlantic killing grounds where the Condors ranged. The censors suppressed reports of the mounting losses at sea, though there was talk of dreadful carnage among our poorly-protected munitions ships and tankers.

One morning we found ourselves in calmer, warmer waters south-west of the Azores. Few of us knew this below decks; the troops were kept in customary ignorance. Apart from the occasional weather bulletin over the mess-deck loudspeakers and the crackly BBC relay at supper time, we plodded on oblivious to the world. Rumours rippled through the mess-decks – the convoy was being diverted to Singapore, to Java, to Hong Kong

– and there was even talk of an unscheduled call on the United States. I thought it best to find out for myself. I requested permission to see the captain.

'The *who*?' sneered the assistant purser, '*You* want to see the *captain*?'

I might have been in Heaven asking for a quick word with God. 'The captain,' I repeated patiently. 'He's a friend of my father's.'

'Your father?' The sneering face became a gothic gargoyle.

'My father,' I said, staring the bastard straight in the eye, 'is Captain Frank Spurr, P&O.'

I've always been a great believer in connections. They did me proud, years later, in China. Connections were useful in this case within the Peninsular & Oriental Steamship Company. A P&O captain was someone of consequence. The P&O was a snobbish, hierarchical outfit. It considered itself a cut above your common shipping companies. Its officers once applied to the Admiralty for permission to wear swords with their dress uniforms.

'Certainly,' came the tongue-in-cheek reply. 'But your swords must be worn on the *right* side.' The idea was quietly shelved.

The P&O was conscious of its role as a lifeline of Empire. For nearly a century its ships had been the chosen conveyance of British pro-consuls eager to assume the white man's burden in Egypt, the Indian Raj and further east. It was this haughty clientele who coined the slang word 'Posh', an acronym for Port Out, Starboard Home, to define the ultimate symbol of status among status-conscious colonials. Before the advent of air-conditioning the choicest berths were always to be found on the port or starboard sides of the ship, coming or going, during passage through the furnace-hot Red Sea.

'*Your* father's a P&O captain?' The assistant purser scowled doubtfully at my lance-corporal's uniform. Picking up the phone he called the Chief Officer.

'So you're one of Frank Spurr's brood!' bawled the Chief Officer, a stout red-faced man, slightly deaf, who looked remarkably like my father. 'Been boozing with him many a time.' He rewarded me with a knowing wink. 'Lucky he isn't in this damn ship. All I ever do is poke my head down blocked lavatories. No job for a sailor.'

My father then commanded one of the P&O freighters transporting munitions. It would shortly be sunk beneath him by E-boats in the English Channel. The old chap survived, but only just. Father's senior colleague, the captain of the *Strathallan*, turned out to be a scholarly man who collected butterflies and stamps. The war with Japan irritated him no end. It had interrupted his regular trips to Yokohama.

'Great pity,' he complained over lunch in his cabin. 'I was finally getting into some marvellous post-Meiji stuff.' He was referring to stamps. As a schoolboy collector I knew what he was talking about.

'This voyage seems to be going on for ever,' the captain later confided over his private chart table. He was doing clever things with rulers and dividers. 'Been wandering all over the place to keep out of trouble. Way up past the *Titanic* route. After all this time we're not even into Freetown.'

The captain assured us later that we should make Freetown for Christmas. 'Provided we don't suffer any more shocks, that is. Reckon we still haven't got the measure of those wretched Japs,' he said.

The main port of Sierra Leone, on the West African coast, Freetown was the place where Graham Greene then worked for British Intelligence. I cannot think of anything else unusual about the place. It was a frequently-used refuelling stop for convoys taking the Cape route to India after long evasive sorties into the remoter stretches of the North Atlantic.

The Japanese army had lately been described by the Associated Press correspondent in Manila as 'an ill-uniformed, untrained mass of young boys between fifteen and eighteen years old, equipped with small-calibre guns and driven forward by desperate determination to advance or die'. Assessments of this sort, by supposed experts, were meant to reassure the Western world. It was rapidly becoming apparent, however, that these same youthful soldiers were a cut above the 70th Argylls, if our desperately worded communiqués were any guide; the 'Banzai Boys', as one of our jokers called them, were presently making unbelievable headway both in the Philippines and against the British garrison in Hong Kong.

The weather grew so hot during our second week at sea that we were ordered into tropical gear. There was a sense of excitement, of delicious anticipation, as we unpacked the light-weight clothing most of us would be wearing for at least the next five years. We looked a dreadful sight. Our khaki cotton shirts were cut too large. Our long, baggy shorts had huge turn-ups that hung down, when unbuttoned, well below the knees. Capping this ludicrous attire was a moulded cork sun helmet (the infamous colonial 'topee') worn at all times, by order, out of doors. Then current mythology insisted that anyone mad enough to go out bare-headed 'neath the blazing sun was a cert for sunstroke. We had all seen a chilling sequence in the pre-war film *The Four Feathers* where poor old Ralph Richardson was struck down and blinded in the Sudan for pursuing his reconnaissance hatless at high noon. Noël Coward sang comic songs about 'Mad Dogs and Englishmen', but to us innocents abroad, sallying forth bare-headed invited trouble.

Naturally, I ignored (or forgot) the rules. So excited was I on Christmas Day, entering steamy Freetown, that I rushed up on deck dangerously uncovered. I was frantic to get my first view of foreign soil. As a boy in Essex I had watched the boat-train clattering past to Harwich and the Hook of Holland. It was with bitter envy that I glimpsed the privileged passengers at lamp-lit tables in the Pullman car. Throughout my youth I had ached to break beyond the boring bounds of suburban Britain, beyond seed cake at the rectory and Wurlitzer nights in darkest Odeon.

It's impossible today to recapture that initial sense of achievement as the first spit of alien land slid into view. There wasn't much to see, come to think of it – no more than a sliver of muddy soil graced by one small, tatty palm. The harbour, the distant houses, the backdrop of jungle-covered hills hid behind a curtain of depressing tropical mist. But never mind: this wasn't Essex, England, anymore.

Someone slapped me on the backside. An officer behind me gesticulated angrily beneath an enormous sun helmet. It was a moment before I realised he was pointing to my naked head. Rambling on about the lethal effects of sunstroke, he sent me below double-quick for my forgotten topee. I dashed down to F-deck and snatched the ugly thing from my junk-stacked bunk just as an announcement broke through the Christmas carols. Halfway back topside I realised what I'd heard. There'd been another unthinkable happening. The British garrison in Hong Kong had surrendered to the Japanese.

I can't honestly say I've had *that* many miserable Christmases. The season of goodwill and, occasionally, peace, is the one time of year I try to be truly cheerful. And I expect everyone around me to act that way even if they don't feel it.

Elated I might have been, making my first landfall overseas, but cheerful I was not on Christmas Day, 1941. I was deeply disturbed by the news from Hong Kong. The Anglo-Canadian garrison had surrendered to the Japanese after little more than two weeks' fighting. The poor devils had done their utmost, we now well know, though in those days their heroism was seriously underrated. The facts as we saw them, swinging round a buoy in Freetown harbour, were that British soldiers – the best, I'd been brought up to believe, bar none in the whole wide world – had given in to a bunch of cartoon characters no one could be expected to take seriously. The one consolation, perhaps, was that the Americans in the Philippines weren't doing all that well either. Their flamboyant commander, Douglas MacArthur, had quickly been bottled up in a minuscule peninsula that juts out into Manila Bay. Still, what could one expect from a bunch of Yanks? Technicians they might be – bankers and movie czars – but fighters? The doughboys couldn't punch their way out of a paper-bag. Or so we told ourselves.

Another depressant was Freetown itself. The fault in this case was probably mine. I suppose I'd been expecting too much. The wide West African anchorage scarcely fitted my romantic concept of your typical tropical lagoon. The harbour was muddy, awash with debris. The tin-roofed townships straggling along the water's edge looked singularly uninviting. Not that there was any chance of exploring further. Shore leave was ruled out. We were due to sail immediately the fuel tanks had been topped up.

It was blisteringly hot. I had never known heat like it. The sticky, steamy, sauna-like heat I was to endure off and on for much of the rest of my adult life was initially a sharp, physical shock. Somehow I never grew used to it. The temperature in our quarters deep on F-deck topped the one-hundred mark. That's close to 40°C in this metric age. Humidity hovered around 95 per cent. A kind of cooling was attempted: fetid air was pumped in through ducts from the malodorous outdoors. The thermometer remained obstinately unmoved. Reduced to melting point, there was nothing for it but to scuttle topside and spend our days and nights on open deck. Definitely not my idea of Christmas.

The one bright spot in Freetown was the armada of African canoes that swarmed around our troop-ship selling bananas and oranges. Tropical fruits had disappeared from Britain since the beginning of the war and the Freetown fruit was especially welcome now that we had eaten all the steak and other luxuries the *Strathallan* had picked up in Canada. Turkeys were reserved for the officers in the first-class accommodation. So was a dwindling stock of liquor, fine wines and champagne. The rest of us received a celebration lunch of the greasy stew that had become our daily fare, washed down with one bottle of lukewarm Canadian beer. Men mutinied for a damned sight less, I'm sure, aboard the *Bounty*.

Someone organised the inevitable concert party, staged on a hold-top in the forecastle. Everyone attended. The various India-bound drafts included a number of actors and vaudeville players now in uniform and one of the cadets in our draft had acted a bit part in *Knight without Armour*, the Marlene Dietrich epic about the Russian Revolution. He'd appeared for one minute as a telegraphist in Siberia blurting out: 'The war is over!' It was the only line they gave him. And in the end, I think, they dubbed it over with someone else's voice instead. The same man now put on a far lengthier concert performance, reciting a lewd monologue attributed to Noël Coward about a female member of the aristocracy who turned to prostitution.

'It nearly broke the family's heart when Lady Jane became a tart ... [shrieks of crude male laughter] ... And so to save the family's face ... and all that goes with such disgrace ... they bought her the most *exclusive* beat ... on the southern side of Jermyn Street ...'

The chief officer, sitting with the colonel in charge of troops, laughed until he cried. It was just his kind of show. I thought it was awful. The acts included a stand-up comic who kept prat-falling on the makeshift stage, a fumbling conjurer who became famous on post-war television, and a transvestite chorus-line whose boobs kept falling out and rolling into the footlights. 'Les Girls' were upholstered, as you might have guessed, with oranges.

Table Mountain loomed up one humid dawn. The weather had grown noticeably hotter despite the temperate latitude. South of the Equator, I was amazed to learn, people were in the middle of *summer*. The mountain disappeared again, scotching rumours that we would go ashore at

Capetown. We sailed on instead to Durban where I first set foot on foreign soil. It was an impressive initiation. Durban looked wonderful. There was no blackout, no shortages; evidence on every hand told of a splendid lifestyle. Splendid, that is, for the whites. Our welcome was slightly muted. Australian reinforcements had just passed through bound for the Western Desert and Tobruk. The bars were all closed, pending massive repairs. My mother was Australian-born but up to that time I had never met any honest to goodness Ockers. They were a tough lot, Durban folk said ruefully, mighty hard fighters and mighty hard drinkers.

'But they didn't bother us girls,' a pretty young nymph advised me. 'All they wanted was beer and a punch-up.'

Ann started chatting me up on the beach. She looked deliciously brown. So did the other white girls lolling decoratively around. They seemed bored out of their minds, only too ready to talk to a young soldier with whitewashed face and rumpled tropical uniform.

'I'll get the houseboy to press your clothes,' Ann offered kindly. She led me down the empty beach. The only blacks we saw carried bottles of fresh water to wash the white folk's feet.

'The blacks don't seem to like swimming,' I remarked in all my innocence.

'They swim all right,' she said. 'But not on this beach. This beach is zoned for the BAAS. Kaffirs aren't allowed.'

We were close to her house. I was telling her comic stories about my days in the Argylls. A little Indian boy scout was approaching us. The boy's hat blew off. I ran over and retrieved it from the gutter. A fat white policeman strolled up. 'You shouldn't do that, son.' The man spoke a peculiar kind of English. 'Whites don't fraternise with the coloureds. This is South Africa, y'know.'

Ann laughed indulgently. 'You *have* got a lot to learn,' she said. 'You'll get quite a shock in India.'

Anti-aircraft watch was abolished directly we left Durban. An announcement declared the danger of air attack finally over. The Japanese would never reach the Indian Ocean. It was too far from their home islands. Again we had much to learn; despite the débâcle at Pearl Harbor and the almost unbelievable loss of the *Prince of Wales* and the *Repulse*, our commanders were still underestimating the mobility and efficiency of the Imperial Japanese Navy. The pep talks we were given predicted that the main Japanese battle fleet would shortly be meeting its first real opposition. A combined Dutch, British and American task force had assembled in Javanese waters to halt the enemy's southward drive. There was more good news. According to the communiqués, the advancing Japanese land forces had been blocked by Indian troops at the Slim River, halfway down the Malayan peninsula. The day our convoy left South Africa the new regional supremo, General Sir Archie Wavell, had flown to Singapore to prepare the counter-attack that would throw these impertinent Asiatics back into the sea. The man who had humbled Mussolini's warriors would have no difficulty pulling off the same trick against the Japanese.

It may sound odd, but I missed my perch in the upperworks abaft the funnel. For close on a month I had cleaned and oiled the twin Lewis machine-guns – never firing them, even in practice; ammunition was too scarce – and had leaned back against the gun-shield enjoying the sight of sea and ships and the smell of clean, salt air. I had escaped torture. My fellow cadets were roughed up by Father Neptune in that ridiculous Equator-crossing ceremony. Being the youngest member of our draft I'd have been a prime target had I not been on watch.

Officer cadets we might be, but so far our draft had received precious little of the officer and gentleman treatment. The final indignity for many was the order to sweep the decks, causing some to fly into hysterical tantrums. No one would deny that the longueurs of the voyage were taking their toll of our tempers. Peer pressure compelled me to pack up my portable gramophone. One more blast of *The Meistersingers* might have consigned me to the sharks. The boy on the bunk below me, a young Sherwood Forester called Frank Schofield, played jazz trumpet. He too accepted a modicum of restraint. A burly Mancunian ex-policeman threatened to shove the instrument down his throat. Nearby bridge players, led by a sergeant of the Coldstream Guards, quarrelled, with increasing ferocity.

After lunch one day the captain took me out on to the bridge. An Indian lascar was at the wheel, a cadet helping him to keep station astern of the *Queen Elizabeth*. The giant liner towered over the rest of the convoy, a veritable whale among minnows. Over on the starboard wing of the bridge the watch officer was struggling to acknowledge flag signals from *Warspite*.

'Haven't seen so much ruddy bunting since the Coronation!' the harassed officer complained, thumbing through the signal book. 'Oh hell, there goes another bloody load of washing!'

Strings of brightly-coloured flags were fluttering from the battleship, going up and down with surprising speed. Those who could read them – with or without the signal book – knew that a course change was being ordered. Never would I have guessed that within a year I too would be conversing in this peculiarly nautical language.

'Our escort could easily beat off the Japs,' the captain nodded confidently towards *Warspite* and her untiring attendants. 'This is the strongest force I've ever sailed with; we're protected by a lot of firepower.'

It was the wrong kind of firepower, though none of us then realised it. The Japanese strike against Pearl Harbor had made battleships redundant. The key from now on would be air power. Ships of the line had become sitting ducks without carrier support. Lessons from the sinking of the *Prince of Wales* and the *Repulse* had not yet been thoroughly absorbed and within weeks, a Japanese carrier task-force would be terrorising the Bay of Bengal (on the other side of India), driving *Warspite* and her surviving squadron back to the coasts of eastern Africa. There they would shelter, helplessly, for the few nerve-wracking months that the Imperial Navy ruled the waves.

January 1942 marked the end of my childish innocence. While it would be absurd to suggest that I was any more ignorant than your average, present-day teenager, I was conditioned, misled, even blinded by the hoary old myths most members of the British public genuinely shared. Those myths may sound laughable today: I recall them solely to emphasise how much our perceptions have changed this past half-century.

Of all of them, the one myth that now sounds silliest was our belief that the United States would never be a superpower. It's easy, mind you, to sneer with hindsight. Flamboyant antics in the pre-war US Congress, where isolationism reigned supreme, obscured the latent strength of the Americans. The United States had become, in fact, the predominant force on the world stage since 1916 when the British government, appalled at the slaughter on the Somme, aware that the treasures of the Victorian era were nearing depletion, was forced to go cap in hand to Washington and Wall Street and beg for help. The US return to isolationism after the frustrations of Versailles maintained the flawed illusion of apparent British might. The true weakness of Britain had lately been exposed by the fall of France. Fresh shocks would shortly come in the Far East.

None of this was immediately apparent as we reached the end of our Odyssey. The nearness of India roused everyone to frenzied activity. Shaking off our shipboard torpor, sublimating the tensions of a month of close-quarter living, we leaped into gymnastics. The polishing of boots and brasses began for a major on-deck inspection. Parading in the dazzling sunlight, we looked downright shambolic in those absurd helmets and ungainly shirts. The unpressed, turned-up shorts overlapped our pink-kneed, half-stockinged legs. But we were keen ... mad keen. The weather had turned strangely cooler. We were not to know that Bombay, our port of disembarkation, was luxuriating in its brief cool season. The temperature in January can occasionally drop to 10°C 'which brings the inhabitants out on to the streets', to quote one home-spun wit, 'swathed in furs, with charcoal burners slung between their knees'.

We were as yet ignorant of all things Indian. History classes at my school had touched on the exploits of Robert, Baron Clive of Plassey – delicately, as if he were an embarrassment – and I'd read lurid stories by Victorian boys' writers like Henty about the Mutiny and the Black Hole of Calcutta. Modern India was largely a blank. There was supposed to be a chap called Gandhi whom Churchill had dubbed 'a half-naked fakir'. But what was a fakir? I hadn't the faintest clue.

What knowledge I had was gleaned from Louis Blomfield's *The Rains Came*. A dog-eared copy had passed and repassed around our mess-desk.

The novel had been written, the blurb informed us, after a six-month visit to the Raj. It reflected the modish views of American liberals who abhorred British rule and patronised the Indians. I thought the book was brilliant. Months would pass before I realised the author had latched on to every imaginable cliché to produce a Hollywood fairy-tale.

The film, starring Tyrone Power, was as unbelievable as the book. All Indians wore turbans and huge beards which made it look like the land was inhabited exclusively by Sikhs. Unlikely bit-players said, 'Salaam, *say-hib*' and grovelled demeaningly to anyone in authority. The only half-human character in the book was an Englishwoman who made love on the floor in a Maharajah's palace. That sounded promising. I prayed someone like her would still be around reserving a little of the action for a soon-to-be-launched subaltern in the Bengal Lancers.

We reached Bombay on 8 January 1942 and anchored in the roadstead. It was too far out to see much besides the Arab dhows with their triangular white sails beating gently past. Small boats besieged us, offering a range of fresh fruit; I got my first taste of custard apples, guavas and pomelos, passed up in a shallow, rattan basket by small boys who dived alongside to retrieve the last of our English pennies.

An announcement over the loudspeakers summoned the cadet draft to the first-class smoking-room. It was a huge place, filled with card tables and restricted until now to the officers. A stout major in beautifully starched drill uniform introduced himself as Adjutant of the Officers Training School, Bangalore. He looked us over with sympathetic eye.

'I am here to welcome you to India,' he declared, 'And to welcome you to the King Emperor's Army. Here you will find an entirely different life. Some will like it. Some will not. That's up to you. But let me be perfectly straight about one thing: the Indian Army will be the most serious challenge of your lives. I wish you the very best of luck. My pleasure will be watching you become officers ... and *gentlemen*.'

It was late afternoon before we docked. For the past two tantalising days our overcrowded troop-ship had been swinging at anchor in the outer reaches of Bombay harbour. From there we could just make out the misty shape of the Gateway to India, the extravagant waterfront welcome for a previous King Emperor who had come here decades ago to receive the homage of the Raj. The *Strathallan* had scarcely secured alongside when news came through that Japanese troops had stormed the British defences on the River Slim, central Malaya, and were pressing southwards to Singapore. The 11th Indian Division had been holding the River Slim line. It was 'pulling back in good order', according to the official communiqué. The formula for concealing military disaster was becoming unpleasantly familiar. Soon we would be hearing nothing else. The censors glossed over the fact that in the River Slim battle, the 11th Division had been decimated.

Members of the Indian Army cadet draft were allowed ashore on a four-hour pass. We were condemned to sleep aboard the *Strathallan* one more night, then disembark and entrain the following day for the Officers' Training School in Bangalore. None of us had ever heard of Bangalore. The young chap who bunked below me, Frank Schofield, spotted it in a school atlas. It seemed a long haul from Bombay; way off in the south of India.

Troop officers issued the direst warnings before contact was permitted with Indian soil. Top of their official 'Don't' list was *no* sex with the natives. Penicillin was not yet freely available and we were led to believe that virulent strains of venereal disease were rampant everywhere. Other scary prohibitions included *no* drinking unboiled water – 'whisky kills the germs, old boy' – and absolutely *no* consumption of fruit that couldn't first be peeled. The repercussions were said to be dreadful. Then there were my own personal phobias. Especially about snakes: cobras and kraits writhed deep in my subconscious, along with imaginary swarms of poisonous bugs, vampire bats and such-like unmentionables. The Indian nights would long be alive with my unfounded fears.

The sun had set when I descended the gangway – still crowned by that irrelevant sun helmet – and stepped on to the grubby Bombay dockside, cautious as any lunar astronaut. A minuscule step it might have been for mankind, avoiding greasy puddles on the wharf, but for me it was an enormous leap into the future. It was the launch-pad into an obsession with Asia that would enslave me the rest of my adult life ...

The first thing I noticed was the smell. It was an unique smell, more intriguing than unpleasant. The aroma of oil and cordage, the kind you come across in any port, overlaid by whiffs of cooking-oil and spices which sprang from the food stalls huddled outside the dockyard gates. Men and women in unfamiliar dress tended a variety of portable kitchens, hawking snacks I could not for the life of me identify. There was a strong, overlying scent of perfume, which must have been jasmine. Girls wearing the white jasmine flowers in their hair fluttered past in multi-coloured saris like clouds of chattering butterflies. Out in the teeming streets impressions were less romantic, though. I was mobbed by beggars. Men, women and children, all ragged, many horribly deformed, quickly snatched every coin of small change, the strangely-shaped *annas* and *pice* I had managed to obtain on board, and were still pressing around, piteously wailing, while I feebly apologised for my further lack of funds.

A heavily tanned British sergeant burst through the beggarly ranks. His crisply laundered uniform shamed the crumbled clothes in which I'd come ashore.

'*Jao! Jao!*' he bellowed at the clamant throng. They fell back sullenly.

Turning to me, the sergeant added, 'When you've got your knees brown you'll give these bastards a clip round the ear!'

He strode off leaving me aghast at his lack of manners. This was surely no way to address the King Emperor's loyal subjects. Relations between the rulers and the ruled in India were not as genial as I had imagined.

'British imperialist!' somebody yelled at the sergeant's retreating back. The yells came from a bespectacled student about my own age. A green, white and saffron badge was pinned on to his long, shabby coat. I was as yet unable to identify the colours of the Indian National Congress. 'Imperialist pigs! All of you!' the young man kept shouting. The spectacles slid down his nose as he jumped up and down trembling with rage. The more excited he became, the more he attracted my attention. A crowd closed in around us.

'You, you,' the student spluttered, tapping my chest with an accusing finger. 'All of you ... robbers, exploiters ... imperialists!'

The poor chap seemed to be exaggerating. My reasons for coming to India might not have been strictly altruistic, but robbery and exploitation were not among them. I had voyaged voluntarily to Bombay, pledged to defend freedom – and the Empire. The two were to me synonymous. Naïve it might sound, but my adolescent ignorance was shaped by Hollywood, Kipling and the *Boy's Own Paper*. The thought that any Indian could reject the benefits of British rule had never entered my mind. Some years before, while still at school, I had joined the crowds in London to cheer King George VI in his coronation coach. Close behind the monarch rode splendid cavalrymen and bejeweled princes shipped in from India to represent a grateful Raj. So what could this fellow be going on about?

Vague memories stirred of paragraphs in the British press. There had been limited agitation against Britain by members of an opposition group, the Something or Other Congress, in the two restless decades since the First World War. The malcontents were dismissed in Britain as 'a handful of hooligans'. The same, telling phrase is still used by tyrannies today. One of the leading agitators I recalled was a man called Nehru. The blighter should have known better, my father always said, because he had been given an English education. He'd actually been taught cricket at Harrow. Father's political views were brutally basic. Towards closing time in our local pub he could be heard blaming the world's woes on 'Yids, Nigs and RCs.' Or 'those of the Jewish persuasion, blacks and Catholics', as we would put it in our more enlightened age. The old man sincerely believed it. Now I was encountering something entirely different, standing at the kerbside of a Bombay street, listening to the out-pourings of this excitable student. The young man's views were outrageous. He was waxing so indignant and, as it seemed to me, so inaccurate, that I felt urged to argue.

'Hold on a moment, sir,' I said. The chap might be deranged. Without careful handling he could fly right off the handle. 'If you'll pardon my saying so,' I spoke slowly and pompously as if to a retarded person, 'I cannot help feeling you are under a misapprehension. I am neither here to rob nor to exploit you. I am here to defend you from fascism.'

I know, it sounds crazy today. But back in 1941 I genuinely knew no better. Human beings can be extraordinarily stupid. It was another time, another place, and, more especially, another me. Troop officers had warned against sexual cohabitation but failed to mention the folly of indulging in political debate, solo, in downtown Bombay. The spot I had inadvertently selected, the Flora fountain, was in those days a favourite venue for protesters. It was here the Indian nationalists expressed their antipathy to the Raj and to the sahibs who ran it.

My reference to fascism stopped the student dead in his tracks. His eyes bulged. He appeared on the verge of apoplexy; writing with hindsight I now realise he thought I was taking the mickey.

'*From* fascism!' the student shrieked. Turning to the crowd, he babbled something I did not understand. People nodded in agreement. The student rushed on into a lengthy speech. People cheered. Several young men jostled me in an unfriendly manner. They grabbed my arms while the student brandished an English-language newspaper under my nose. Headlines proclaimed the defeat of 'fascist forces' in Malaya by the 'liberating' Japanese.

'*Fascism*!' screamed the student. 'Japan will destroy *British* fascism!'

It was my turn to be indignant. This was barefaced treason. Such nonsense demanded an answer.

'You can't talk like that. You don't know when you're well off,' I blustered. 'Our people rescued India from chaos – ' It was the usual British apologia but I did not get much further. The crowd closed on me with a furious roar. Fists beat me to the ground. Police whistles shrilled and a band of men in strange blue uniforms – braided shirts, shorts and puttees – rushed to my rescue, laying about them with long bamboo staves. A British police officer helped me to my feet.

'What the hell d'you think you're doing?' he demanded. Suspiciously he sniffed my breath. 'Sober too, but why are you picking a fight?'

'I was discussing politics,' I replied with all the dignity at my command. My shirt was torn. The top of my sun helmet was stove right in.

'Discussing *what*?' cried the officer. He stepped back a pace, looked me up and down. 'I see,' he said finally. 'A new boy. Well there's one thing you'll find out when you've got your mucking knees brown. You don't talk politics. Not with the bloody *wogs*.'

The who? I had been in India for one hour. Already I was grappling with the vocabulary of colonialism.

Around breakfast time we boarded the troop train for Bangalore. A large steam locomotive with red-painted driving wheels hauled the specially-built khaki carriages – 'other ranks, British, for the use of' – on to a siding beyond the loading cranes. Without regret we extricated ourselves from the maw of the *Strathallan*, our home for the past four weeks, and staggered across the wharf loaded with the most unlikely paraphernalia. My own kit comprised underwear and uniforms, tropical and winter, heavy-issue socks, towels and blankets, plus an expensive pair of brown brogues and an officer's raincoat which proved too heavy ever to be worn, purchased at a snooty store in the West End of London, and obtained with the loan Mother managed to wring from an unfriendly bank manager. Along with that went several Hemingway novels, Steinbeck's *Grapes of Wrath* (I'd given up trying to decipher Robert Burns), my precious portable gramophone and its two shellac records. *The Meistersingers* would yet again belt out into the Indian night.

The bulk of the stuff bulged through the top of my kitbag and seemed to weigh a ton. The *Strathallan* might have been uncomfortable as a trooper but I felt twinges of regret when the news finally came through that she'd been sunk during the North Africa landings.

It was chaos down on the dock. Our draft of five hundred officer cadets was hardly a homogeneous military unit. Everyone held the same, tentative rank, fostering a degree of egalitarianism that made orderly manoeuvre difficult. We were eventually marshalled in alphabetical order, arbitrarily divided into platoon-sized groups, and introduced to the sergeants who would shepherd us through Officers' Training School. There was no such thing as an OTS in Britain. Potential officers went to OCTU: an Officer Cadet Training Unit. The difference was subtle but profound. Those who went to OCTU knew their chances of ever becoming an officer were no better than evens. Out in India it was *assumed* you were already an officer. And you'd certainly be one after three months' training.

'Gentlemen, permit me to introduce myself.'

The speaker was a short, stout man with sergeant's stripes on his immaculate drill uniform. He had one of those pudgy Irish faces inlaid with flecks of red; the veined bulbous nose would have lit the way into any doctor's surgery.

'The name is Loosely. Sergeant Timothy Loosely. And I'll be in charge of you until you graduate in April.'

Sergeant Loosely peered pleasantly at the thirty of us cadets whose names began with the letter 'S'. We must have looked a mangy old mob but the sergeant did not bat an eyelid. He'd seen it all before.

'You, sir' – he pointed at me – 'what's your name?'

'Spurr, sergeant,' I replied.

'Well, Mr Spurr,' the sergeant smiled. 'You need a new shirt.' The one I was wearing had been ripped in the political contretemps of the previous night.

'It got torn,' I said lamely.

Everyone laughed. The whole draft knew about my brief encounter by the Flora Fountain.

'Ah yes, you're the politician,' the sergeant observed mildly. 'A subject you would do well to keep clear of. I trust there'll be no more arguments with the *wogs*?'

That word again: the same obnoxious term of contempt for the King Emperor's loyal subjects. I remembered the colonel's advice on leaving the Argylls: 'Keep your bowels open and your mouth shut'. It was time, I reckoned, to shut up.

'Not to worry, Mr Spurr,' the sergeant went on. He sounded like a butler glossing over his master's most minor peccadillo. I couldn't believe my ears; no sergeant had ever spoken to me like this before. 'The tailor will soon fix you up, sir.' He dazzled the whole group of us with a mighty set of flashing dentures. 'The tailor will fix you *all* up. Pardon me for suggesting that you badly need it.'

The tropical gear issued in Aldershot had not been improved by the primitive laundry facilities aboard the ship. We looked as if we'd slept in our clothes – as some of us had – and smelled like we hadn't bathed in a week, which wasn't far from the truth. Hordes of coolies overran the wharf to relieve us of our baggage. They would have taken our money as well but the sergeant began yelling in what we came to know as Hindustani. It was the *lingua franca* between rulers and the ruled.

'It is unfortunate,' Sergeant Loosely apologised, ushering us aboard the train, 'but there are too many of you on this draft to travel the way you should. This troop-train, I'm afraid, is for BORs.'

It was another expression commonplace to the Raj. BORs were British Other Ranks: it distinguished them from the IORs, the Indian Other Ranks. Other ranks – that is, enlisted men – we soon learned, whether British or Indian – were way down the totem pole.

'But don't worry,' the sergeant added breezily, taking a small coupé marked 'Sergeants Only'. 'Once you reach Bangalore you'll be treated like gentlemen.'

We did not seem to be doing too badly already. The coolies had stowed our kit and were now unravelling bedding rolls with clean sheets, blankets and pillows on the carriage bunks. Waiters in white turbans and flowing white robes handed out lunch-boxes of cold chicken, hard-boiled eggs and grey, sour bread. Barbers appeared brandishing frothy brushes and awesome razors. There was plenty of time, we were told, for a trackside haircut and shave.

'Make sure they sterilise those bloody razors,' Sergeant Loosely advised. 'Otherwise you'll get God-knows-what skin complaints.' You could see he enjoyed telling the new boys to watch for unseen horrors.

A man put a basket on the ground and coaxed out a cobra with his wailing pipe. It was the first time I had ever seen such a thing. Maybe someone would perform the Indian rope trick? Women with pan-stained mouths sold us baskets of miniature bananas. Small boys clamoured to shine our boots. They grabbed our small change and melted away as the train trundled tardily out of the docks.

There's a special magic about travelling by an Indian train. The railways that reach from the Himalayas to Cape Comorin have long been an institution, almost a ceremonial part of the Indian way of life. And why not? The routes built by the British to consolidate imperial rule ended up unifying, transforming and pretty well creating the present-day republic.

There are plenty of things I've done in my misspent life – like wearing a kilt, studying Chinese painting, hearing Gigli in the Teatro Romano, seeing the Taj Mahal by moonlight, catching the first flush of dawn across Kanchenjunga or the Yangtse Gorge – all things I've done and never regretted. Yet pride of place in my memory still goes to crossing India by rail. I can picture my first Indian train journey as if it were yesterday, coupling on the extra locomotive on the outskirts of Bombay. Drivers in battered leather caps leaning out of their cabs shouting gibberish, lit by the flare from their coal-fired furnaces, while barefoot track staff leaped like death-defying picadors to thrust coupling hooks between the converging buffers, and several men in topees and dark-glasses (the eternal badge of Asian authority) ran pompously about waving flags and blowing whistles. Two locomotives were needed to help us negotiate the Western Ghats, the steep mountain chain that overlooks this part of India.

We pulled out of Bombay, through miles of suburbs, past satanic mills and factories, and inlets speckled with fishing craft. Out on the coastal plain farmers pecked at the soil with inadequate wooden ploughs. Groups of drably-dressed women swung scoops of irrigation water on to the fields. Children frantically shooed the cows that wandered, chewing mindlessly, into the path of our train. Slowly the pictures begin to blur: the first of so many farming villages ... a huddle of thatched-roof cottages, dung pats drying on the whitewashed walls ... oxen hauling water from a farmyard well ... the occasional temple dome peeping through the trees ... peasants winnowing grain by tossing it into the wind ... tiny shrines daubed with red, bedecked with yellow flowers ... washermen beating the clothes on stream side rocks.

It was late afternoon when we reached Poona. The Indians spell it differently these days – *Pune*, I think – perhaps because the old name recalls too much of a best-forgotten past. Poona was the largest British Army base in western India. The comedian Spike Milligan was brought up there as a child – his father was a BOR. The town was notorious in the dying days of the Raj as the breeding-ground for red-faced blimps. Cartoonists created mustachioed colonels declaring: 'Gad, sir, I'd horse-whip you – if I still had my horse!' The place was eminently forgettable, yet it remained well-known in Britain. The joker in the music hall had only to say: 'When I was in Poona!' and people fell about laughing. British Army slang was particularly marked by a century and a half of garrison duties in such a city. Tommies all over the world brewed up their cups of '*char*' (tea), talked of a '*cushy*' (soft) posting, dropped a '*gooli*' (a bollock, that is, made a mistake) and sat on the *bungalow verandah* in *pyjamas* – all words acquired in India.

'We've made a *bando* here for a *pukkah* late *tiffin*,' Sergeant Loosely announced. We were busy stretching our legs on the Poona platform. I did not quite know what he meant but, as it turned out, an excellent late luncheon had indeed been arranged. Bearers in loose-fitting green *ashkans* (jackets) served a light curry in our compartments. The food arrived on brass trays called *talis*, and the various ingredients – rice pillau, lentils and mutton – were contained in separate brass bowls or *katoris*.

The bearer who brought my tray offered to show me how to eat rice with my fingers. There is quite an art to it, rolling the rice into a ball and popping it into your mouth with a flick of the thumb, but the sergeant cut him short.

'Your job isn't to eat *Wog*-style, Mr Spurr,' he sighed. 'You've come to India to teach these buggers table-manners.'

The Mogul emperor Akhbar, first setting eyes on Kashmir, is said to have exclaimed: 'If there be paradise on earth, it is here, it is here, it is here!' I said much the same on seeing Bangalore, though not in the same poetic Urdu. It was forgivable hyperbole. Anyone acquainted with the former administrative capital of Mysore state in central southern India, knows it as a perfectly ordinary town. Like Calcutta and Bombay, Bangalore is largely a product of the British Raj. Unlike either of those other great cities, its origins are more bureaucratic than commercial. The real value of Bangalore, as far as the British were concerned, was its altitude. It lies mid-way across the Indian peninsula, on the lower part of the Deccan plateau, 949 metres (or 3,113 feet) above sea-level. High enough, that is, to provide a cool refuge from the sweltering coastal plains, though not as cold as places higher still, the so-called 'hill stations'. It was this coolness that enabled the sahibs to enjoy a healthier lifestyle in the days before air-conditioning when the death toll among the foreign community was still depressingly high.

The air was positively chilly the morning our troop-train drew into Bangalore. The auxiliary locomotive had been uncoupled at Poona after hauling us up the slopes of the Western Ghats. A cold night had followed our lunch halt at the notorious old garrison town, and then came an interminable, dusty day, chugging through fields of new-sown wheat, mustard and oil-seed, before the sun shot itself down in flames again and left us shivering in our skimpy tropical gear. The bridge school pulled blankets around their shoulders and entered their umpteenth hour of play. The rest of us clustered around the periphery, waiting for the bickering to start.

'For God's sake, partner, how can you go four no trumps on a hand like that?' It was enough to put you off bridge for life.

One of the more learned cadets, swotting up on his Urdu (the official language of the Indian Army), got off at a night stop to try out his phrases on the locals.

'*Kitna dur Bangalore hai?*' he faltered. The locals shook their heads. They spoke only Telegu.

'You want to know how far Bangalore is, my dear fellow?'

The speaker was a neatly-dressed Dravidian with an Oxford accent. He wore a blue college blazer and grey slacks. His flashing white teeth would have qualified for any toothpaste advertisement.

'From here I'd say it's about as far as Evesham to Edinburgh,' the man went on. 'As an extraordinarily slow crow might fly.'

Sergeant Timothy Loosely brought a strong whiff of alcohol on to the platform. He glowered as the well-spoken Indian vanished into the night.

'Familiar bastard,' he sneered. 'It's the educated ones I can't stand.'

Nobody slept much that night. It was too cold. And we were too excited. Frank Schofield fished the trumpet out of his pack and belched a few quavering bars of *I wish I could Shimmy like my Sister Kate*. He was brow-beaten into silence by a chorus of complaints. The opening burst of *The Meistersingers* on my portable gramophone was dispatched with equally short shrift.

'You two deserve each other,' one of the bridge players snarled. He spoke truer than he knew.

We disembarked at dawn with stiffened limbs and chattering teeth in the cantonment station. The word 'cantonment', derived from the French, originally meant a place for quartering troops. In British India it meant a great deal more. The rulers of the Raj could never bring themselves to live in the old Indian cities. Accommodation was cramped, and sanitation and plumbing were practically non-existent. The sahibs preferred to build their own adjacent ghettos where the streets were wide, the housing spacious and the taps ran near-potable water. Barracks naturally went up in these areas, as did the splendid club houses for socially acceptable residents. These, we soon learned, were an exceptionally exclusive élite.

Buses transported us to the Officers' Training School. Anywhere else we'd have been loaded on trucks. Porters relieved us of our heavy baggage, and my gramophone and other trivia were borne off on the back of a little, wizened man old enough to be my grandfather.

We drove down wide, dusty streets past pretty bungalows smothered in bougainvillea. There did not appear to be anything very Indian about the town, but that, after all, was the general idea. It was an oasis of Englishness in an alien desert, the kind of isolated spot where the British could pull up the drawbridge (metaphorically speaking) and fend off foreign encroachment.

Our draft debouched on to an immense parade ground boxed in by long, single-storey buildings. A scattering of sergeants, our minder among them, sorted us into alphabetical platoons and distributed maps we were meant to memorise. They revealed an enormous encampment. There was a barber's shop, I noticed, a tailor, shoemaker and, would you believe, stables. Shades of the Bengal Lancers!

'Surely we don't need horses?' I asked our sergeant hopefully. Perhaps this was the way to get into the cavalry. 'After all,' I went on, 'we're infantry.'

'Not here, you're not,' Loosely replied. 'In India, *all* officers ride.'

He must have been talking about peacetime officers. Throughout my brief Indian Army career I never got near a horse. The best they could do was try to teach me to drive a beaten-up truck until I mashed the gear-box attempting to double-declutch. Nevertheless, it was entirely different from any cadet training establishment in wartime England. The courses back there were more an endurance test – bad as any detention centre – with chances of graduating, for people as incompetent as myself, predictably poor. The Bangalore OTS was for gentlemen destined to become officers. There was next to no doubt about it. You would have to do something appalling to be rusticated. Similar, sprawling camps were springing up at that time all over India. But the ambience of Bangalore made it particularly pleasant.

'Before you do anything else, gentlemen,' Sergeant Loosely was intoning, 'you had better get breakfast.' He assumed his oiliest Jeeves-style manner. 'I can particularly recommend the kidneys.' He indicated a small army of Indians waiting on the side-lines. 'After that I'll introduce you to your servants. They can't wait to get to work on your boots.'

Mess waiters in vivid turbans helped us to our chairs. The menus waved beneath our noses proffered an amazing selection of foodstuffs, some of which stood steaming and bubbling in burnished chafing dishes. All around me cadets, brutalised by troop-ship swill, were tucking into porridge, kippers, kidneys, sausages, and thick-cut marmalade. The range of choice unnerved me.

'Three-minute eggs, master?' inquired a wizened waiter with a drooping white moustache. I'd never heard of a three-minute egg but eagerly I nodded agreement. Four semi-soft-boiled eggs appeared with plenty of hot, buttered toast. 'And after this, kidneys, master?' the waiter inquired.

Many a good meal I've eaten in my life but this was among the most memorable. The ample servings, the white linen, the tableware, the solicitous service ... it was unbelievable the way the waiters dashed around to do your bidding, their bare feet loudly slapping the polished teak floors. My one fear was that I might wake up and find it all a dream.

We strolled to our quarters in the residential lines. One-room apartments had been built with attached baths in long, single-storey strips. No wonder they were called 'lines'. Each shared apartment contained two beds sprouting poles for mosquito nets, two plain, softwood desks, two chairs and a large *almirah* (closet) for our clothes. Frank Schofield and I were billeted together – 'the child musicians', someone derisively called us – and were presented with armbands bearing our personal number, and gleaming new bicycles to get us round the extensive school facilities.

Our personal servant greeted us with a polite '*salaam*'. He was an amenable young Dravidian who whisked away our boots for polishing. We called him Bop. It was the nearest we could get to a long and unpronounceable Telegu name. Bop's younger brother (and full-time assistant) unpacked our gear, while the *dhobi*, or washerman, vanished with our grubby clothes. Everything came back that evening cleaned and ironed and crisply starched. The *beesti* (shades of Gunga Din) poured our baths while the *jemadar*, or sweeper, an untouchable of extremely dark complexion, spruced up the loo. I was trying to remember all their names when our minder, Sergeant Loosely, bustled past.

'Never call servants by their names, Mr Spurr,' he said reprovingly. 'Only by their occupations. That man – ' he glared at our servant, ' – should be addressed as "Bearer". Otherwise he'll just get bloody familiar.'

Bop looked at me and winked. 'Him one of old school,' he whispered after the sergeant had gone.

'Don't you find his manner objectionable?' I asked.

Bop shrugged. 'This India,' he said. We continued to call him by our version of his name.

It didn't take long to get adjusted to our privileged new lifestyle. That first morning the shoemaker, a slight, bearded Muslim, measured us for new footwear. He opened a fresh page of his foolscap order book and drew a pencilled outline round our bare feet. We were expected to wear suede half-boots for walking out – the type that came to be known as 'brothel creepers' – because heavy, regulation boots were worn only on parade or in the field. The tailor came next to measure us for smart new servicedress, paid for from our clothing allowance. The tropical uniform issued at Aldershot was entirely recut, the absurd turn-up on the shorts lopped off, and supplemented by the peculiarly Indian bush shirt, nowadays known as the 'safari jacket'. It evolved from the Indian custom of wearing an ordinary long-sleeved shirt outside the trousers to avoid sweating too much around the waist.

'Officers used to buy uniform out of their own pockets,' Sergeant Loosely remarked with traces of nostalgia. 'They needed a private income to join most regiments. But of course, it's different in wartime.'

I mentioned my interest in the Bengal Lancers.

'They don't exist,' the sergeant told me. 'Only in Hollywood. The nearest thing to them is the Bengal Light Horse. Cavalry's the élite, you know, even today. Most of the regiments have gone armoured, though they keep their horses. You still need money there. Polo ponies cost a packet.' He cut me down with a patronising smile, 'I reckon you'd do better in some not-too-fashionable regiment, Mr Spurr,' he confided. 'Not the Gurkhas. They're much too demanding. Something like the Frontier Force. You'd have fun shooting up the Afghans.'

My enthusiasm waned perceptively. The North-west Frontier sounded a bit savage. My ambitions ran no further than some quiet little outfit assigned to garrison duty in the Middle East. Palestine struck me as an attractive possibility. It was so peaceful in those days and a fair old distance from the Libyan desert where a German called Rommel had lately taken over from the Italians. Since Rommel's début, the Middle East communiqués had grown markedly less exultant; rumour had it that this zealous German planned to toughen up the desert war.

Ten minutes before reveille, Bop brought a tray of *chota hazri* – tea, a biscuit and a small banana – and laid them on our bedside tables. Neither Frank nor I had slept too well. That first night we had omitted to draw mosquito nets from the stores, and the bugs had a ball. But now hot baths stood ready, clean uniforms laid out on our chairs. Bop dressed us, helping us into shirts and shorts and fitting the boots on our feet. We were much too embarrassed to refuse.

The commandant delivered his welcoming address in the lecture hall. He was a tense, wiry man with the rank of brigadier, and a DSO among his medal ribbons. The words hadn't varied, someone told me later, since the OTS had opened the previous year. Great stress was put upon gentlemanly conduct and regimental honour. There were warnings against signing too many mess chits ('an officer must never renege on his bar bill') and the expected standards of behaviour ('an officer knows how to hold his liquor'). It reminded me of Lord Rowallan's parting advice back in Scotland. I was doing my best, although my bowels were taking it a trifle literally. Already I had contracted what was known as 'Bangalore tummy'. Calls of nature grew increasingly frequent. I squirmed uncomfortably in my seat while the commandant droned on.

'Gentlemanly behaviour in the mess … before entering, be sure to remove your cap and Sam Browne belt … never mention a lady's name …'

There was no mention of the war. No mention of the Japanese. You would have thought we were there on vacation. Weeks passed before we realised that the good, soft life in Bangalore was inadequate preparation for the coming conflict with Japan; it wasn't until a year after our graduation that the training course was drastically amended to produce officers and gentlemen better fitted to fight a jungle war.

The common wisdom before the Japanese burst on to the scene was that military campaigns could not be conducted in the jungle. Our training emphasised desert warfare. The Officers' Training School was located on a dusty plateau with plenty of open country and few trees; the ideal place, we found, to learn the wiles of campaigning in, say, Libya. Indeed, the Indian Army had done particularly well in desert terrain since the outbreak of the Second World War, entirely in the Middle East and Africa, kicking around an ill-assorted selection of Iraqis, Iranians, Vichy French and Italians.

'We had begun to build up that most valuable of all assets, a tradition of success,' wrote General (later Field Marshal) Bill Slim, reviewing the Indian Army's efforts in the two years before Pearl Harbor. 'We had a good soldierly conceit of ourselves.'

Most of those successes had unfortunately been achieved over demoralised or ineffectual opponents. And successes bought cheaply can prove dangerously misleading. The army's greatest triumph was the storming of Keren, an Italian stronghold in Eritrea which fell to frontal attack on 26 March 1941. The ponderous if gallant action was then chosen as the set-piece strategy lecture at Bangalore. It was a peculiarly colonial-style affair fought without much air support or armour; the antithesis, unfortunately, of the new modes of war – the doctrines of blitzkrieg – lately demonstrated by the Germans and soon to be verified by the Japanese. The art of blitzkrieg, to quote an authority like Charles Messenger, was the exploitation of mobility ... 'the psychological dislocation of the enemy through the use of shock action on land and in the air along the line of least expectation.' The ugly truth was that the Japanese were by this time doing plenty of dislocating in the Philippines, Malaya, Borneo and the Dutch East Indies. Japanese troops, trained in jungle warfare on Hainan Island off the coast of occupied China, stuffed into troop-ships tighter than sardines and equipped with tanks the Allies thought unusable in jungle terrain, were infiltrating supposedly impenetrable country with extraordinary speed. They advanced on foot, bicycle and occasionally by boat, rewriting the rule-books while those of us destined to confront them were still learning to be officers and ... sahibs.

The euphoria couldn't last. Less than a month went by, wallowing in the comforts of Bangalore, before I was moaning my fool head off. I was not alone; the entire draft of officer cadets who'd arrived with me from England was criticising the quality, indeed the direction, of our curriculum. The Officers' Training School didn't take kindly to our complaints. The staff considered us positively ungrateful. Nothing would convince them of our concern. The approbation was taken personally. The whingeing of younger cadets, myself among them, could be dismissed as irresponsible. Fair enough: the staff believed, with some truth, that 'the kiddies', as they called us, had come to India only for the fun. It was not so easy to shrug off the criticisms of maturer cadets who regarded the challenge of the Japanese, and our prospects of defeating them, with growing alarm.

The war situation hadn't looked too bad the day we arrived. The Japanese had in a matter of weeks seized the International Settlements in Shanghai, overrun Hong Kong and occupied most of the Philippines, but none of the garrisons in those places could be considered formidable. And the Yanks retreating into Bataan weren't worth a monkey's, in our biased view – as we'd have said in the Argylls, they 'couldnae punch their way oot o' a paper-bag'. The first serious newspaper I had seen since leaving Britain was a two-day-old copy of the Calcutta *Statesman*, then the chief British-owned daily in India, whose editorial line was pro-government without being unduly subservient. The lead story described Commonwealth forces regrouping in new defensive positions closer to Singapore. Nothing to worry about there: the Japanese would run smack into the Australians under the command of the audacious General Bennett.

'They'll teach the little buck-toothed bastards a real lesson,' Frank Schofield chuckled. I saw no reason to disagree with my room-mate. The pair of us had been weaned on racist clichés. We took it for granted that Chinese soldiers couldn't fight, any more than Italians, while the toothy, bespectacled Japanese couldn't see well enough to aim a rifle. The Australians, on the other hand, were unbeatable. My father had served with them at Gallipoli and considered them the best shock troops in the world. We felt confident that Fortress Singapore, with its leavening of Australian defenders, was the anvil that would break the Japanese hammer. No one for a moment believed, in those innocent, tightly-censored days, that the colonial powers would themselves be broken. Amazement spread around the mess as successive editions of the *Statesman* unravelled a tale of woe. 'Allied forces fought ferociously,' the paper faithfully (and inaccurately) reported, 'but ...'

The Japanese landed in the Dutch East Indies on 11 January and took Tavoy in Burma eight days later. By the end of the month they had bottled up the Commonwealth forces in Singapore, and pushed into Upper Burma after scoring a stunning victory at Moulmein. Soon they would be racing to the very frontiers of the Raj, scattering the Indian Army before them.

Some of the maturer cadets in our draft got the message more quickly than I did. Many came from crack regiments like the Brigade of Guards and most had seen action in France. They understood the implications of the word 'blitzkrieg'. They knew what it was like to be on the wrong end of a Panzer tank or dive-bomber. The equipment these men had handled in combat, like the very latest anti-tank rockets and heavy mortars, had not yet arrived in India. Resentments flared when OTS staff tried to prepare us for battle with wooden weapon replicas and canvas-covered trucks made to look like tanks. There was universal dismay at the approach our instructors took to modern war.

Perhaps I should make it perfectly clear that the sumptuous, somnolent condition of the Bangalore OTS was not entirely typical of the Indian Army. A splendid force had been created during one and a half centuries of British rule. There were plenty of regiments with proud traditions, first-class fighting men and devoted officers. The general lack of urgency apparent to newcomers from Britain was perfectly understandable. India, up until then, had been a backwater remote from actual combat. Campaigning had been confined to African and Middle Eastern colonies with less of the fluidity and – how shall I put it? – the blood-curdling impact of suicidal, sword-swinging samurai. Out-flanked by this new, apparently irresistible foe in unfamiliar jungle surroundings, Indian troops resorted to unruly retreat.

The Japanese were decimating the 11th Indian Division on the Slim River defence line in Malaya about the time we were being introduced to the intricacies of desert navigation. The bigwigs in Delhi had earmarked most of our draft for North Africa to deal with the upstart Rommel. The training course with its overemphasis on desert warfare remained unaltered during the whole three months I was there. An undue degree of attention was also devoted to the North-west Frontier; shooting up tribesmen on either side of the Khyber, on what is now the border between Afghanistan and Pakistan, had been something of an Indian Army speciality since before the First World War. The last tribal uprising in the mid-1930s, led by a fundamentalist fakir from a place called Ipi, had tied down five British-Indian Divisions, backed by aircraft, for two costly years. The bombing of Afghan villages, so hotly condemned when the Russians were doing it, dates back to that nasty little war.

The majority of our instructors had served against the fakir's tribal fanatics. Embarrassed by the combat experience of those they were supposed to be teaching, the staff was keen to reassert authority by impressing us with its superior knowledge of this one highly-specialised type of warfare. There was a spate of forced-marching over rocky hills, as well as lectures on the heliograph and other oddities. The Indian Army had come into its own, sonny, and you'd better believe it.

Sergeant Loosely seemed to have spent his whole service career swapping volleys with 'the tribals' at God-forsaken spots like Landi Khotal. To hear him, you might have been in Hollywood. Talking and sounding like an MGM bit-player, he told us: 'Don't never get captured, gentlemen. Them tribal women 'as a nasty way wiv knives.'

Mutilation and a slow, painful death were hopefully to be avoided by a kind of stylised warfare. We dubbed it fighting-by-numbers. It had evolved over many years of combat along the North-west Frontier, the main aim being to repel ambush. The Pathan tribesmen had the disconcerting habit of leaping, screaming, from nowhere, knives bared, guns blazing, and hacking a hapless patrol to bits before anyone could aim a rifle. We were taught to hit straight back by going through several oft-rehearsed, numbered drills: shouting, 'Five!', for example, brought the patrol bunched together firing rapidly in all directions. If that sounds a bit Kipling-esque, well it was. But it seemed to work. The Americans could have done a lot worse employing similar drills in Vietnam. They would have been even more useful to the Russians fifteen years later. The cardinal rules were cautious advance, command of the heights and refusal to rely over-much on aircraft and artillery. And the way to go about it was graphically demonstrated to us by a squad of young Eurasians drawn from the local volunteers, a kind of Home Guard, who staged some cleverly choreographed displays among nearby rocks and nullahs. The volunteers formed squares and executed rapid fire (with blanks) while fellow squaddies in tribal dress emerged unexpectedly from concealment. It was spectacular to watch but unfortunately unreal; irrelevant too, since the North-west Frontier was reportedly quiet. The Raj had bought a temporary peace with gold and, strange as it may sound, with rifles.

Jungle training wasn't entirely omitted, though suitable sites were difficult to find on the rocky wastes round Bangalore. The major jungle exercise was delayed until we went to camp. The object was to spend three days and nights in casserina woods some miles from the OTS, getting a taste of conditions in the field. The woods were a pale substitute for tropical rain forest but were clearly the best to hand. Camp was going to be tough, the training staff warned us, and I was inclined to believe them.

Marching out there the cadet in charge of our squad lost his way and led us across a firing range. Machine-gun bullets crackled about us. We were too inexperienced to know what was happening. Officers raced up on horseback shouting, while the squad blundered blindly around the range. It was a taste of things to come. The American acronym 'snafu' (Situation Normal, All Fouled Up) was just infiltrating the British military vocabulary.

The woods appeared ahead of us late that afternoon as we toiled out of a dusty nullah. We were hot, tired and apprehensive. It was the first time we had been cut off from the comforts of the school. We need not have worried. Something white beckoned from afar: tents had been erected within the tree-line and the mess waiters were there in force, appropriately robed, arranging the silverware on portable picnic tables.

'Ready for a beer, master?' asked a familiar voice. It was our personal servant Bop. 'We got plenty bottles here on ice.'

Frank and I sat drinking in the shade while Bop removed our boots. We washed in warm water and changed into fresh uniforms. The pair of us lay back in the undergrowth puffing mild Madras cheroots.

'So this is war,' Frank said thoughtfully. Our minder, Sergeant Loosely, pottered past, a wooden model of a machine-gun in one hand, a chota peg in the other. Ice tinkled inside his whisky glass.

'Maybe this is the time to quit,' I said, equally thoughtfully. 'While we're ahead of the game.'

PART THREE

Trust me to hanker for a change within weeks of joining the Indian Army. Typical, though, of the way things worked out; virtually the opening chapter of an absurdly misspent life. For the next forty-odd years, during a lengthy, picaresque career, I would face new challenges, grapple briefly with their complexities, only to flounce off, or be booted out, into fresh, ever-transitory fields. I would take a stab at being a journalist, an author, a photographer ... a TV reporter, presenter, director and combat cameraman ... oh yes, a soldier and a sailor as well ... each tackled with questionable degrees of success. The proverbial jack-of-all-trades, you might accurately say, who never mastered one of them.

Soldiering was undoubtedly my worst shot. The army wasn't my scene. The romantic view I had entertained of military life – the swirling kilts, mess night in the Bengal Lancers – was no better than a mirage. By the time that fantasy was played out my rating as a soldier on any scale of one to ten would hardly hit two. I did do slightly better as a sailor, though, despite a disastrous start. And it took me a long time to live down the dhow I hit in Bombay harbour. But let's not get ahead here ... right now I am still an Indian Army cadet, a whingeing, somewhat slothful creature more interested in dancing than campaigning, a wimp on the assault course and an embarrassment to my fellow men.

Strange as it may seem, my chance of a change appeared on 15 February 1942. That day the unthinkable happened. Singapore surrendered. Its Commonwealth defenders outnumbered the Japanese two to one yet the enemy general, Tomoyuki ('Tiger') Yamashita, brow-beat his British opponent, General Percival, into brandishing the white flag. Troops were still disembarking in the docks, bound ultimately for the River Kwai, as the wretched Percival grovelled in the Ford factory beside the Bukit Timah road. Things went crazy from then on. The Japanese bombed Darwin, the main city in northern Australia, arousing fears Down Under of imminent invasion, and two weeks later the combined Dutch, British and American fleet – the force we all expected to redress the balance of sea power in South-east Asia – was wiped out in the Java Sea. The Dutch East Indies vanished for ever from the map. Burma went next. Rangoon was evacuated on 7 March 1942. Resistance almost immediately collapsed. The main defending force, the British-led 1st Burma Division, threw away its arms and scuttled home. Some of the deserters switched sides and turned on their retreating rulers. That left the 17th British-Indian Division, already badly mauled, isolated south of Mandalay. Twice it was nearly encircled, though the survivors managed eventually to make their way to India, losing the bulk of their guns, tanks and transportation in the process.

The Imperial Japanese Navy felt compelled to get its share of the limelight. Its hated army rivals couldn't be seen grabbing all the headlines. First Air Fleet ('the folks who gave you Pearl Harbor') swept into the Bay of Bengal, sank the British carrier *Hermes* and the cruiser *Dorsetshire*, and bombed Colombo, the naval base at Trincomalee on the other side of Ceylon, as well as Vizagapatam on the East Indian coast. And dive-bombers from the same task-force caught a large convoy of merchant ships fleeing to Calcutta and sank the lot.

The 'black Friday' sinkings, plus the raids, caused panic in India. The immediate effect, as far as I was concerned, was a softening of the older sahibs' attitudes to the so-called 'temporary gentlemen' – people like me – sent from Britain to flesh out the Indian armed forces. The expatriate community plainly loathed us. The way they went on, you'd have thought we had upset the ecological balance. Some monocled fool in the Bangalore Club once brayed within my hearing, 'Simply can't get near the bar for these new fellas.' Thanks to the Japanese, he bought me a drink next time I dropped around.

'Got to put up with a few hardships, I suppose,' the same man mused. 'Might even have to admit bloody Indians ... officers, naturally.' But still greater hardships awaited these irascible old fools. The worst blow was the disappearance of Scotch whisky and imported beer. Supplies of the real thing quickly dried up. Indian substitutes trickled on to the market. There was a kind of gin, for instance, made in Madras:

> Before you drink your Parry's gin ...
> ... please fill in your next of kin.

Hottest topic of club conversation was the impending invasion of India. Any moment now, the old-hands reckoned, the Japanese would bestride the land.

'Glad to have you around, Mr Spurr: can I call you up another gin?' Occupation of the Andaman Islands, the old penal colony in the Bay of Bengal, by Japanese amphibious forces on 23 March, was seen as the first step to a landing on the coast near Calcutta. It would link up with an overland drive, the monocled club member confidently predicted, through Burma into Assam and Bengal.

Already, the stampede was on to get out of eastern India. Trains bound for Delhi and remoter spots west were booked for weeks ahead. Hotels filled up with refugees from the coast – even in Bangalore – where dust-covered cars appeared loaded with memsahibs and their more portable possessions. Squawking women added to the overall unease by spreading horror stories about 'ungrateful' Burmese butchering British civilians as they tried to quit the country. Much the same thing could happen in India, the memsahibs muttered in their cups, since most of the nationalist leaders, Mahatma Gandhi among them, appeared ready and eager to welcome the Japanese as liberators. The Indian National Congress certainly stirred up a storm with its ill-considered 'Quit India' campaign a few months later. The fear in Delhi was that a Japanese landing anywhere along the coast could touch off a powder keg. The ghosts of the Indian Mutiny were back again, haunting the British Raj.

The vulnerability of India's lengthy coastline became suddenly apparent. Delhi had assumed that Britannia would always rule the offshore waves. The uncontested depredations of the Japanese First Fleet – and the Royal Navy's ignominious withdrawal to Eastern Africa – now gave an unwonted impetus to Indian coastal defence. Patrol craft of all kinds were pressed into service in the Sundarbans, the swampy region south-east of Calcutta where the Ganges meets the River Brahmaputra; it was through there that any seaborne assault upon the city would probably have to proceed. The army took to the sea, forming its own defence flotilla, while efforts were made to expand the Royal Indian Navy.

The Royal Indian what? To be perfectly honest, I hadn't heard of it either. For nearly two centuries, British defence efforts in India had concentrated on the land. It was not until the mid-1930s that British financial stringency prompted the Delhi government to transform its coastal survey service, the Indian Marine, into a minuscule navy. The Royal Indian Navy ('Gandhi's navy', we called it) boasted three or four frigates by 1942 and a shoal of small armed merchantmen. Calls for a full-blown Indian coastal defence force modelled on the British forces operating in the English Channel increased the demand for officers. The shortage was so acute that an appeal went out to army cadets training at Bangalore to transfer, on commissioning, to what was in Indian terms the 'junior' service. The chance was too good to miss. My father was, as I've said, a sea captain, and since childhood I'd been involved with ships and shipping. My fondest memories were the tales my father told of his apprenticeship in sailing ships around Cape Horn.

'Once I was nearly washed overboard.' It was one of his favourite stories. 'I landed up entangled in the shrouds. Alongside me, caught in the same way, was a great big sealion. He looked as surprised as I was.'

'You've been drinking, Frank,' my mother would complain. 'I can see it by your eyes.' Father would protest feebly and slip me books of naval lore. Sitting beside the sitting-room fire on a winter's night I would help hoist Nelson's signal before Trafalgar, and I would take my place on the bridge as Beattie's battle-cruisers emerged head-on from the Jutland smog into the concentrated shellfire of the German battle fleet. The Royal Indian Navy did not offer anything so dramatic. But the prospects were irresistible.

'I think it's a great idea,' declared my room-mate Frank Schofield. He added his name to the transfer list at the bottom of the OTS notice-board. I did the same. There'd be no more route marches. No more heat and dust and thirst. Warships took their refrigerators into battle. I pictured myself bearing down upon the Japanese, battle-flags at the fore – or was it the main? Horatio Nelson, telescope to blind eye, nodded approvingly.

Transforming a nascent second-lieutenant, marked for posting to the Frontier Force Regiment, into a midshipman, Royal Indian Navy, proved more painful than I had anticipated. The act of changing horses in midstream, of reconditioning Pavlov's dribbling dogs, was child's play by comparison. Layers of army lore had to be stripped away, and much that replaced it appeared contradictory. Take drill, for example. Sailors cannot stamp around wooden decks the way soldiers do on the parade ground. Boot-bashing was out: so was the crashing of rifle butts. Sailors loped through soldiers ceremony: or so it seemed to me. The navy joked openly about it: 'Ship's company will advance in column of route from the right, led by a stoker on a bloody great 'orse, taking their time from the dockyard clock ... January, February, *march*!'

The language was different. You didn't get a rocket from a senior officer, you got a 'bottle'. A bottle of acid was supposed to drip from the exalted-one's tongue. Receiving an order in the army, you replied 'Very good, sir'. In the navy it was 'Aye aye, sir'. 'Very good' was reserved for your superiors when you humbly reported completion of whatever you had been told to do.

'Very good, Number One. Now that the sea cocks are open you may give "Abandon ship".'

'Aye aye, sir! Coxswain, pipe "Abandon ship".'

Emergencies like this were dutifully enacted at training school. The boatswain's call (whistle) would shriek out a set of piercing notes. It was my impression that there were any number of variations, each imparting some special meaning. I never did find out. My ploy was to wait until someone bellowed 'Abandon ship' before shinning down the sheets of rope-netting draped across the assault course in the Gunnery School yard. Fortunately, it was an exercise I never had to enact in real life. Surely it was pardonable to appear confused? The orders, the procedures, the technicalities were so unfamiliar I couldn't help standing around looking stupid. But no. Excuses weren't acceptable. You were *supposed* to understand.

There's a marvellous passage in *The Caine Mutiny*, where the newly-commissioned US ensign takes his first turn on deck-duty. The destroyer is putting out paravanes. The executive officer ('Number One' in the RN) gives orders to the work party ('work detail' in the USN).

'Fix the mumble-grumble to the gizzet, petty officer, before warping out the whatsit. Then roodle the caboodle round the flipflop ... ', or words to that effect.

Absolute gibberish, you tell yourself, until gradually the terms take on meaning and you find you're using them too. I should have grown used to it in the Zagreb Hussars ... sorry, the Argyll and Sutherland Highlanders. But for a long and embarrassing period I was condemned to stagger around shipboard like a deaf-mute out of touch with my immediate surroundings. It was the price of being a 'pongo'. One of the first bits of argot I picked up was naval slang for someone in the army. The thirty or forty of us who had transferred from Bangalore were 'pongos' to a man. Mixed in with several hundred trainee officers who had mostly transferred from the Royal Navy, many after service on the lower deck (as enlisted men), we were the butt of endless jokes.

'Hey, pongo! Run down the engine-room and fetch me a bucket of steam.'

'I need a marline-spike to stir my gin.'

'See if the surgeon's got a running Turk's head.' It turned out to be a knot on the end of a heaving line.

Add to this the ignominy of age. I was well into my nineteenth year: too young to commission as a sub-lieutenant and stuck with the equivocal rank of midshipman. It was, in naval parlance, the lowest form of animal life. Having been the youngest, brashest cadet in Bangalore – my elders called me *chokra*, a contemptuous term for youngster – I was now addressed as 'Snotty', the implication being that I was nothing but a runny-nosed urchin. The three buttons on the sleeve of the midshipman's winter uniform were said to encourage creatures like myself to use a handkerchief. That, at least, was the naval tradition.

('Naval what?' Churchill is once said to have exclaimed. 'I'll tell you what's naval tradition. It's rum, sodomy and the lash!')

The Royal Navy's attitude to midshipmen was adopted by the rapidly-expanding RIN. The Indian service was, after all, a carbon-copy of the RN with only the merest sprinkling of curry powder. Aboard the bigger British ships, for instance, midshipmen were not permitted to mess with their seniors in the ward-room. They were assigned a separate gunroom. There they could be thrashed like naughty schoolboys (with a dirk scabbard) for trivial misdemeanours. The RIN had no big ships in 1942, and hence no Gun Rooms; yet midshipmen were accorded scant respect. I was ordered about mercilessly by my betters, running messages, standing the most uncomfortable watches and, on occasion, mixing the Number One's pink gins.

The most cruel disappointment was the uniform. Or rather, the apparent lack of it – midshipmen's summer whites bore no rank badges. The short-sleeved white shirt was without epaulettes. It meant walking around looking like a cabin steward. Hardly the kind of rigout, I thought, to attract the girls.

My attitude was reprehensible. I make no apology. At this awkward, adolescent stage of my life I was frivolous and obnoxious. I was also touchy, insecure, pompous, defensive of my personal dignity and more indifferent than I should have been to the task at hand. The task, that is, of becoming an efficient and effective naval officer. It's a dreadful thing to admit but at the time I really didn't care. The war was a convenient escape, as I've already repeated, from the constraints of suburban life. Another year would pass before I took things seriously. The penny would only drop after the trauma of a typhoon in the Bay of Bengal; by then I would be shamed into doing my duty.

Naval training was interrupted by the gravest challenge to British rule since the Indian Mutiny. I had already savoured the discontent simmering below the surface that first, frightening night in Bombay. The mini-confrontation with a nationalistic student at the Flora fountain warned me of the revulsion felt by many Indians, especially the younger ones, towards their British overlords. The Raj, I had been conditioned to believe, was a wholly benevolent institution. The revelation that the King Emperor's subjects – or maybe a vocal minority – did not share my childish view, left me surprised, indignant and more than a little uneasy.

Returning to Bombay four months after my arrival in India to join the RIN I found the political discontent more marked than ever. Frustrations reached boiling point in August 1942, when Mahatma Gandhi launched his Quit India campaign. I can't help feeling to this day that the Indian leader made a major mistake. His attempt to oust the British at the very moment the Japanese were threatening invasion across the Burma border was the whim of an impractical politician, unbefitting the image of a great spiritual figure; it was a wilful, quixotic gesture long since glossed over by history. The episode scarcely figures, for instance, in Richard Attenborough's starry-eyed rewrite of the Gandhi story. Perhaps it's just as well.

Fortunately for everyone, the Indian Army stood firm. The slightest defection could have toppled the Raj and distorted the course of history. The Second World War would have been prolonged. The Churchill government was realistic enough to recognise the gravity of the situation. A Labour member of the coalition government, Sir Stafford Cripps, a public advocate of freedom for India, had been sent out from London in March to offer the nationalists self-rule after, but only *after*, the defeat of the Axis powers. He haggled for weeks on the cool upper terraces of Simla, the Indian summer capital, before Gandhi broke off the negotiations. The Cripps proposals were dismissed as 'a cheque on a failing bank.' The Mahatma retreated to his *ashram* at Sevagram, a village in central India, took up his symbolic spinning-wheel and told the British to pack up and go home. Should the British refuse – and in view of the circumstances they could hardly do anything else – they would be faced with nationwide non-violence.

The practice of non-violence, or *satyagraha*, requiring demonstrators to offer no resistance when the police closed in wielding their brass-tipped *lathis*, had thoroughly embarrassed the British during the Gandhian campaigns of the 1930s. Protesters against the salt tax meekly allowed themselves to be clubbed over the head by impotent British police officers, thereby winning the support of influential pacifists throughout Europe and America.

But the world was now at war. It was one thing to call for a peaceful boycott of British goods and taxes in times of peace; quite another to demand British abdication at a peculiarly critical hour.

Satyagraha was supposed to be a subtle form of protest. Seldom, in fact, was it ever completely non-violent – human reactions being what they are – especially in the highly-charged, hysterical atmosphere whipped up in India following the fall of Singapore. The Quit India campaign led inevitably to violence. Mobs stormed through most of the major cities, Bombay among them, attacking Europeans, looting and burning. Out in the countryside, especially in the north-east, trains were halted and searched. Anyone with a white skin was hauled off and hacked to bits. Four Canadian Air Force officers, trapped in their compartment in Bihar, tried to explain that they had nothing to do with the Raj. They had come to fight the Japanese, not the Indians. The mob took them apart with machetes. Blood spurted from floor to ceiling. Most alarming was the destruction of rail links to the Burma border. Great stretches of track were torn up and military traffic came to a halt. Fighter aircraft were called in to patrol the main lines and mobs caught tampering with the track were machine-gunned.

It was a period of which no one could be proud. Casualties were kept down, overall, by judicious use of military force. Troops supported the civil power under strictly controlled conditions. There were no Tienan-men-style massacres. But there were some nasty moments.

I was caught on the top of a bus shortly after joining the Royal Indian Navy in Bombay. Armed police rushed a crowd of demonstrators around the now-familiar Flora fountain. The policemen in their pale-blue uniforms carried rifles with fixed bayonets at the high port; from the look of them (I was beginning to discern the differences) the police were northern Muslims. They had mean, fanatic looks on their faces as they ploughed into the largely Hindu crowd, lunging at the ringleaders with their bayonets and kicking the others with hobnailed boots. It was monsoon time. A storm burst overhead dousing the mêlée, and the area round the fountain suddenly emptied. Sodden demonstrators melted away into the side-streets, dragging their injured behind them. The vengeful policemen halted, panting and cursing, glowering at the retreating mob.

Their blood was up. They would gladly have gone in for the kill. But it was a golden rule of riot-suppression never to push blindly into back alleys. In conditions like those a disciplined force could get completely out of hand. It could also be broken up in the narrow streets and counter-attacked piecemeal.

Things looked so fraught for a day or two that all officers undergoing naval training were called off their courses to practise bayonet drill in a field near Malabar Hill. It was a welcome relief from the intricacies of semaphore and such-like mysteries. The exercise struck me as absurd, having just come out of the army, until I managed to clout myself under the chin in a moment of over-confidence with my own rifle butt. Our task, we were told, was a last-ditch defence of naval installations. We would be issued with ten rounds of ammunition, and permitted to fire only under supervision of a magistrate, following recitation of the Riot Act. Not the complete Act, of course; the first four paragraphs were thought to be sufficient.

'After which, you shoot to kill.' Our instructor, a grizzled old Scottish police superintendent, spoke with chilling conviction. 'Never shoot in the air,' he went on. 'That won't stop a mob. Pick out a target, one of the obvious leaders, and let him have it through the heart. Then you stop. No random firing. One volley is usually enough. If another is required, you'll be ordered to fire again.'

It was a carefully conceived drill which took account, as the superintendent put it, 'of the superiority of armed troops over unarmed civilians'. The British hadn't always acted that way. Machine-guns had been used years before in notorious incidents in places like Amritsar. The biggest worry in any civil disturbance, the instructor told us, was keeping tabs on the magistrate. It was his unpalatable duty to validate your actions. The majority of magistrates were poorly paid Indian officials seldom noted for their martial disposition. The tougher the going, the more frantically they would try to flee the scene.

Many mistakes were made all over the country that frenetic August. There was vast confusion. But with Gandhi, Nehru and thousands of other nationalists clapped in jail, the Quit India movement quickly petered out. The reason was that many Indians had a vested interest in the war effort: industry was expanding, the foundations were being laid for India's industrial revolution, and opportunities were being created in administration and in the armed forces. The officers who commanded the three services after Independence all learned their trade, or honed their skills, in the Second World War.

The crisis over, it was back to training; attempting to learn in the classroom what could only, genuinely, be learned at sea. Someone must have guessed what was wrong. All 'pongos' were suddenly hauled off their various courses and posted to the fleet. It made considerable sense; there's nothing like on-the-spot tuition. Two weeks before my twentieth birthday, I found myself handling flag signals on the bridge of the converted coastal steamer HMIS *Padmavati*, heading out of Calcutta for enemy-occupied Burma.

'Haul up "Apples",' the signals officer shouted. His voice was shrill with excitement. A siren sounded below decks. Men scampered topside, clamping on steel helmets. There were clicks and clacks as the guns were loaded. I hauled feverishly on the signal halliard, watching the 'A' flag break free at the yard. We called it 'Apples' in the old phonetic alphabet. My naval knowledge was limited but already I knew the meaning of that flag: enemy aircraft were approaching. We were as helpless as a sitting duck, with no air cover, patrolling the inner reaches of the Bay of Bengal.

His Majesty's Indian Ship *Padmavati* was classed as an armed merchant cruiser. More accurately, she was a sheep in sheep's clothing. Built during the early 1930s, well before the world went mad, the 800-ton coastal steamer provided ample passage for sahibs and memsahibs between the western ports of India. The Goanese stewards still gossiped about the adulterous couplings induced by pink gin and the seductive zephyrs blowing nightly off the shore. Smearings of green and blue camouflage now effaced the peacetime paintwork. Every inch of holystoned teak decking, once the coxswain's pride, was daubed a concealing grey. A six-inch gun protruded from the forward deck and some half-dozen light machine-guns cluttered the midships section pretending to offer defence against enemy aircraft. Nobody was fooled. Nothing could effectively turn this comfortable coaster into a fighting ship. She would always be envied for the comfort of her cabins, for the handsome stateroom converted into a wardroom worthy of a battleship and the gargantuan Sunday lunch – heaped-up helpings of delicious curries that left everyone comatose – which was the sole survivor of a palmy, half-forgotten past. The armaments were mere window-dressing. The forward gun threatened to tear loose from the mountings every time it was fired. The anti-aircraft machine-guns frequently jammed, and their sights were unsuitable for aiming at aerial attackers. Boxes full of their cursed ammunition lurked in ambush around the deck waiting to trip you in the dark.

Ship and crew had together been co-opted into naval service on the outbreak of the Second World War. Most of the deck-hands were Lascars: that is, Muslim sailors recruited from the Chittagong area, in what is today Bangladesh, or from Ratanagiri, along the Indian west coast. Lascars had a long and honourable tradition as merchant seamen. The P&O and its related shipping lines were almost entirely manned by them. My father, whose political views lay somewhere to the right of Genghis Khan's, swore Indian sailors were superior to what he contemptuously called 'bolshie white crews'. They also happened to be a great deal cheaper. And that was no mean consideration during the Depression among the moguls of Threadneedle Street.

Lascars were not noted, however, for their martial qualities (who was?), so the naval authorities saw fit to infiltrate a handful of gung-ho Punjabis to man the guns.

Few of the Punjabis had ever seen the sea and they suffered agonies of sea-sickness. There were frequent squabbles down on the mess-decks because they despised the lascars, especially those from Chittagong, as a bunch of 'rice-eating monkeys'. The Punjabis preferred wheaten *chapattis* with their meals and disdained those who ate rice. The Urdu words *bund* (water front) and *bander* (monkey) are so similar that some comedian from Lahore would invariably find himself unable to resist making a cruel pun about the lascars whenever they started to tie up alongside a wharf. The lascars would storm off ashore shouting picturesque insults.

It is a measure of the gravity of the situation in north-east India, midsummer 1942 – and of the daunting lack of genuine warships – that anything as unsuitable as HMIS *Padmavati* should be chosen to patrol the approaches to Calcutta. Pardon me if I appear to malign the poor old thing; after all, she was the first ship in which I ever served, no matter how briefly, in my tortuous transmutation from soldier into sailor, and hence has a special place in my affections. But even I could see that a recycled seaborne hotel, noted for the deftness of its Chittagonian Mugh cooks, was scarcely the ideal choice for providing early warning of any Japanese invasion from Burma. You might just as well have ordered the Show Boat to take on the Federal Navy during the American Civil War.

I reported aboard without giving thought to the Japanese menace. Insulated as I had been in Bangalore and Bombay, both far from enemy threat, I was surprised to find Calcutta partially blacked-out and bordering on hysteria. Night raiders had struck at the city, causing minimal damage but an almighty panic. Royal Air Force Hurricanes were taking off from the Red Road, the short triumphal carriageway downtown which in those days was lined with imperial statuary.

The general gloom did not prevent a party of us younger officers from spending an uproarious night at Firpo's, the popular Calcutta night-club. Beer and Scotch were no longer available but I was getting used to the locally-made gin. Next morning the stewards were serving highly-spiced mulligatawny soup for breakfast, the traditional Anglo-Indian cure for a hangover, when the signal came through ordering us to sail into the teeth of the enemy. Or thereabouts.

Our job was to patrol the Bay of Bengal off the north-east Indian coast. Somewhere in this region the Japanese were expected to make amphibious landings as part of their plan to invade India. We were supposed to flash a radio warning and, possibly, poop off a few rounds from our single six-inch gun before it tore clear of the deck or the Imperial Japanese Navy blasted us out of existence. It wasn't quite the role I had dreamed up for myself on volunteering for transfer to the RIN. My dream posting was some place like Bombay near one of the military hospitals where nubile young nurses were said to welcome the company of handsome naval midshipmen. It hadn't occurred to me that I might land up in the Bay of Bengal where an unchallenged Japanese carrier fleet had lately sunk everything in sight. The *Padmavati* patrol sounded distinctly dangerous. A kamikaze mission if ever there was one ...

The Japanese had just completed their conquest of Burma. They had taken Akyab, the most northerly port and chief town of the Arakan, the coastal strip that ran southwards from the Indian border. From there they were expected to launch a seaborne assault into the Sunderbans, the wild, swampy region south-east of Calcutta. The only foe so far encountered by river patrols in the Sunderbans had apparently been tigers.

Burma, on the other hand, was more lethal. The RIN had suffered its first (and only) serious loss there. The elderly frigate *Indus* had put into Akyab around May 1942, hot-foot from abandoned Rangoon. She should have gone straight on to Calcutta but the extent of the military débâcle had not yet dawned on the Indian High Command. The captain was ordered to hang on in Akyab and show the flag. Japanese bombers caught the frigate as she was raising anchor. None of the enemy planes scored a direct hit but a near miss jammed the rudder, sending her careering round in circles, while further near misses stove in the elderly hull plates rendered fragile by excessive over-scaling. The doomed ship capsized in half an hour. Survivors swore she was loaded with loot from Rangoon. Her decks were crammed with stolen motorbikes. Gold from the Bank of Burma was supposed to be secreted in the captain's safe. I made for the wreck, bottom-up in mid-harbour, directly we retook Akyab in 1945. But someone had already cut through the hull and removed the safe. The motorbikes had vanished too.

Bombers were not our immediate fear as we headed down the River Hooghly towards the sea. The Hooghly is an offshoot of the Ganges. The Ganges debouches through several mouths into the Bay of Bengal, along with the River Brahmaputra, forming the Sunderbans delta. The Hooghly itself has been a major waterway since Job Charnock founded Fort St George, Calcutta, in 1689. Sailors have never liked it: the river is a navigator's nightmare.

'The Hooghly is the arsehole of the earth,' my father used to say. 'And Calcutta is seventy miles up it!'

The river runs alarmingly fast and it's at its worst during the rains. The moment you cast off, the tide race can flick your ship into midstream where all kinds of havoc are liable to be created among the milling tugs and lighters. It is vital to gain immediate steerage way which isn't always easy in a following current. Ships have to steam faster than the current in order to use the rudder – at times this means steaming more than fourteen knots. And that demands quick decisions because sandbanks shift overnight, popping up where they are least expected, while barges filled with straw and produce, looking much like floating haystacks, have a nasty habit of looming up, unannounced, in midstream. Fishing boats sweep under your bows when you get closer to the estuary. They are frail canoe-like affairs, operating in shoals without a warning light between them.

An élite corps of eccentrics, the Bengal Pilotage Service, handled most of the merchant shipping. They were highly paid, highly skilled and, in many cases, perpetually high. A member of the service once told me his mess was unique in serving gin with breakfast.

'It's the drink that keeps you going,' he said. 'I couldn't face the mucking job stone cold sober.'

Drunk though some might have been, these men did wonders piloting ships up and down one of busiest and most hazardous rivers in the world. Their services were not available to naval vessels which carried their own trained navigators – fortunately, the man aboard *Padmavati* had made the run plenty of times in the past. Nevertheless, there was an element of nail-biting before we reached the outer anchorage of Diamond Harbour.

By this time it was late afternoon. Half a dozen merchantmen were nervously waiting to sail upriver. They feared an air attack. One of them querulously signalled by Aldis lamp, demanding to know when pilots would be available. Having proceeded this far through unfriendly waters, the merchant captain had no intention of being pipped at the post by marauding Japanese.

A tense situation grew tenser a few minutes later when a wireless operator rushed up to the bridge with an urgent signal. A flight of Japanese bombers had been detected heading towards Calcutta. They would be overhead, we reckoned, in about seven minutes.

There's nothing quite so unnerving as air attack at sea. It's bad enough when planes attack you on land. But at least there, the moment they start bombing and strafing, you can hopefully duck into a trench or press yourself into the naked earth, praying the next bomb or bullet has some other poor devil's name on it. Chances are you won't suffer much harm. At sea, there's nowhere to duck. You're trapped at your post, inside an isolated, often thinly-armoured target, zigzagging madly perhaps, engines belting flat out, all guns firing in every possible direction, but hopelessly obvious, hopelessly vulnerable in the wide open sea; a bull's eye, you convince yourself, for any determined bombardier.

It's even worse if you land up in a converted coastal steamer never meant for war. The raucous call to 'Action stations!' brought the *Padmavati*'s crew stampeding to their posts. There was a clanking of steel helmets hurriedly assumed, of ammunition boxes wrenched open and readied. The breech of the forward gun clicked and clanged as its Punjabi crew thrust in a six-inch shell.

'Number One gun ready for action, sir!' the petty officer in charge called up to the bridge. He did not mean anti-aircraft action. Number One gun was intended for use against surface targets; its barrel could not be elevated above 40 degrees.

Confirmation that someone had a round up the spout should have sounded reasurring. Instead, I was terrified. I kept asking myself why I had ever left the Indian Army. The old lags' saying, 'Never volunteer for anything', struck me now as the wisest truism. I kept remembering that an all-conquering Japanese carrier fleet had lately been raging around the Bay of Bengal, where we were venturing, tentatively, on picket patrol.

'The bastards will be here in no time,' the navigator murmured when the radio warning arrived. We were as yet innocent of radar.

The signals officer set me hauling up the aircraft warning flag, from my post among the flag-lockers on the starboard wing of the bridge, and there was immediate consternation among the merchant ships anchored around us. The merchantmen were already jumpy. Ships had quite recently been attacked in the open reaches of Diamond Harbour by Japanese bombers based in Rangoon. Signals blinked, flags flapped and steam billowed from half a dozen forecastles as crews hurriedly raised anchor.

The alarm siren brought the commanding officer hatless on to the bridge. The first-lieutenant handed him a steel helmet. 'Keep it!' yelled the CO. 'Can't see a mucking thing with that tin pot on my head.' The skipper was an eccentric but competent Bengali called Chakravatee. Old 'Chuckers' as he was known (behind his back) was one of the first Indians to command a RIN ship. And a right old terror he was too.

'You! ... snotty!' he yelled at me. 'Don't stand there gawping. Take charge of the starboard Lewis guns!'

The half-dozen Lewis guns – our so-called anti-aircraft defence – might have deterred Blériot or any of the other string and paper pioneers; they proffered little but gnat-bites to an attacking Japanese. Still, control of the guns gave me something to do. I raced down to the promenade deck to get my first taste of giving orders. Lack of naval training for once presented no difficulty. I had trained on Lewis guns in the Argyll and Sutherland Highlanders. And manned them aboard the troop-ship *Strathallan*.

Lewis guns dated back to the First World War and were notoriously unreliable. A circular magazine was supposed to rotate, feeding rounds into the chamber as the weapon fired. That was the theory, anyway. It was, in fact, a mechanical contradiction: rotation combined uncertainly with thrust. As the magazine turned, the thrusting bolt action jammed with ominous regularity.

'Where are the enemy aeroplanes?' asked the senior Punjabi gunner. He spoke Urdu in his excitement. The Urdu word for 'aeroplane' is *hawai jahaz* and translates literally as 'air ship' and for a moment I peered wildly forward expecting to see a Zeppelin. There wasn't so much as a seagull in sight.

The *Padmavati* had picked up speed – every bit, I suppose, of her full fifteen knots – swinging wildly to leeward of the moored merchantmen.

Fishing boats scattered from our path. Commander Chakravatee had hit on the clever idea of shielding the freighters with smoke. This would come from a weird-looking gizmo, rather like a moonlighter's still, mounted on the stern, which squirted chemicals into our wake to create a smokescreen. As long as we stayed on the right quarter the wind would blow the smoke across the merchantmen, hiding them (we prayed) from enemy aircraft.

Ten minutes went by … the smoke rolled across the anchorage in a woolly grey cloud much to the annoyance, we soon learned, of the harassed merchant captains. The last thing they wanted, it transpired, was our protection. The captains' instinct, once their anchors were free of the harbour bed, was to head upstream beneath the protection of shore-based anti-aircraft guns. The captains were mistaken. There were no such guns for a good fifty miles but we could not explain that. The smoke made it impossible to communicate visually. And radio contact was expressly forbidden until you were actually sinking.

A freighter slid sideways out of the murk. Another followed it, moving crabwise. The two ships' anchor chains were inextricably snagged. Their forecastle crews were working desperately to slip the chains into the sea. The skippers stopped abusing each other with their loud hailers to turn their invective against us.

'What the muck d'you think ye're doin'?' boomed an irate Scottish voice. 'Can't see a hand in front of ma muckin' face!'

'The Japs won't see you either,' Commander Chakravatee yelled back. He had an expensive Oxbridge accent. 'Be good chaps and keep under cover of the smoke.'

Another bank of our man-made fog blotted the interlocking ships from sight, though curses and imprecations continued to echo across the water. There was a distant clunk as two steel hulls collided sharply together.

'Where's the enemy, sahib?' my Punjabi gunner asked expectantly. I could see from the look on his face that this man couldn't wait to start blazing away into the wild blue yonder. But there was nothing to blaze at. The blue was turning deep indigo as the tropical night came rushing in upon us. The muddy shoreline, knotted with mangroves, grew misty purple flecked by a wisp or two of evening fog. Only a skein of wind-blown cirrus, high above, now caught the dying sunlight.

'Look there!' shouted the gunner pointing high on the starboard beam. There was a standard form for reporting a sighting but he seemed to have forgotten it. 'Bombers bearing one eight zero,' the gunnery officer intoned more correctly over the ship's speaker system.

A group of golden specks gleamed in the sky several miles away. There were twelve twin-engined specks marshalled in three neat diamond formations. The Punjabi gunner let fly despite my attempts to stop him and others followed suit. Tracer arced uselessly into the sky. Something banged loudly inside the smokescreen. A shell whistled overhead. One of the freighters was armed like us with a six-inch deck gun and our haphazard firing had encouraged its crew to join in the fracas.

'Check, check, check!' bawled the *Padmavati*'s gunnery officer. 'Stop it, for Christ's sake! Don't waste mucking ammunition.'

The planes were Mitsubishis, code-named 'Nell', a naval Type 96 attack bomber. They altered course towards us with the precision of parade-ground soldiers. Despite the smoke, we must have presented a tempting target – so tempting, in fact, that the enemy pilots overlooked the squadron of Hurricanes diving out of the sun like cavalry to the rescue.

The Japanese must have grown over-confident, as they were attacking in near-daylight without fighter protection. And here at Diamond Harbour they were within the admittedly limited range of the RAF defences. The bombers broke formation as the lead plane blew apart in a burst of flame. Another tipped over on one wing and fell, smoking, into the mangroves. Several others emptied their bombs as they fled the anchorage, churning up harmless geysers of mud and water. The only slight damage on our side was suffered by the entangled freighters in the fog.

The whole thing was over in less than five minutes – the longest five minutes, I can honestly say, of my entire life. Most of that time I was too busy helping to clear jammed Lewis guns to feel much fear. It's always helpful, in brief, hysterical bursts of action, to have something useful to do.

My Punjabis felt ten feet tall. They claimed two, possibly three enemy bombers. Their fusillades had fallen a good mile short, I reckoned, but it was impolitic to say so. Morale is an intangible quality, wonderful when high, lethal when low.

'*Sharbash*,' I said. Well done.

Old Chukkers was off his head. On this, Jesudasen and I were firmly agreed. We weren't agreed on much else: my fellow midshipman aboard the *Padmavati* happened to be a committed Indian nationalist whose party piece was an unkindly accurate impersonation of the King Emperor, George VI, stammering through his traditional Christmas broadcast. It left me amused but scandalised. The Japanese were not the only ones, half a century ago, to regard their monarch as sacred. Mother had brought me up to view the throne with a kind of religious awe. She made us all stand to attention at the Christmas dinner-table, still wearing our party hats, when the national anthem rumbled out at the end of the royal broadcast. A great patriot, my mother. She particularly hated Germans. That foot-in-mouth politician, Nicholas Ridley, would have won her vote any day.

It was naturally a bit much, I told myself, expecting the same sort of patriotism from a young, educated Indian. My main objection was that 'Jesu', as I called him, had sworn loyal service to the same, stuttering crown. And here he was spending his time sniping away at every aspect of the British Raj.

'India's being looted by the British,' he would reply accusingly. 'D'you know what RICH stands for? Rob India, Come Home.'

The rupee was being held down to an artificially low rate against the pound, he stoutly maintained, to the financial benefit of expatriates shipping their money back to England. It may or may not have been true but the belief was strongly held by Indian nationalists in the run-up to independence. Arguments like this shocked but intrigued me. I enjoyed arguing politics, and ideology never ensnared me. It was power and the exercise of power that I found fascinating. My discussions with Jesudasen on watch, in the small hours of the night, when the officer in charge was nodding over the chart table and the look-outs were doing their darnedest to keep awake, were my first on-going dialogue with an Indian who opposed British rule – apart from that brief, unfortunate encounter at the Flora fountain in Bombay – and I quivered with self-righteous indignation: 'Why ever did you join the Royal Indian Navy?' I would demand indignantly, 'if you feel such hatred for the government?'

'The chance of a lifetime,' was Jesudasen's invariable reply. 'My chance to prepare for *swaraj* [independence]. Indians are getting commands these days. Just like Old Chukkers.'

He was referring, covertly, to our lord and master, skipper of the *Padmavati*, now carrying us boldly into the Bay of Bengal. Commander Chakravatee was a Bengali of mercurial temperament whose undoubted ability, energy and sarcasm terrified officers and crew alike. Especially now. Overnight, Old Chukkers seemed to have gone stark, staring mad. Fresh from the brush with Japanese bombers at the approaches to Calcutta he had set course, without hesitation, for a patrol route off Chittagong, close to the Burma border. Orders from FOCRIN (Flag Officer Commanding, Royal Indian Navy) were to establish ourselves as an early warning system – a picket ship, the sailors called it – to detect any moves by air or sea against Calcutta. A Japanese amphibious invasion was still thought likely to cash in on the political unrest aroused by the first serious setback to British rule in Asia for a century. A hundred years before, almost to the day, a British doctor had stumbled, bleeding, into Jalalabad with a Union Jack wrapped around his body. He was the sole survivor of the British column slaughtered in the disastrous retreat from Afghanistan.

The skipper didn't have to take FOCRIN's orders *that* seriously, Jesudasen and I agreed, because the skirmish in the mouth of the Hooghly had revealed our lethal lack of armament. This far east, out braving the monsoon squalls, there would be no Hurricane fighters galloping to our rescue. The area we were patrolling was at that time beyond the reach of RAF fighters.

'Don't worry,' I heard Chakravatee telling the navigating officer. 'Lightning never strikes the same place twice. The Japs won't be back for a while.'

The navigating officer looked doubtful but wisely held his tongue. It didn't do to argue with Old Chukkers.

The RIN was a modest force, some 35,000 men strong, its largest and newest ships being modified Black Swan class sloops built in wartime Britain. The main expansion was in the inshore component, landing craft and coastal forces, the arm I was destined to join. Officers were recruited from all over the Commonwealth, mostly from Britain but also from Australia and New Zealand, and there were among us Frenchmen, Poles, even one White Russian, working in India, who had left the tea-trade to volunteer for 'Gandhi's Navy'. They were paid more than their Indian colleagues: an overseas allowance was awarded on the grounds that life for Europeans in India was expected to be more expensive.

Terminologies change but in those days everyone with pink skin pigmentation was referred to as 'European' whether they came from Soho or Sydney; the Americans were not yet thick enough on the ground to force adoption of that ghastly word 'Caucasian'.

The Indians were understandably prickly about the overseas allowance. 'Bloody robbery,' Jesudasen grumbled. And privately I agreed with him. It was an incredibly insensitive piece of legislation. Buzz words like 'discrimination' had yet to infiltrate the political vocabulary.

'Don't worry,' I assured Jesu. 'You'll do better than me in the long run. You'll end up an admiral.'

I think he did too.

'I've got to survive first,' Jesudasen groaned, hastily crossing himself, as 'Action stations' sounded for the third time in a day. Nothing happened but we were by this time uncomfortably close to Burma. Japanese Bomber Command might have been licking its wounds but there were plenty of enemy fighters capable of giving our apology for a warship an extremely hard time. You couldn't help feeling a trifle jumpy. Commander Chakravatee decided to boost morale with a spot of drill.

A primitive apparatus known as ASDIC kept pinging away inside a darkened box on the bridge. It was supposed to pick up lurking submarines. The Americans later dubbed the equipment SONAR – trust the Yanks to hit on a more marketable name – and developed it to an astounding degree. The primitive gear we carried appeared incapable of detecting anything but shoals of fish. One extra-large shoal gave the commander his excuse to put us into attack mode. A persistent underwater blip about a mile away brought us to 'anti-submarine stations'. The alarm sounded and deck-hands assembled aft checking the depth-charges. There were a dozen of these barrel-shaped canisters packed with an exceptionally powerful explosive. They were rolled overboard from rails mounted on the stern. A depth gauge set the charges off at anything between two and five hundred fathoms. The least we could drop them was at the one hundred fathom setting because the *Padmavati*, flat out, could only manage fifteen knots. Anything set for less than one hundred fathoms could have gone off before we were clear of the area.

The skipper knew we hadn't picked up a Japanese submarine. There were plenty of submarines of all shapes and sizes in the Imperial Navy but they were seldom used for long-range marauding like, say, the Germans' Atlantic 'wolf-packs' or the US submarine force deployed against Japan. 'We've got to show a bit of aggression,' Chakravatee explained to the first-lieutenant.

And psychologically he was right: the exercise did wonders all round. The ship thrust forward, engines racing, and one after the other four depth-charges plopped into our wake. For a minute or two nothing happened. Then a white circle of spray flashed across the surface of the sea, the water boiled and finally erupted with a heavy, muffled thud into a towering column of water. Not a sign of a submarine – nobody expected it – but so many fish were blown to the surface that the whaler was launched to the shrilling of the bosun's call and shouts of 'Away, sea boat's crew'. Down it went into the water, ropes screeching through the pulleys, to a stream of incomprehensible orders. It was a time-honoured routine as old as the navy itself. (The Americans had their own nautical language. A few years later, aboard the US carrier *Midway* I was amused to hear the ship's speakers shriek: 'Now hear this. Now hear this. Away *gasoline gig*!')

The crew of the whaler were plucking fish out of the sea when the sharks attacked. A floating fish close to our beam disappeared in a swirl of water. Another, then another and another. Sharks swarmed around us, large, grey and clearly visible. The oily swell was swarming with them.

'God save us,' whispered Jesudasen. 'That could be me out there.' He crossed himself, aghast. 'Let's get back to Calcutta.'

This once, I was firmly in agreement.

A lot of people loathe Calcutta. Kipling called it 'the city of dreadful night'. Most of my friends who've stopped there, bound for Benares, or for Darjeeling and the high Himalayas, couldn't wait to get away. One glance from the bus window during that squalid ride from Dum Dum airport, one encounter with those peculiarly persistent beggars around the entrance to the hotel, is usually enough to send the most seasoned traveller clamouring for onward bookings. Maybe I've had more time than most to get acquainted with the city's unsung charms: I went back to live there for two years after the Second World War. Our eldest son was born in a nursing home on Elgin, correction, Acharya Jagadish Chandra Bose Road – but friends declare that's no excuse. Nobody of sane mind and discerning taste, they say, can possibly *like* Calcutta.

Sorry, I must insist: to me, Calcutta is one of the most fascinating cities in the world. I've been convinced of that for close on fifty years. I would be the first to admit, however, that you've got to work at it. Love can't come at first sight. My own affair with this steaming, teeming monument to imperial acumen – yes, and greed too, one must admit – almost got off on the wrong foot.

Calcutta in the late summer of 1942 was at its least attractive. The Japanese were on the Burma border, some four hundred kilometres away, spasmodically bombing the Calcutta docks; word had sped round a highly politicised population that at long last the British were on the way out. British and Indian troops had arrived in vast numbers with the dual role of defending the city and suppressing dissent. I found myself engulfed in soldiers, most of them British, streaming listlessly down the broad sidewalks of Chowringhee, the thoroughfare that links the ghetto beside the south-eastern bank of the Hooghly, where Europeans and wealthy Indians choose to live, with the slums that ooze along both banks of the river up and beyond the old French enclave of Chandernagar.

The British soldiers were unarmed, sober and helpless-looking; thankfully released from barracks now that the Gandhi Rebellion – the ill-considered Quit India campaign – had spent itself in hopeless protest. These were the so-called British Other Ranks, the depressed and bedraggled BORs, overlooked and neglected in a land they had begun to hate. Many of these soldiers had been in India for a year or two. They were doomed to sweat it out three more years, until the defeat of Japan gave them gradual release; already the 'Dear John' letters from neglected wives and sweethearts were playing havoc with morale. The randy reception their loved ones were giving the Americans back in Britain went delicately unmentioned by the Indian press.

Swarming about this legion of lost and lonely men, and around us youngsters enjoying shore leave fresh from the Burma patrol, were crowds of pimps and touts and shoe-shine boys tootling home-made bamboo flutes. The shrill, mocking flutes of Chowringhee drowned out the importuning and the wheedling that propelled the foolish and the lovelorn into the dozens of decrepit bars dispensing bath-tub booze. The attraction wasn't the booze. It was the girls. Pretty young Eurasian girls had been astutely hired to sit behind the bars – tantalisingly out of reach – to draw in the British soldiery. The girls did not do anything but sit there. Drinks were served in the traditional manner by turbaned bearers. The girls simply smiled into space while the BORs paid ridiculous prices for glasses of greasy gin. Men starved of female company tried desperately to strike up a conversation, even to make a girl's acquaintance. They tried in vain: the girls knew their price, and it was far more than any BOR could pay.

I sympathised with the soldiers: I wasn't doing too well with the women myself. Dreams of donning the kind of dashing uniform that would lay 'em out in rows did not, regrettably, materialise, and a midshipman in the Royal Indian Navy did not cut a particularly glamorous figure. The absurd preponderance of men over eligible women made courting a cut-throat scramble. Custom did not permit Indian girls to mix with foreigners, or anyone else outside the home for that matter. The politest, most innocent attempt to help one of them down from a bus could be seriously misunderstood. European men had always outnumbered their womenfolk in India, hence the pre-war 'fishing fleet' searching for husbands, but the natural shortage was exacerbated by the wartime influx of hundreds of young men like myself. Only a handful of young Eurasian and European girls would condescend to fraternise, even with officers. The ones who did were for the most part snooty wee things, known sourly among my fellow wolves as 'Miss Sahibs'. A promising marriage was in those days the height of female ambition, which led them to guard their chastity closer than the crown jewels.

Officers were at least allowed into the social clubs, the more fashionable restaurants and night-clubs. The most popular spot in Calcutta was Firpo's, a large dance hall-cum-restaurant, founded by Greeks who made a fortune out of the war.

Fortunes were being made aplenty. The war was a windfall for Indian manufacturers. Factories were churning out millions of uniforms, boots, shells and rifles. The Indian-owned steel mill at Jamshedpur produced more steel than any mill outside the United States. Wartime expansion laid the groundwork for the industrial revolution (and for the large-scale corruption) that followed the British withdrawal. The blatant profiteering turned me off at first. Indians were out for all they could grab, or so it seemed to me; I saw no sign of the serenity and culture I now associate with Bengal. The Bengalis, I later found, were a sadly-misunderstood people. Other Indians actively disliked them.

'When walking through the jungle, should you meet a snake and a Bengali,' a Sikh once told me, 'kill the Bengali first.'

The Bengalis were in fact a vivid, volatile people committed to the concept of freedom. Their concept verged occasionally upon anarchy but freedom it was, nevertheless. They reminded me in some ways of the Cantonese. Like the predominant racial group in southern China, the Bengalis were the first to make considerable contact with the encroaching Europeans. They led, then lost, control of the nationalist movement. Leadership passed westwards to the Hindu heartland – as it passed northwards in China – leaving Bengal partitioned and aggrieved.

My introduction to a more civilised Calcutta came through a kindly aunt and uncle. Their large, airy apartment down by the Anglican cathedral provided my first insight into the comforts of expatriate life. Uncle Guy had been in India for forty years. He made a good living selling automobiles, but within the hierarchical ranks of the British business community in India – the men we called the 'box wallahs' – my uncle was, unforgivably, in 'trade'. The leading clubs admitted only those in 'commerce', offering access to men hawking insurance but slamming the door on anything as paltry as a car-salesman. My uncle was naturally bitter and, while thoroughly enjoying the Anglo-Indian lifestyle, he regarded his country of chosen exile with deeply jaundiced eye. The political scene, in his view, was a farce.

'Gandhi, Nehru, the whole bloody lot of them can be bought off for a couple of *lakhs* [200,000 rupees]', he stoutly maintained.

It was not true. The Indian leadership could never have been snapped up for the equivalent of £16,000. Or ten, or any number of times that sum, in my opinion. But this was a belief widely held by expatriate businessmen.

'The minute we leave, the tribesmen will be down from the hills,' Uncle Guy would growl delightedly. 'There won't be a virgin left in the Ganges valley.'

The thought seemed to give him enormous satisfaction.

'Too many liberals mucking about with our India policy,' he would declare, fixing me with an accusing stare. I'm certain he thought me one of them but was too polite to say so.

'Look around you. Learn a bit. You'll see we're here to stay.'

Looking around convinced me of the opposite. But it was my turn to be polite. I changed the subject or went off to talk to Aunt Marjorie. My aunt told a different story. Knitting on the apartment verandah, after her afternoon nap, she told me about the Great Durbar of 1912. It was then that George V announced the removal of the capital from Calcutta. The moment the King Emperor declared that a fresh seat would be found for the government of the Raj at an entirely new site outside Delhi – what we now call 'New' Delhi – a murmur rose from the crowd. A soothsayer had predicted that British rule would come to an end when the viceroy vacated Calcutta. The prediction came true, but not for another thirty-five years.

Personally, I was unimpressed by the Raj. The British are an odd bunch and I should know, being one of them, but prolonged exposure to power seemed to expose unpleasant aspects of their character. Perfectly pleasant people from Surbiton or Shrewsbury become prickly and pompous beneath a feathered cocked hat; an unduly harsh judgment, perhaps, but that was the way things struck me after a matter of months in India, still glowing with self-righteous liberalism and sympathy for the underdog. I moved for the most part, mind you, in the narrowest service circles. The British I had so far met were bigots to a man. Most of the women were too, as far as I can remember, though I did not meet as many of them as I'd have liked. An extended stay in Calcutta did not entirely dispel my prejudices, but contact with that extraordinary city widened my perspectives. Some errand took me to Writers' Building, the government headquarters, in what was then Dalhousie Place. It's since been renamed Bendy Bagel Dinesh Bag.

Writers' Building was a scruffy, red-brick rabbit warren bulging with *babus*. This is the generic term for the sub-species of Indian clerk that was peculiar to the Raj. It was created to ease the administrative load of the

1,300 men who ran India. The covenanted officers of the Indian Civil Service (ICS), 'the steel frame' as they immodestly called themselves, were an élite handful selected by examination after the manner of Chinese mandarins. Their reputation for incorruptibility is still a byword in independent India.

The ICS men I met in Writers' Building were urbane, civilised and somewhat scholarly, deeply committed to the people they served. None of them used the dreaded word 'wog'. It was my first encounter in India with Britons who were neither racist nor reactionary – members of an élite bureaucracy, dedicated to the well-being, not the denigration, of the people they ruled – and they aroused in me an interest in the imperial past. Surely, I began to ask myself, it couldn't have been *all* bad? Nor was it, on examination, though the disaster that winter left me profoundly depressed.

The ICS officers I met in Calcutta in 1942 were, however, losing heart. They knew their time was running out – not, as I had been led to believe, because of the Japanese or the Gandhi rebellion, but because the India Act passed by the British parliament in 1935 had set irrevocable course for self-rule. The provinces of India had been made self-governing under political (mainly Indian National Congress) administrations. Members of the ICS, by this time almost half of them Indian, some controlling districts a third the size of England with millions of inhabitants, were obliged to operate at the behest of politicians who plainly hated their guts. The experiment, known as 'dyarchy', produced a contradictory form of dual control, with ICS and politicians constantly at each others' throats. It ended in September 1939, when the Congress administrations resigned in protest against the tactless British failure to consult them over the declaration of war against Hitler. The clock could never be put back, however; the reforms had signalled a march, indeed a gallop, towards independence that nothing could possibly stop.

Around the end of 1942, a bumbling British attempt to retake the strip of coast adjoining India, known as the Arakan, was mercilessly repulsed by the Japanese. The political temperature in Calcutta hovered at boiling-point. The nationalists, believing that independence was within their grasp, sensed the sweet scent of victory. Two fresh targets had lately been found for their calumny. One was the Muslim coalition government of Bengal. The Muslims were a comparatively new force in Indian politics. Their agitations were sadly destined to result in the political disaster of Pakistan. They emerged from obscurity when the provincial Congress administration resigned at the outbreak of the Second World War. Muslim politicos stepped sleazily into the vacuum in Calcutta, led by a fat, fatuous manipulator, one Fazil Haq, who looked like he bathed perpetually in axle grease.

The other object of nationalistic loathing was the British writer, Beverly Nichols, described by one of his many detractors as 'a graduate to journalism from the bed of Somerset Maugham'. Nichols had come out briefly at the beginning of the war and written a book called *Verdict on India*. It was an ill-timed, arrogant and superficial work that dismissed nationalist demands for self-rule and sneered at many aspects of Indian life.

Many Indians objected vociferously. The Nichols 'verdict' whipped up a storm of protest. I caught a whiff of it one spring afternoon, lolling around the *maidan*, the long strip of parkland that separates the smarter sections of Calcutta from the River Hooghly. It was a beautiful day. The flame trees were a blaze of crimson. People dozed and chatted in the little pepper-pot pavilions beneath the tall tower now known as the *Sahid Minar*, the base of which provided a handy platform for speakers at political rallies.

Demonstrators began gathering as I sat there enjoying the sunshine. Banners appeared condemning the British Raj, the Fazil Haq administration and Beverly Nichols – plenty there to keep any rabble-rouser gainfully employed. Political demonstrations had been banned since Gandhi launched the Quit India movement. Well, not exactly banned, but as the authorities politely put it, meetings were 'permissible only under police licence'. The licence, needless to say, was never granted. On this particular afternoon the speakers had hardly gotten into their stride when riot squads rolled up by the busload, brandishing brass-tipped staves. Coolly and efficiently they set about dispersing the crowd. Before they did so, charging in, beating the fleeing demonstrators, I caught one of the speakers condemning the onset of famine.

India had suffered dreadful famines in the past. Those in Mogul times depopulated large areas of the country. Famines had recurred under the British but a system established in 1908 was supposed to make such things impossible. The plan was to rush in food supplies from reserve stores whenever shortages developed. But the system broke down towards the end of 1942. Rice shipments from Burma had been cut off. There was panic buying. The price of rice, the staple diet of Bengal, increased five times in as many weeks. Speculators made fortunes. The greediest and most notorious were hand in glove with the Fazil Haq administration. Chief Minister Haq refused for a long time to face up to the crisis. The over-worked British bureaucracy ('file-flattened', one columnist called them) failed to move relief supplies in time. The bureaucrats blamed the administration for failing to provide sufficient warning. The politicians in their turn blamed the bureaucrats.

The Bengal famine cost more than half a million lives, with the poorer peasantry being particularly hard hit. They streamed into Calcutta in their thousands and the streets were soon strewn with dead and dying. It was 'a shame and a reproach,' wrote Philip Woodruff, 'to men of English blood'. British bureaucrats in Bengal blamed 'dyarchy', the lately-introduced form of government. Before then the Raj had been autocratically ruled by a handful of expatriates using a mixture of bluff and *hikmatali*, best translated as cautious, judicious management.

'Responsibility was blurred [under dyarchy],' Woodruff declared years later. 'Neither Englishman nor Indian felt it was his failure but the other man's when he saw a pregnant woman lying dead of starvation in the streets.'

The Bengal famine was the final blow to ICS morale. The long drawn-out experiment in power-sharing had paralysed an already over-loaded machine. Expatriates who had given their lives to the Indian service gave up in despair. Woodruff knew it was the end. The political reforms might be flawed, he regretfully concluded, but they had set the British upon 'a road on which there was no going back; they must go forward; that meant they must leave India'.

Historians see the Second World War from a loftier perspective. The books I've read about the struggle with Japan emphasise the victory of superior technology over a less-developed economy. It all sounds a bit strange today. Some praise the efficacy of western educational systems that churned out fighter pilots and similar technocrats faster than the more formalised schooling in Japan. I'm sure that no longer applies. My school didn't do much for me when it came to turning out a well-honed fighting machine: though I must have been a special case. A dip into my one surviving diary (for the year 1943) reveals nothing more than an obsession with girls. The diary creates the impression I had no other interests. Not a word emerges from those early pages of the efforts I should have been making to perfect my seamanship in readiness for my first patrol; not a mention either of the burgeoning struggle then being planned by the Indian High Command to win back Burma. I can't even find mention of the 75-foot harbour defence motor launch (HDML) to which I'd been assigned, or of the skipper who plainly hated my guts.

Lieutenant Harry Revell RINVR was what we called 'pusser' through and through. He was thoroughly imbued, in other words, with the traditions of the Royal Navy. His father had been killed at Jutland. He'd lost a brother, I think, aboard HMS *Hood*. A volunteer from the outbreak of the war, a veteran of the Atlantic convoys, the man who commanded HDML 1076 had forgotten more about arcane naval matters than I would ever know. The chap was deep into mysteries like rust-inhibiting red lead ('a few dabs here and there are the sign of a well-kempt ship'), the use of sounding lines, semaphore signals, foresprings and backsprings and flexible steel wire rope. The sort of dedicated professional who rightly resented being stuck with an idle, indifferent youth who cared only for *navel* knowledge of the most carnal kind. The lieutenant's sole reason for joining the RIN had been to impart some of his considerable expertise into a new and over-expanded branch of the Indian imperial services. It was his cruel fate, he often complained, to have me landed on his deck as green as an unripe tomato. About as useful too, I might add.

Having completed my training period aboard HMIS *Padmavati*, I had been sent from Calcutta to Bombay to serve at sea with Coastal Forces. Coastal Forces – or 'Costly Farces' as the regulars sneeringly called us – had been formed, largely by yachtsmen, to combat German E-boats in the North Sea and the English Channel. High-speed, short-range boats had been specially developed to fight a vicious little war at close quarters with an extremely skilful enemy.

The same sort of conditions did not exist around India where similar wooden motor launches (MLs) were used either for harbour defence or, in a larger size, for offensive operations down the Burma coast. Acting as second-in-command (or 'Number One' in naval parlance) aboard one of these launches struck me as a piece of cake. And for a long time nothing would induce me to take the job seriously. The time I should have been perfecting my abilities as a gung-ho nineteen-year-old midshipman was spent largely in pursuit of equally youthful nurses in one of the main city hospitals.

I was not alone in my incompetence. Most of our twelve-man crew had never been to sea. One of them, a fierce-eyed Muslim from the Punjab, had never even *seen* the sea until he took the King Emperor's rupee. But we pottered about Bombay harbour trying to look like sailors, hoisting flag signals (the wrong way up), heaving the lead (and losing it) and attempting, without great success, to operate our Asdic anti-submarine gear. Our task (as the brass would say nowadays) was to establish an impenetrable defence ring, day and night, around the outer approaches. Our young Singhalese Asdic operator, fresh out of training school, never got a single 'ping' out of the equipment. He was hastily transferred after an embarrassing night's debauch with a Sikh petty officer, but that's another story.

My first problem once we had made it out into the harbour was finding out where we'd got to. Or to quote the skipper, getting a 'fix' on our position. The chart down in the wheelhouse was marked with certain navigational points. They could be a lighthouse, a buoy or a monolith on a prominent headland. All you had to do was take bearings from three of these points with a prismatic gizmo on top of the bridge compass and back-trace them across the chart. The place where they intersected would form a triangular 'cocked hat' which gave your approximate position. The first time I did it, Harry Revell ordered me to take off my hat.

'Why?' I asked.

'Because according to you this ship is smack in the middle of Bombay Cathedral,' howled Revell. I know you've heard the story before but it really happened to me, cross my heart and so forth. The first night on patrol the skipper stayed on the bridge until the small hours.

'I can't keep awake a moment longer,' he finally told me. 'I've just got to lie down. She's all yours, God help us.'

Experience, they say, is the most expensive thing in the world. I got plenty that night. I took my stand alone, untried and dangerously unskilled, as HDML 1076 surged around the outer reaches of Bombay harbour at all of fifteen knots. Not all that fast, you might say? Fast as light when you don't know how to stop the wretched thing in her tracks. Of course, I'd learned a few basics. Things like helm orders – 'port', that's left, I think … 'port five', … that gives you five degrees of port rudder … and, hold on to your hat … *'hard a' starboard'*, which spins her to the right pretty damn quick – oh yes, I vaguely knew how to steer.

What no one had taught me, as far as I can recall, was how to slam the brakes on. And as the tide-set carried me down, inexorably, on to a cluster of moored dhows I knew that sometime in the next few minutes I would need to halt this ship. Desperately I ordered the coxswain down in the wheelhouse to steer us around the bows of the sleeping sail-boats. It was hopeless. The only way to pass moored vessels, I learned that night, is *astern* of them. If you try to creep close around their bows the tide will carry you to inevitable collision, and the tide in Bombay is very strong indeed. 'Port five, port ten,' I ordered. 'Port twenty, *hard a' port!*'

Not a bit of use: the tide was too fierce. A bowsprit loomed overhead chewing into our starboard shrouds. At the moment of impact I remembered the depth-charges. Coming up on watch I'd set all their primers (pressure fuses) to six feet. Why not, we were in shallowish water, weren't we? There was a loud splash as the bow of the boat I'd hit swept one of the explosive canisters overboard. You were supposed to be a good two hundred yards away when one of those went off. I braced myself for the imminent explosion underneath our hull …

Harry Revell came rushing back to the bridge when he heard the crash.

'Full astern two!' he yelled to the coxswain. The engine telegraph clanged. The engines went into reverse. The patrol boat stopped dead and began to back away. Now why didn't I think of that?

'The depth-charge,' I said guiltily, pointing to the empty cradle on our starboard quarter. It should have gone off in two or three seconds, blowing us all to kingdom come.

'Some bloody fool set the primers to six feet,' Revell said, staring hard at me in the darkness. 'Fortunately I set them all to *off* before I turned in.'

'That was smart,' I gulped with relief. 'I wonder who could have done such a stupid thing?'

We should never have sailed. To this day I can't think why we did. Exigencies of the service and all that guff, one can only presume; more likely the sloth of some weather-watchers forgetting to warn sailors of approaching peril. Whatever the reason we slipped moorings in all innocence, ordered southwards to Madras, way down the Indian east coast, despite the fact that there was ample time to abort the trip. Calcutta slipped astern in streaming rain, while the full-flooding Hooghly hustled us downstream. Diamond Harbour murkily appeared. We passed the anchorage patrolled by *Padmavati* and bombed by the Japanese and headed blithely into the Bay of Bengal smack into the teeth of an approaching cyclone.

The scene was entirely different from the way it looked the year before. Merchantmen had wisely quit the anchorage, seeking shelter upriver. The fishing boats had cut and run. Rows of them lay beached on the alluvial shoreline, held down with stones and rope, while the palm trees bowed close to breaking point and frightened villagers fled inland from the encroaching sea. A howling wind blustered in loaded with lukewarm rain. At first it sounded like a roaring lion. Later it became a thundering express train. Its gusts scalped the wave-tops, knifing off volleys of stinging spume. Mountains of muddy ocean heaved up on every hand, dropping us into troughs deeper than the cross-yard, dousing our battered boat with booming waves that bent the forward gunshield and stove in one of the wheelhouse windows.

Most of the crew were already paralysed with sea-sickness. Groaning bodies carpeted the lower deck. I was sick myself, struggling with the wheel while the coxswain checked below for damage and the waters sluiced through the broken wheelhouse glass and swirled around my knees. Much of my vomit had trickled inside my shirt, retaining sour memories of breakfast lost and I pleaded with my new skipper, Charles Bradshaw, to let me sneak below and quietly expire. The skipper refused to listen. He held grimly to his perch atop the bridge assisted by Denis, a Eurasian midshipman with two years' sea service. The boy's undoubted knowledge of seamanship was proving far more valuable at this critical hour than anything I had bothered to pick up.

I did not realise it at the time – there was too much else to think about – but this was my moment of truth. On 25 May 1943, Sub-Lieutenant Russell Spurr RINVR, an officer of notorious incompetence, was face to face with the facts of life. This was no longer a game. Play-school was over. There could be no more fantasising, no more fooling around. Commitment, dedication and a great deal of hard work were finally required. It's the sort of challenge, I suppose, that eventually confronts us all. A lucky few learn their lesson early on; I was a regrettably slow learner. But out in the storm-swept Bay it looked for a while as if realisation had come too late. Any moment now could be our last.

Earlier in the year I had been promoted from midshipman, on age rather than merit, and transferred from futile patrol in the Bombay approaches to the star performer of Indian Coastal Forces, the 55th ML (Motor Launch) Flotilla. The MLs in question were bigger than those I'd known before. They were 110-foot Fairmile 'Bs', equipped with two Hall-Scott engines, maximum speed nineteen knots, and fitted out as motor gunboats (with anti-submarine capability) for operations down the Burma coast. Before I joined, the flotilla had been rampaging through the Arakan region, interdicting Japanese supply barges close inshore. Publicity pictures had shown a skipper painting Rising Sun flags on his bridge housing: one flag for every enemy craft destroyed.

The operations sounded dangerous to me – and absurdly ill-timed. After long and patient effort, in blatant disregard of my duties, I had managed to engineer what is nowadays called a relationship (we used a more explicit term) with a teenage nurse in a Bombay hospital. The question of my transfer to the flotilla had been the subject of furious debate, I subsequently learned; my reputation for casual uselessness had reached influential ears. Word gets around when skippers go scuttling to the powers-that-be begging them to post an officer to anybody's boat but *theirs*. Manpower was at a premium, however, and I was transferred with some misgivings to ML 475, brand-new, and about to be commissioned from a Calcutta shipyard. I was received with polite reserve by the skipper, Lieutenant Charles Bradshaw RINVR, and Denis, the midshipman, who had originally served in the merchant navy.

Charles was another new arrival from the Royal Navy. He had heard plenty about his new second-in-command. I don't think he liked what he'd heard. He took me under protest; strictly on trial. It did not take him long to get the measure of me. He was particularly unimpressed by my performance during the cyclone. Taking a turn at the wheel might sound heroic but the myriad jobs I should have been doing – to check the straining hull, rouse the crew and relieve the skipper on the bridge – were being done better, and without question, by the boy appointed as my junior.

My fate was decided even before we clawed our way out of the storm. I had spent several unthinking hours on my bunk, leaving Charles and Denis to weather the elements, bothered only by the ungainly pitching and by the mosquitoes that swarmed out of our flooded bilges. While I idled below the pair of them fought the boat into a sheltering lee shore. We spent a nightmare night, constantly dragging anchor, drifting close to pounding surf, before limping back next day to the dockyard in Calcutta. Denis spent the time up-river preparing a damage list that should have been my responsibility. Charles said nothing. He had made up his mind to get rid of me as soon as we joined the flotilla in Madras.

The resumed trip south was smoothly uneventful. The cyclone had blown itself out leaving the inevitable trail of damage. We entered Madras harbour at 1545 hours, Saturday, 5 June 1943. My diary shows I'd no idea of the fate awaiting me. There is an art to disposing of unpleasant situations with the minimum of fuss – I've been knifed often enough since to know that confrontation is the last thing executives desire – but I can't help remarking that on this occasion my removal was exquisitely arranged. I stayed aboard sorting out my dirty laundry, blissfully unaware of what was going on, while Charles was putting the hard word to the flotilla leader. Three days later a signal came through from the shore base, HMIS

Russell Spurr, the young RIN officer armed with a camera

Frank Worth on entering the Navy at the age of 19 as a midshipman – the lowest form of naval officer life! Naval rules permit the holding of the rank of sub-lieutenant only after the age of 20. But soon after his combat coverage Mountbatten arranged the special promotion of Worth to sub-lieutenant – still at the age of 19

Russell as a young Argyll and Sutherland Highlander

Midshipman Worth dreaming of his future exploits

Russell captured at a rare moment – with a non-alcoholic drink, coconut milk!

Sub-Lieutenant Frank Worth

RIN MLs lead in the landing craft to an assault on the enemy's coastal defences

*The 'ball of fire' which Frank captured at rather closer quarters during one of the
RIN's amphibious swoops on the northern tip of Ramree Island*

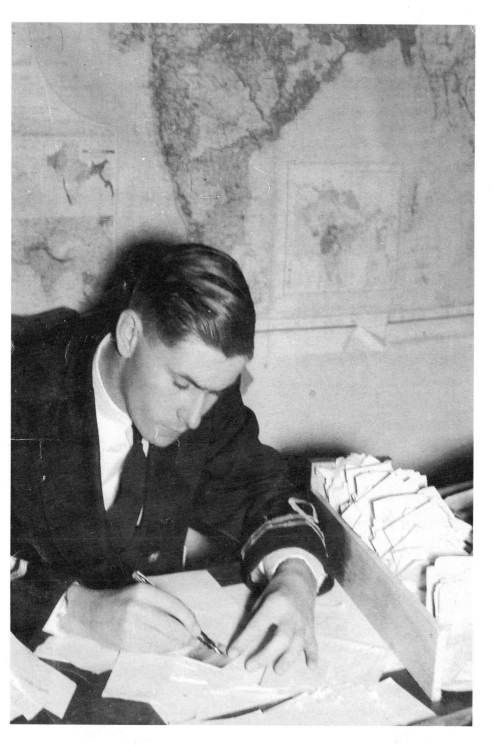

Russell hard at work cropping pictures at the PRD office in Delhi

Frank poking his tongue out at Russell as there was no room for him in a spotter plane off to observe explosions of naval shells on Japanese positions

An RIN ship moored alongside Rangoon docks. They were devastated by the RAF in the course of the war

Romulus and Remus, Frank and Russell: the Heavenly Twins and the Terrible Twins – but which is which?

Mahseer, announcing that Denis would get my job as second-in-command of ML 475, while I would be transferred elsewhere.

'A terrible blow!' my diary records. 'I am transferred to ML 476.' It was, I realise, the end of the line. ML 476 had just returned from action in Burma. Its hull and upperworks were still streaked with camouflage and dirt. The crew were a bolshie lot who despised their officers. But that wasn't the half of it. 'ML 476 is bad enough,' I went on, 'but Peter Lawrence has (just) got command of her and that's a bit more than *anyone* can bear.' It was a widely-held view among junior officers in the flotilla that Captain Bligh outdid Lieutenant Peter Lawrence in the popularity stakes. It was well-known that he did not suffer fools gladly; especially idle fools like me.

It was some time before I realised that his chilly aloofness was partially defensive. The poor man was cursed with a pronounced stammer of which he was painfully self-conscious. He eyed me, when I reported aboard, with unconcealed loathing.

'Your r-r-reputation has p-p-preceded you,' he managed to spit out. His cold blue eyes flashed angrily. 'You either sh-sh-shape up in this sh-sh-ship or ashore you go into the m-m-motor pool.'

The motor pool in an Indian naval base was considered the kiss of death. You couldn't sink any lower. The prospect didn't convert me overnight into an estimable officer, but it jolted me hard enough to transform ML 476 into a clean and efficient ship. It set me studying signalling, rope and wire splicing, seamanship and rudimentary navigation until I had won a measure of respect from my peers.

Things started disastrously, however. The flotilla put to sea the afternoon I reported aboard for signal exercises. My job as first-lieutenant was to supervise raising anchor at the small forecastle capstan. The boat's anchor chain was too small for the capstan teeth (the 'gypsy', I think we called it) and had to be hauled in by hand without protection of the ratchet that stops the winding handle flying back. A sudden strain came on the chain and it did precisely that: flying into the face of the seaman who was manning it. He was terribly injured, bleeding all over the deck. We were late leaving harbour while the injured man was rushed ashore. Lawrence told me next day that a court of inquiry would be held. He implied that I was to blame.

'How fed up I am with him and his bloody ship,' I wrote in my diary. It could have been his chance to dump me. But to my surprise he took my side and I was tentatively let off the hook.

The 55th ML Flotilla was led by a lieutenant-commander called Heather. He was one of those marvellous eccentrics the British seem to produce in wartime: an officer in the mould of Wingate, the lunatic then leading the Chindit irregulars in Burma. Like that unorthodox brigadier, who once received the Commander-in-Chief, India, wearing a topee and nothing but nothing else, Heather inspired fanatic loyalty among his underlings and loathing among the higher brass. None of us in the flotilla had any doubt that during the last operational period in Burma he had forged the 55th into an effective fighting instrument; yet this was certainly not the view of Captain, Coastal Forces, an unimaginative four-ringer who barely concealed his contempt for amateur sailors. Seen through peacetime spectacles he may have been right. The way we conducted ourselves, like seaborne guerrillas, was often unorthodox in the extreme.

The so-called 'big ship sailors' – those serving in the RIN's small fleet of frigates and AMCs – were often the object of our ridicule. Their lives seemed lapped around with bullshit. As far as we were concerned naval regulations were meant to be bent, if not broken. Defiantly, we scrounged stores to which we weren't entitled. The army had given us 3-inch mortars which were mounted on our after-decks. Our lockers were stuffed full of unauthorised Bren guns, boxes and boxes of grenades and strictly forbidden objects like fake Japanese flags, flown covertly behind the lines, which mocked the Geneva convention. Worst of all, from the viewpoint of the regulars, we displayed a pride, a panache, that could only be construed by tight-laced time-servers as plain impertinence.

Heather was relieved of command early in July. I never knew why. His enemies swore he had gone mad. Checking in at naval headquarters, Karachi, he is alleged to have kicked the admiral's Pekingese – a sure sign of madness, we were told. The day of his departure all ships' companies were paraded on the quayside. Heather made a short speech and then with true showmanship ordered his flotilla leader's pennant lowered from the yard. Some wept.

Most moved was my new-found friend, Mickey Tong, the flotilla engineer officer. A pre-war racing driver, Mickey thought the world of Heather. He thought the world of Vera Lynn, incidentally, and regularly wept when she sang *White Cliffs of Dover*. That night I accompanied Tong to a fashionable hotel in Madras where he proceeded to lay one on. He went through his regular party trick, munching glasses in the bar, to the astonishment of the other drinkers, leading someone to complain about his conduct. I got the blame, of course. The newly-appointed flotilla leader, Lieutenant-Commander 'Ram' Derbyshire, felt I should have restrained my colleague. The Ram knew me from Bombay. He did not like me one little bit. I saw the confidential report he wrote about me at the end of the war. 'Lacks sense of responsibility', it said with masterly understatement. It took time to convince him of my bona fides.

It took time to convince Lawrence, as well. Relations between us were never cordial. A man so private, so cultured, so essentially stiff-upper-lip, found my personal brand of flamboyance deeply offensive. Lots of others have since, so who am I to complain? The extraordinary thing was that this biting tension produced a profitable partnership, earning the least popular boat in the flotilla a novel reputation for smartness and efficiency.

As far as I was concerned, the penny had finally dropped. Overnight the cheerful lay-about was abnormally businesslike. Some thought I overdid it. I prowled the boat, noting defects, setting everything to rights. Rusted bottlescrews were cleaned and oiled – a minor matter noticed only by real sailors – and those much-needed repairs were made to the capstan. Wire brushes cleaned the tattered guard-rails. Dabs of red lead appeared all over the place. Painting became an obsession. The hull, the upper works and our one squat funnel gleamed battleship grey. Cockroaches were hunted from the galley with caustic soda (at some risk to the wiring) and fresh splinter mats arranged around the bridge. Things that experience alone can teach – the set of the tide, manoeuvring on twin engines, keeping station at night without ramming the boat immediately ahead – began falling into place. Technical language, once gibberish, gradually made sense. A new-found pride stung me into learning the seaman's trade; it might not have produced a superb sailor but the reformed girl-chaser was a great deal wiser, and cleverer and, dare I say it, more sure of himself, when the flotilla sailed for Burma in November 1943.

A green flare arched up above the palm trees. It could have meant we'd been spotted. The gun crews tensed. Up on the bridge we held our breath: any moment now could come a sudden burst of gunfire. Nothing happened. The rubber dinghy pulled steadily towards the surf, paddles dimly flashing in the starlight. I watched it anxiously through binoculars. The skipper, standing beside me, checked and rechecked his watch. According to our information we had half an hour before the Japanese beach patrol returned. The last word we had been given was that it came and went with uncanny precision. The Japanese, we now knew, were superb soldiers. They'd thoroughly earned the sobriquet 'Prussians of the East'. We hoped that, like their Teutonic counterparts, they would now display a helpful inflexibility.

It was three o'clock on a cold morning in late November. We were on our first mission down the Burma coast. A spy-drop. Three men had come aboard at Chittagong, one British, the other two Burmese. All were members of the Royal Burma Police returning to their old bailiwick south of the occupied port of Akyab. Landfall was a gorgeous stretch of beach in a picture-postcard bay, close, but not too close, to a once-thriving fishing village. The fishermen's boats were almost out of sight beneath the dense hedge of fringing palms. And though a hostile force would be thoroughly well concealed within such vegetation, it was unlikely any were here, since all indications were that this stretch of coast was lightly held. And unlike most Burmese the local fishermen were friendly. They had been badly hit by the war and wanted out. Fishing boats seldom ventured to sea these days. Any form of offshore activity was hazardous. The coastal barge traffic our boats had encountered earlier in the year was virtually at a standstill. We were being forced further and further behind Japanese lines in search of targets.

The 55th ML Flotilla, eight boats strong, had been given the job of inshore harassment from the main Allied base at Chittagong. A handier forward base had been established at Teknaaf on the northern bank of the Naaf River (the present border between Burma and Bangladesh) but the moorings were too exposed to ship in fuel and ammunition. Japanese fighter pilots took to shooting up our river-craft when there was nothing better to do.

Our spy-drop was conducted under strict security. The three policemen spent the trip in the ward-room, speaking to Peter Lawrence and no one else. They were given twenty minutes to paddle ashore through the surf, hide the dinghy and give us the get-away signal with a blue-shielded flashlamp. My job was to watch them safely through the surf. It looked simple; the sea was reasonably calm. The six-foot surf should pose no problems. The plan was that we should do our best to rescue them if they got into difficulties, or the enemy made a surprise appearance. Meanwhile we would hover offshore, almost aground in the shallow waters, until that flashlamp signal. We should beat it, fast. No one wanted to get caught.

Army intelligence had given us a lecture back in Chittagong on special escape procedures. Clever little devices were demonstrated to navigate us back to friendly lines – the cleverest of all were magnetic fly buttons which spun north when detached from your pants and hung by a cotton thread. As far as I know they were never issued. Personally, I couldn't see myself fiddling with my flies if we were unlucky enough to get wrecked this far behind enemy lines.

Little help could be expected from the Burmese, our lecturer warned us, and we could face at least a week's walk back through areas the Japanese tightly controlled. The likelihood was that we'd be captured (a thought that struck dismay in every heart), in which case it was advisable to play things cool and conserve your strength. The Japanese had set ways of dealing with captured personnel. They roughed you up and starved you for a couple of days before you were considered weak enough for them to relax their vigilance. That was when the attempt should be made at a breakaway although we were advised that retribution, on recapture, could be severe. Decapitation by samurai sword was fairly common. If it was any consolation, the Japanese felt that particular form of execution conferred some kind of honour ...

The dinghy hit the surf and promptly capsized. Three heads appeared beside it in the water striking out for the shore. They staggered up the beach dragging the upended dinghy with them. Another flare rose, this time a red one.

'T-t-twenty minutes gone,' Peter Lawrence stuttered. 'I w-w-wonder if they've l-l-lost their stores?' One of the men carried a heavy pack in his hand.

'Maybe the flashlight will be useless,' I suggested helpfully. I found myself regarding the scene with uncanny detachment. It was as if I wasn't personally involved.

'It was waterproof,' Lawrence replied. He always lost his stutter when situations grew more worrisome. 'But I hope to Christ the buggers hurry up,' he added.

One of our most experienced seamen was taking soundings with the leadline. His muttered readings could hardly be heard above the low throb of our idling engines.

'By the mark *two*!'

We were safe enough in a couple of fathoms. Anything less than a fathom and a half and the Asdic dome slung uselessly below our bow would bump sea bottom. A tiny blue light winked from beneath the trees.

'That's it!' cried Lawrence, heaving a sigh of relief. 'Number One, it's time we f-f-fucked off!'

Nobody asked the Japanese to wish us a merry Christmas but they did so, regardless. Their brown camouflaged bombers came in low across Chittagong harbour – twelve of them, all holding perfect formation – low enough, in fact, to spot the red suns and the oil streaks on their wings and, directly overhead, the bomb doors deliberately opening ... It wasn't fair, of course, but in their place I would probably have done the same. You could almost imagine their Harvard-educated intelligence officer spelling out his audacious plan for catching the hated *gaijin* with their pants down. Right down. Trust me to be in that position, down in the heads, at precisely that moment, wondering why some practical joker was sounding the air-raid siren.

It was three o'clock on Christmas afternoon. The Japanese had chosen the perfect time to strike. Everyone had wined and dined a mite too well. The Japanese caught us, incapable of coherent action, swinging from a buoy in the fast-flowing River Karnapuli, looking foolish and feeling completely helpless.

We had returned to base the previous evening from a further spell in the River Naaf, inviting the occasional mortar-shell from the embattled Japanese as they fell back before the Indo-British offensive. Moored off Teknaaf we had watched the gun flashes as the 25th Indian Division fought its way out of encirclement.

We did not know it at the time but this was an historic action, the turning point, in fact, of the Arakan campaign. The Japanese had followed their traditional tactic of attacking to stave off our advance, temporarily surrounding the division and cutting off its supplies. This would ordinarily have thrown our side into retreat; on this occasion the Division stood and slugged it out, amply supplied by air. Now it was the turn of the Japanese to retreat as their supplies ran out, taking the first stumbling step in a rout that was to carry us back to Rangoon, while we sat sipping army-issue rum

on the after deck, speculating how long the war would last. Three more
years at least, most of us reckoned.

I had bought a record player and a collection of shellac records.
Tchaikovsky's First Piano Concerto was a current favourite, thanks to a
Hollywood film that portrayed Stalin's Russia as Paradise Regained, but
the night of the battle I favoured the Moonlight Sonata. Tum, tum, tum ...
Tum, tum, tum ... the rum passed around, the moon glistened on the wide
river waters while a mile away on the southern bank men fought with
unbridled ferocity. Every yard along the forested estuary was bitterly
contested. The Japanese threw away their lives in hopeless assaults while
Tum, tum, tum ... the pianist was Moiseiwitsch, the recording monaural,
made in Carnegie Hall about 1937. Dum, de, *Dum* ...! A vehicle went up in
flames close to the riverbank, burnishing the dark waters with billowy
orange light.

'Another poor sod's bought it,' a colleague murmured.

'Tough luck,' someone else said callously. 'If your number's on it,
you've had it.'

We weren't as hard as we made out. But most of us were deeply
fatalistic. So much depended on *kismet*, on fate, on the luck of the draw.
Our war so far had been relatively painless – that was fate too. One boat
should have been written off already. It had run aground within sight of an
enemy shore battery, leaving it the proverbial sitting duck. Shells started
whining in, closer and closer. A Eurasian officer named Jordan, a devout
Catholic, fell on his knees on open deck proclaiming: 'Fifty chips (rupees)
to the Shrine of Saint Somebody if we get out of this alive.' Mist
immediately drifted in, spoiling the enemy gunners' aim. From then on we
talked (but never laughed) about 'Jordan's fifty chip mist.'

Another boat, way down the coast on an interdiction raid, was
whiling away the afternoon anchored off-shore. It was flying the Japanese
flag. We found it safer to lay up in the daytime, displaying enemy colours,
and doing our dirty work mainly at night. A Mitsubishi bomber appeared
from nowhere. He flew low over the boat waggling his wings in
recognition. The false flag must have convinced the pilot that this boat was
one of theirs – it should have been, that deep into enemy territory. The
ML's most experienced gunner, a Baluchi fundamentalist called Ahmed
Khan, was drowsing alongside his Oerlikon cannon. Totally disregarding
orders, muttering something about *jihad*, he leaped into the harness and
loosed off a magazine full of cannon shells at the intruding plane. The
Japanese was obviously astounded – as was the ship's company. The plane
turned back towards the ship on a bombing run while the crew tried,
frantically and vainly, to ditch the anchor. Suddenly smoke spouted from
the Mitsubishi's starboard engine, the plane wobbled, gingerly reversed
course and headed back inland. Much against everyone's recommendation
the mad Baluchi won a mention in dispatches.

The main topic as we tied up in Chittagong on Christmas Eve was the next day's lunch. Our Goanese cook, De Souza, managed to scrounge a couple of scrawny chickens from the late-night bazaar. It certainly made a change from an endless diet of bully beef. We ate bully beef until it was coming out of our ears. We ate the wretched stuff curried, stewed, fried and most often as a liquid sludge straight from the can.

My job was to rustle up the booze. Borrowing a jeep from our shore-based staff I drove to the nearest Gurkha encampment and crossed a few palms with rupees. I ended up with three bottles of Indian-made gin. I also managed to purloin two dozen bottles of Rosa Triple X ration rum, enough to keep the non-Muslim members of the crew paralytic for the next forty-eight hours. De Souza was an excellent cook but he did have a drinking problem. His price for producing Christmas lunch with all the trimmings was one bottle of rum to himself.

We were starting in on his mince pies (and I had nipped out of the ward-room to answer a quick call of nature) when the Japanese arrived. Our enemies reckoned, quite rightly, that the defending forces would be feeling little pain. Anti-aircraft fire turned out to be wild in the extreme. All but one of our newly-arrived Spitfires remained grounded, and the only one that managed to take off ploughed into trees at the end of the runway. It was being flown, if that is the word, by an accounts officer who ran whooping from the mess, jumped into the cockpit and trundled off, terminally, before anyone could stop him.

Clutching at my trousers, I scrambled across the upper deck to help slip the mooring ropes. The crews of two other boats beside us were trying to do the same. Everybody shouted, staggering about. The only inactive figure was De Souza, bottle in hand, slumped beside the Oerlikon gun.

'Jesus save us!' he gasped, gaping at the bombers. At that point he passed clean out.

Our boat drifted in mid-stream while the engineers tried to start the engines. Being cold and cussed the huge Hall-Scotts took their ponderous time. I stared up as the coxswain juggled with our forward gun. The three-pounder did not have the elevation but he loosed off a round or two for the fun of it. Dead overhead the bomb doors of our evil-looking attackers cranked open and large, black cylindrical shapes drifted lazily down towards us. During moments like these I have always tended to believe myself the sole target. Fortunately, I was wrong. The Japanese were aiming at the supply ships moored further down-river. Their bombs landed harmlessly short of the target sending up fountains of tea-coloured water. A second or two later it was all over. The coxswain put De Souza to bed. We finished the mince pies, the gin and most of the rum. It wasn't until evening that the fear hit me. Again I saw those bomb doors opening. Cold shudders shot through my stomach. I felt very, very sick.

Two weeks later we nearly bought it. Our orders were to interdict enemy coastal craft off the port of Sandoway. It was a long haul from Chittagong, two thirds the way down to Rangoon, and much of the trip was in broad daylight without hope of air cover. Nothing could be done to help us, we were told, if our boat got into serious trouble. Operating distances were too great for our short-ranged Fairmiles, designed originally for the English Channel, so we carried additional fuel supplies. The after-deck was covered with cans of high octane petrol that made us smell like a floating service station. Naturally, nobody smoked. One spark, one incendiary round from a patrolling Japanese aircraft guaranteed instant cremation. The very idea sets me shuddering today. But back in '43, being young and reckless, I never gave it a thought. '*Kismet hai*,' ('it's fate') we used to say. You have to be old to worry.

We arrived off Sandoway on a calm moonlit night and commenced our sweep along the coast. Our MLs were not equipped with radar but my night vision was exceptionally good and I was given the job of target-spotting through powerful binoculars on the bridge. Soon I picked up what appeared to be sampans.

'Sampans fine on the port bow,' I reported. The skipper ordered full speed ahead.

'I can see more of them!' I exclaimed excitedly. 'More, more!'

I lowered the binoculars to wipe the perspiration from my eyes. Glancing to port I got the fright of my life. A hump-backed rock – a 'sampan!' – was sliding past our beam about fifty yards away.

'Oh my God! Rocks!' I yelled.

Peter Lawrence slammed both engines full astern. Too late. The bow hit the rocks ahead with a terrible crash. ML 476 hung there grinding in the surf for two or three interminable minutes. Then she shuddered and slid astern. I rushed below decks to check the bilges. With that impact the hull must have been stove in. The thought of being wrecked on a reef three hundred miles behind Japanese lines was too dreadful to contemplate. Why, oh why, hadn't they issued those magnetic fly buttons?

But to my surprise the bilges were dry as a bone. We anchored at dawn in the lee of an off-shore island, flying the Japanese flag, and swam underneath to inspect the damage. An anti-submarine (Asdic) dome was ordinarily suspended beneath the bow. It was useless in these waters. Now it was gone, sheered off by the rocks, leaving the hull unscathed.

'Our l-l-lucky night, N-n-number One,' Lawrence remarked wryly. He did not laugh. But he did not upbraid me for incompetence. I must have been making progress.

A few weeks later, led by the flotilla leader with one other boat, we launched a hit-and-run raid on Ramree Island. It was a boringly routine affair. The Japanese were constructing beach defences every night, intelligence told us, using large numbers of unpaid local labourers. The island was to be seized next year by our amphibious forces and the Japanese were taking what proved to be useless precautions. Cloaked in total darkness our three boats crept close into the surf, fired off hundreds of tracer and immediately withdrew. There was no return fire, no way of knowing whether we had hit a thing. The idea was to scare the labourers and paralyse construction work. Word came through later that three days after our raid the entire labour force was still running inland.

'N-n-nothing to it,' Lawrence yawned. 'A p-p-piece of cake.'

This once he was wrong. The pair of us were breakfasting next morning in our tiny ward-room when something began knocking, near at hand, underwater. My first thought was that one of our propeller shafts had snapped. But that didn't explain the water still cascading around us when we rushed up on deck. Our boat was stopped, rolling immobile in the water. The officer on watch was Midshipman Sethna, a Bombay Parsee, one day to become a leading figure in India's nuclear development programme.

'Mines!' he shouted. 'I've stopped both engines. We've run into mines!'

'M-m-mines be b-b-buggered,' stuttered Lawrence, pointing overhead. Right above the masthead, just out of range of our puny anti-aircraft guns, droned a diamond-shaped clump of camouflaged Japanese bombers.

'Full ahead two. Hard a'port!' Lawrence ordered from the bridge. Once again all trace of stutter was gone.

ML 476 veered away from the other two boats to present a less concentrated target. The first bombs had fallen ahead of us, uncomfortably close. There were splinter marks in the bridge housing of the flotilla leader. The 'A' flag, warning of approaching aircraft, had been cut from its yard and was trailing in the sea. The bombers loosed another eight-bomb stick, which fell wide, and vanished over the horizon unperturbed by the futile barrage put up by our Oerlikon cannon.

Another group appeared half an hour later and took more careful aim. The first stick drifted down on our boat and the explosions marched steadily towards us. Six, seven – a fountain of water gushed up two hundred yards away – the eighth would hit us direct. Lawrence gave a quick, clipped helm order and the boat heeled over to starboard. I ducked behind the splinter mats certain this was the end. My last thought was of my mother. One last bang would take us to eternity ... but there wasn't one. There wasn't an eighth bomb in the stick. The Japanese kept coming all day in a determined effort to destroy us. But they never got that near again.

Spitfires had recently arrived in Burma and there was a squadron based in Chittagong. Their range was too limited to tackle the Japanese far south of the River Naaf but, as the day progressed and the frustrated enemy pressed his attacks, the time came when the Spitfires could pounce. Way out of our limited vision twenty-one Japanese planes were shot down and the back of the enemy bomber force in Burma was permanently broken.

Senior officers in Chittagong, who had feared our boats were a goner, now ran around congratulating each other. 'Operation Singed Beard' was promptly renamed 'Operation Decoy'. It had been planned that way from the start (or so the final reports made out) and medals went out to all and sundry. Staff officers got most of them, come to think of it.

That night we pulled into the River Naaf utterly exhausted. Fighting continued on the southern bank. The Japanese had fallen back but were far from beaten. Their fighters flew in low at dawn and shot up everything on the river. We guessed something was seriously wrong when an Allied supply plane, a heavily camouflaged Dakota, came zooming across the treetops faster than I'd ever seen one fly. The wonderful old workhorse looked fit to tear its wings off. Close behind came the Japanese, who immediately spotted our three boats moored to a couple of flat-topped barges close to Teknaaf village. A Bofors gun on one of the barges opened up as three of the enemy fighters jinked towards us. I was supposed to stand beside the amidships Oerlikon with my *back* to the attackers, scanning the nearby northern shore, in case the Japanese attacked from both sides at once. It was asking a bit much. Nothing could stop me glancing over my shoulder at a scene etched on my memory to this day: the red propeller boss of the fighter that made a beeline for us, the orange blobs at each oil-streaked wing-tip, close enough to touch it seemed as the guns chattered and the pilot pulled sharply away across the river. We went on firing. Bright arcs as our tracer looped up towards the fighter's vulnerable belly without, as far as we could make out, scoring a single palpable hit. Enough though, to put the pilot off his aim. One of the other pilots was less fazed. He made a straight run for the Bofors and raked it with machine-gun fire. It was all over in a matter of seconds, leaving us shaken but exultant.

Getting under way at speed our boat swung suddenly and unexpectedly towards the flotilla leader. The skipper vainly yelled helm corrections.

'Port twenty! Hard a'port!'

The bow of ML 476 turned relentlessly to starboard aiming directly at the flotilla leader. At the speed we were going, we seemed likely to slice it in half. Then it dawned on me what was happening.

'Full astern two!' the skipper yelled.

I dashed down into the wheelhouse. Just as I expected, an over-tired helmsman was setting the rudder to starboard instead of to port. I tore the wheel from his grasp and spun it frantically the opposite way. Through the wheelhouse windows I glimpsed the crew of the other boat gaping open-mouthed in horror as we bore down on them. They shot past on our starboard side as we scraped by with scarcely a foot to spare. Peter Lawrence was very pale when I returned to the bridge.

'F-f-first class, Number One,' he said. 'Th-th-thanks.'

It was the nicest thing he ever said to me.

PART FOUR

I was becoming bored. It was typical of wartime. Moments of frenetic excitement were punctuated by days, weeks and occasionally months of draining monotony. It was also typical of me. The urge for change, the same, oft-repeated urge that would do me no good in later life, grew from an itch to an imperative. Something had to release me from a shipboard routine I had mastered to my own satisfaction – and to everyone else's undisguised surprise. A bespectacled lieutenant arrived from Delhi to give publicity to 'the small boat heroes'. It took me some time to realise he meant us. The lieutenant was a Public Relations officer, the first I'd ever met, and a former journalist in Britain, sent out with some trepidation to praise RIN activity at the sharp end. It sounded like a challenging job.

'We desperately need a photographic officer,' he told me. He produced clippings of pictures he had taken of our flotilla on the Arakan. 'Know anything about the business?' he inquired.

I've been into photography since I was thirteen. I was still a schoolboy, completely penniless, which meant I had to make do with the most modest equipment. A favourite aunt gave me one of those Kodak roll-film cameras that unfolded with a bellows-shaped arrangement separating lens from film. Panchromatic emulsions had recently come on the market, enabling the photographer to register colours more accurately – blue skies, for instance – admittedly in black and white. Real colour was available only in transparencies, and viewing them involved trundling out a projector.

I showed the visiting Public Relations officer some of the shots I'd taken with my own twin-reflex camera. On one occasion, during bombardment of a coastal target, I had left the shutter open, using the muzzle flash to catch a realistic shot of the forward-gun crew. It was a simple trick if you knew what you were doing. The PR officer was impressed. 'You ought to apply for that job,' he said.

I did better than that. Directly we got back to Calcutta for refit I wrote out my own movement order and took the train to Delhi. Applications through customary channels would never get through, of this I was certain, because senior officers were loathe to allow trained men to transfer elsewhere.

New Delhi was every bit as striking as I'd expected. The massive sandstone Secretariat, split into North and South Blocks on either side of the drive to the viceregal palace, shimmered in the harsh, bright sunlight of the scorching Indian summer. The office I sought lay in South Block in a ground-floor office screened with exterior curtains of aromatic reeds. *Bhistis* splashed water on the reeds to cool those labouring inside, since only the most important offices enjoyed air-conditioning. My quarry turned out to be Commander Eric Britter RINVR, an urbane and kindly man who became the first post-war correspondent in Tokyo for the London *Times.* We would later serve together as war correspondents in Korea. Britter was impressed by the initiative I had shown in coming personally to lobby for the job. He sent me for a brief trial with the Inter-services Photographic Unit located in temporary buildings near the old fort, the *Purana Khila.* I had a few days' leave in hand and could well spare the time. But first I had to pass scrutiny by the doyen of Indian press photographers: the former head cameraman of the British-owned *Statesman* newspaper, the formidable Captain Arjun.

The captain regarded me curiously. He was a grizzled old Punjabi, fierce of face but with the pleasantest twinkle in his eye. 'You're very young,' he said doubtfully.

I suppose I looked that way: lean, fit and rather boyish. Not young, though. I was a man. I was every bit of twenty-one.

'You know what you're letting yourself in for?' Arjun pursued. 'Have you ever been in action?' The American term 'combat' had yet to infiltrate our vocabulary. Well, of course, I'd seen action, plenty of it. I had been bombed and machine-gunned and mortared and generally harassed by the Japanese enemy up and down the Burma coast.

'On land, I mean,' said Arjun. 'You see, we belong to an *inter-services* directorate. You're not just expected to take a few pretty pictures of the navy. You're supposed to go ashore with the landing forces and cover the fighting with the troops. Or fly with our bombers if the Indian Air Force ever gets any. It could be highly dangerous.'

I hadn't become involved in the Second World War with any intention of sticking my neck out. Prospects of a splendid uniform, armfuls of girls and luxury mess-night life (plus a brief, breathless encounter with the recruiting officer's daughter) had inveigled me into accepting the King's shilling. But the smell of cordite, the sheer excitement of naval engagement had done something to my metabolism; I was fair panting for a spot more of those gut-chilling moments of pure terror that tail off into the soaring, almost sexual, exhilaration that sets in once danger is passed and you find you have actually survived.

'No bother,' I said nonchalantly. It wasn't entirely true but I wanted the job. There was a glamour attached to the title of official photographer that outdid anything in the Royal Indian Navy's motor gunboats. Someone else entered the scene.

'For Christ's sake, who's this Pommy poofter?'

It was a loud, booming Australian voice emanating from a stocky little major in the uniform of the Royal Indian Service Corps – or the 'Rice Corps' we sneeringly called it.

'The name's Tilley,' the major declared, gracing me with a curt nod. 'I'm second-in-command here. We're a regular League of Nations.' They looked like the wrong kind of nations to me. If first impressions counted with this bloke I was definitely down the tube. Maybe it would be unfair to blame him: brashness made me more enemies than friends in those days.

'I'm checking out this man for the photographic job,' said Arjun. He spoke gently as ever but looked decidedly miffed. Relationships sounded frighteningly sour in All-India Inter-services Public Relations.

'I'll decide who comes in here,' boomed Tilley.

'But I'll decide if he's capable,' Arjun insisted.

Major Tilley looked me up and down contemptuously. I couldn't have looked very macho in my white naval shirt and shorts.

'Then send him to Dehra Dun,' the major commanded. 'See how he shapes up in the bloody bush!'

Arjun steered me off into the equipment room, where he issued me with a Zeiss Ikonta. He knew I did not want to use one of the heavy old press cameras. The Ikonta was a bellows-type folding camera taking 120-size roll film. It was a beautiful instrument, though delicate, and scarcely suited to battlefield conditions. The Germans were said to ship Ikontas to neutral Istanbul in great quantities, along with a few Leicas, where they were snapped up by Allied purchasers (payment in gold) for military use.

'What goes on at Dehra Dun?' I asked.

It was an army test-range, Arjun explained, a night's train-ride from Delhi. All kinds of new equipment was put through its paces in rough, forested terrain. I would be expected to bring back pictures of a simulated attack together with shots of the latest tanks and artillery operating under combat conditions.

First, though, I would be required to shoot off a test film in the picturesque New Delhi neighbourhood. The old fort, a short walk up the road, made great pictures. So did a nearby ruined mosque. A stairway led up to a ledge overlooking the prayer floor. A wall plaque explained that this was the very spot chosen by a would-be assassin who shot the Emperor Akbar through the shoulder with an arrow while he knelt in prayer. I've always been a sucker for the romance of history.

'Not bad,' said Arjun. He examined the prints sympathetically. I had the feeling that he did not like Major Tilley and would do his damnedest to get me into the outfit.

'It will be a lot different at Dehra Dun,' he added. 'They use live ammunition. You won't have time to be very arty.'

The brigadier commanding the weapons testing establishment at Dehra Dun couldn't believe his eyes. He looked closely at my orders, and then closely at me, dressed in my crisp navy whites.

'You're going down the range dressed like *that*?' he demanded.

'Why not, sir?' I replied, cocky as ever. The uniform might look a little out of place but I'd had army training. I was a graduate of the Officers' Training School at Bangalore.

'Watch it,' the brigadier said doubtfully.

I joined an assault-wave of Indian infantry rushing across open fields and into the jungle-covered foothills. Bursts of machine-gun fire from way out on the flank crackled overhead. Leading our assault were half a dozen General Grant-type tanks. They were slow, high silhouette contraptions, unsuitable for use against German Panzers; it was impossible to dig them in hull-down because the main gun was clumsily mounted in a movable turret high up on the left-hand side.

The Indian summer was at its hottest. The temperature stood way above 40 degrees. We charged sweating and wheezing through the undergrowth picking up leeches on the exposed parts of our bodies. Far too much of my body was exposed in my unlikely uniform but I noticed nothing at the time. I can't think what it was, but that day at Dehra Dun fate was kind to me. I was inspired. Blame it on the excitement, the thrilling new challenge, but photographically I couldn't put a foot wrong. A flame-throwing weapons-carrier shot out great bursts of fire. The picture I took became a propaganda poster.

Forward I pressed, close behind the tanks, ignoring shouted warnings from the soldiers. Machine-gun bullets overhead showered down shorn twigs and leaves. The tanks stopped to engage an imagined enemy. The tank gunners were using graze fuses that went off on the slightest impact. I moved in, foolishly, for close-ups. Directly I pressed the shutter release, a shell ploughed into the bushes some twenty metres ahead. The tank crew were safe enough behind their armour but the explosion knocked me down. An Indian soldier helped me to my feet.

'You all right, sahib?' he asked anxiously. At least I think that's what he said – I was temporarily deafened. The soldier lit a cigarette and began burning clumps of leeches off my arms and legs. The brigadier came puffing up, advised that the idiot photographer had stepped too close to the action.

'You're either barmy or brave,' he admonished. 'Play it more carefully next time.' He indicated my soiled and dishevelled white uniform. 'And next time wear something more suitable. The enemy would see you a mile away.'

Permit me immodestly to report that my Dehra Dun pictures caused a mild sensation back in Delhi. 'This young man's got what it takes,' chuckled Captain Arjun.

It was nothing but luck, nothing but *kismet*, in my opinion. Even my Australian ill-wisher, Major Tilley, accepted me reluctantly. 'But get this into your head, sonny,' he said. 'I want pictures of Japs. Close-ups of Japs. Fighting Japs. And don't you forget it.'

He got what he wanted a few months later, though the Japanese I photographed were all decidedly dead. Taking those pictures nearly cost me my life.

Suddenly I was in a completely new world. The 55th ML Flotilla had saved me, arguably, from perdition. Challenges had been presented to my personal pride that pitchforked me into adulthood. Ambition now overrode the cheery hedonism that previously shackled my energies and channelled them down more productive paths. I was undergoing a role-change: from fiddling grasshopper to industrious ant. But the seaborne life had had its limitations. The horizons of the average officer seldom stretched beyond his forecastle. There was an unhealthy preoccupation with gossip, intrigue and naval minutiae.

The job of stills cameraman for the Royal Indian Navy transported me into a wider world of publicity and propaganda. Dozens of different forms of activity, from diving to amphibious warfare, demanded camera coverage. Working with scant supervision I was able to undertake assignments largely on my own initiative. Over the next few months I ranged all over India, often in company with the RIN's only commissioned movie-cameraman, a cherubic nineteen-year-old sub-lieutenant called Frank Worth. The pair of us worked together as a team for what was known as the Joint Public Relations Directorate (PRD). Colleagues called us, enviously and derisively, 'the Heavenly Twins'.

Frank Worth is these days a highly successful award-winning film director and screenwriter, with well over fifty international film festival prizes to his credit, including Grand Prix won both in Europe and the USA. Back in 1944 he was an infant prodigy. His knowledge of movie-making, almost entirely self-taught, was simply phenomenal. This is not idle praise: it's been my privilege over the years to meet plenty of people who've made the big time. None was necessarily blessed with a massive IQ; such people had something more valuable in common. All of them had matured early. While others were playing childish games – or frittering away their time, like me, on girls – the mature ones were seriously confronting life. The sooner they got to grips with it, you felt, the better off they'd be.

Even as a young midshipman Frank was commanding the Royal Indian Naval Operational Film unit, a post tailored for a lieutenant-commander. He wangled himself free of this position to be free for operational duties as a combat cameraman. His abilities soon gained him early promotion to sub-lieutenant, at the exceptional age of nineteen. Mountbatten, who well understood the value of film in war, was reputed to be behind the recommendation.

Frank was a typical early achiever. Born in India of British parents, he was barely into his teens when his mother bought him his first 8mm home-movie camera; from then on he became absorbed in the shooting, editing and production of films. By the time we teamed up he was a seasoned cameraman, operating a hefty old silent camera with a clockwork motor, interchangeable lenses and 35mm film magazines. Off-duty he was as carefree as I was, with quite a knack for chatting up girls. But once his eye was clamped to that viewfinder he became the pictorial perfectionist, oblivious to everything around him.

The pair of us shared a dream of a job. Covering all three services, not merely the navy, gave us a flexibility unusual in the armed forces; within any particular war-zone we could do pretty much as we chose. Which helps explain what happened when the Second World War reached its sudden, surprising end …

The common wisdom was that the Japanese would hold out for years. The Americans were having to fight like the devil for every Pacific island they seized. Enemy resistance in Burma had so far been beyond belief. The commander of 15 Corps paid special tribute, in my presence, to the Japanese squad that stormed one of our airstrips on the Arakan. The last survivor holed up with a machine-gun in a crater in the middle of the strip, effectively suspending all flying. The man had lost a leg and was bleeding slowly to death but he operated a tourniquet with one hand and the machine-gun with the other. A bulldozer had to be brought in finally to bury him.

'In our army,' Lieutenant-General Christison declared, 'that man would have been awarded the Victoria Cross.'

You might wonder why, camera in hand, I did not go straight into combat. The fact was that on the Arakan there wasn't much happening. Naval campaigning in Burma was strangely seasonal. Throughout the monsoon and beyond, the weather hampered naval operations, par-ticularly by smaller vessels. Coastal landings had to be postponed until early 1945, partly due to heavy seas, partly to the persistent shortage of landing craft. It wasn't until three days after Christmas, spent wassailing around log fires in wintry Delhi, that orders came through for Frank and myself to head back to the Arakan.

The first objective of what proved to be the final offensive was the port of Akyab, where the sunken RIN frigate *Hindustan* still lay capsized in mid-harbour. A full-scale assault proved unnecessary. An artillery officer flying over the place in a light plane on 2 January 1945 saw villagers waving in a friendly manner and, seeing no sign of the Japanese garrison, he boldly landed on the airstrip.

The enemy had been gone for forty-eight hours. They had joined a southward retreat that soon would become a rout. The Japanese escape route lay down a single coastal road stretching some seventy miles to the south before switching east at the township of Taungup, across the forested heights of the Arakan Yomas to the Irrawaddy valley. Once there, the Japanese could hope to avoid the main offensive being mounted by Allied forces down in central Burma and reach shelter in the jungles beyond Rangoon. The plan was to trap our retreating foe with a series of landings that cut the road before they could reach Taungup.

It was a bright clear morning. Our landing craft were circling off a narrow beach at the tip of Myebon island. The date was 12 January 1945. There was no marked eagerness to go storming ashore: the frogmen who had risked their necks checking out the beachhead had found rows of sharpened stakes planted across the approaches. The stakes could impale any amphibious craft that rode among them at high tide. Others arriving past the peak were in almost as much danger from the ebb. The Arakan coast was heavily indented with mangrove-infested tidal inlets. The Burmese called them *chaungs*. They were navigable only a few hours each day; any boat unlucky enough to run aground at high water could find itself precariously marooned until the next rising tide. So treacherous could these *chaungs* become, with their hidden rocks and fast-emerging mud-banks, that we considered them the prototype of the oft-quoted, odoriferous creek that trapped the unwary without a paddle. (The expression 'up shit creek' was, in fact, Australian.)

The frogmen established that Myebon 'beach' was nothing but mud. It was probably too soft for tanks, trucks and artillery. There would be plenty of headaches for the engineers. The terrain at this stage of the war was causing us almost as much grief as the Japanese. Reconnaissance reports suggested that landmines had been scattered throughout the area or tied to the tops of those forbidding stakes. Overall, it was an unpleasant prospect.

Yet the island had to be taken. Unless its defending guns were knocked out the Japanese would be able to pick us off as we sailed past to the next and more vital landing, around the corner, so to speak, near the village of Kangaw. The village lay astride the coastal road. Once cut off, the retreating Japanese would be in desperate straits. Somewhere around Kangaw the most significant battle of the three-year Arakan campaign was confidently expected. But at that stage none of us grasped the strategic implications. Our sole concern was surviving Day One at Myebon.

Dive-bombers and offshore warships were softening up the island as we milled around Myebon Bay awaiting the command to run shorewards. The distinct thud of high explosives merged into a single rumbling roar as the bombardment reached its climax. A column of reddish dust rose into the pale cerulean sky. Assessing the sun-lit scene with a photographer's eye I estimated that a pale yellow-green filter would best bring out the contrasts without overdarkening the sky or substantially reducing my shutter speed; it was important to maintain what we called a 'fast' shutter, preferably a 250th of a second, to freeze most movement. Given such sparkling light and a film speed of 100 ASA (the speediest film PRD could then provide), I would expect to be taking my pictures at a 250th at F-8.

It sounds ridiculous, I suppose, making arcane calculations on the fringe of battle. But photographers have to be exceptionally single-minded. There's the classic story of the chap on the *New York Times* who came back to the office with a heart-rending story about a destitute woman he'd met in Central Park. The poor soul was without family, homeless and broke.

'How terrible!' a colleague exclaimed. 'What did you give her?'

'Oh, a fiftieth at F-16,' the photographer replied.

In my case, of course, concentration on the mechanics of picture-taking provided an antidote to fear. Being a born coward I had always worried about my behaviour under fire, though so far, with the 55th Flotilla, I had enjoyed, yes actually *enjoyed*, a misguided sense of exhilaration in moments of high danger. This time, perhaps, it would be different. I was uncomfortably out of my element. Frank and I had to observe (and film) everything around us while standing exposed on the open after-deck of a Landing Craft, Vehicle, a clapped-out old bucket long overdue for the scrapyard. Beside us, tucked inside a tall, steel wheelhouse, stood the coxswain and the LCV commander, a sub-lieutenant younger than ourselves and a great deal more nervous. 'Don't like the look of those bloody stakes,' he grumbled, scanning the beachhead through his binoculars.

I didn't like them any more than he did. And they were only our first obstacle. Directly the LCV touched ground Frank and I were supposed to jump down into the well of the craft, packed not with vehicles but with heavily-laden Punjabi troops, and join them when the front ramp went down in the short, sharp dash to terra firma – a piece of cake, briefing officers assured us. The bay was not particularly deep and there'd be no difficulty wading ashore with our cameras and spare film held well clear of the water.

The bombardment lifted. Up went a signal flare. The first wave of fast, low-slung assault craft, some twenty LCPs (or Landing Craft, Personnel) fanned out in line abreast and raced towards the beach. The lead craft passed close abeam and I glimpsed the Beachmaster, a ruddy-faced naval lieutenant called Kettle, crouched beside the coxswain with his arms full of signal flags. We'd been drinking together a couple of nights before – the man had the most infectious laugh – but now he looked tense and grim. The LCPs were packed with beach staff, engineers and Royal Marine commandos whose job was to clear the way for the main invasion force. In other words, for us.

Bracing ourselves against the steel wheelhouse Frank and I watched the LCPs approach the dreaded stakes, weaving slightly to confuse the defenders. A gout of muddy water shot up ahead of them. Another and another rose within their ranks. The Japanese had the range but not the luck. Two or three medium guns had survived the bombardment in deep bunkers further inside the island but the battering they'd received seemed to have spoiled the gunners' aim.

The landing craft hit the beach unscathed, men began scrambling ashore and on the wave of a green and red flag our idling engines roared into life. Some fifteen crowded LCVs formed line abreast. Vibrating madly, we headed for the beach. There was no time to waste, as the tide was ebbing fast and the stakes already stood a good four feet clear of the receding waters. LCVs drew more water than the assault craft and we could be stranded way offshore if the tide fell much further. The assault craft passed us on their way back. The coxswains looked glad to be clear of the enemy guns. One man leaned out of his cabin and gave us the V sign.

A tremendous explosion threw up sand and mud from the middle of the beach. I grabbed one shot, cursing the lack of a telephoto lens. Considerable cropping (and enlargement) was needed when the film got back to the PRD labs. My old adversary Major Tilley sent me a contact print with crop lines around the explosion. On the back he wrote, 'Why weren't you nearer?'

I wrote: 'Why weren't you?' and sent it back to Delhi.

Without knowing it I had photographed the demise of Beachmaster Kettle. Two or three minutes after wading ashore, establishing a control-point higher up the beach, he had trodden on a landmine. Sappers began racing about with detectors to clear any further mines before we hit the beach. The safest course would have been to stop us but by now it was too late: we were in among the stakes with shells falling on every hand. There was a crash nearby and an LCV spun slowly out of line, smoke pouring from its engines. A near miss had set something on fire below the wheelhouse. I raced round to the starboard side and grabbed a picture just as another craft took a hit on the stern and swung uncontrollably into the stakes. An almighty thump confirmed that we had hit bottom. The craft alongside us dropped its ramp and a Patton tank shot out. It hit the water with a tremendous splash ... and vanished. When the spray cleared, only the turret was visible. The tank commander, who'd leaped out, was trying to rescue the rest of his crew. They had all drowned at the controls.

Our ramp went down and we prepared to wade ashore. One look held us back gaping in disbelief. The beach was a good three hundred yards away. The first of our Punjabis, loaded with full pack and weaponry, jumped into the water and went down without trace. 'We're in ten feet of water!' the landing craft commander shouted desperately. 'Hold back! We must be stuck on a stake.' He gunned the engines full astern. The LCV heaved clear and lunged again towards the beach. A shell burst ahead of us, clearing a path through the stakes, but again we grounded. The men who now jumped gingerly off the ramp were submerged up to their necks. Gamely they struggled through the water. All round us others were doing the same. My picture showing hundreds of men wading ashore appeared in newspapers all over the world.

'Aren't you going?' the sub-lieutenant yelled.

'Not in this depth of water,' I yelled back. Our equipment would be ruined. It would take weeks to find replacements. 'Can't you get in closer?'

'Not a hope,' came the reply. 'I'm getting the hell out of here.' Most of the other craft were already heading back to reload. Our engines again revved full astern. The LCV refused to budge. Another near miss failed to free us.

'We're going to be stuck here!' the sub-lieutenant wailed. 'Stuck like sitting bloody ducks.'

Two or three more shells burst harmlessly in the bay and then the dive-bombers were back on the job winkling out those cursed guns. The shelling stopped. The tide receded, leaving us high and dry.

'Never again,' the sub-lieutenant growled. 'You're the last cameramen I'm going to carry. You're nothing but bad bloody luck.'

'Could have been worse,' said Frank as we floundered ashore an hour later through knee-deep mud. The LCV, the sunken tank, some snapped-off stakes and several drowned soldiers lay around like tidal flotsam. 'Got some great footage,' Frank added. No matter what the cost, in his eyes good footage justified everything.

Ten days later we weren't so certain. The Japanese had us both trapped. It was 22 January 1945. The previous morning the 3rd Commando Brigade had descended as planned on the village of Kangaw. Their task was to block the Japanese retreat from the Arakan. The Japanese fought back. Frank and I, carried away by the excitement of the moment, had joined in one of the commandos' counter-attacks, only to be pinned down by heavy machine-gun fire in a patch of dead ground. I pressed myself into the earth, scared out of my wits, wondering what the hell had persuaded me to get involved. It was a question I was often to ask myself in years to come. Frank was stretched out nearby, weighed down by his heavy equipment, trying to make himself invisible. Several of the commandos around us were already dead; the man at my left elbow had risen to his knees aiming his Bren gun up the slope and taken a bullet between the eyes. He went down without a sound.

Kangaw lay east of Myebon, reached only through more of those tortuous *chaungs*. The initial landing passed off unopposed. The commandos charged up a slimy creek bank thick with mangroves, and occupied a hill marked 160 (feet high) on army maps. With this pivotal position secured, troops of the 25th Indian Division, including a battalion of Rajputs led by the then Colonel Thimmaya, destined to become commander-in-chief of the post-war Indian Army, pushed another mile further inland and blocked the only road through this wild stretch of country, thus cutting the main enemy escape route.

The Japanese reacted immediately. The morning after the landing, as the dawn sun dispersed the overnight mists and the commandos were brewing their breakfast tea atop Hill 160, the Japanese struck with unexpected force. A full-strength reconnaissance brigade materialised without warning, and charged, flags flying, up the tree-cloaked slopes.

'One minute there was nothing below us but empty paddy-fields,' an officer told me afterwards. 'Suddenly the fields were swarming with the bastards, bayonets fixed, swords flashing, battle flags, the whole bloody *banzai* bit.'

Loss of Hill 160 would threaten the beachhead. The commandos knew it. Their bullets ripped through the ranks of khaki-clad figures clawing up towards them. Nothing could stop so suicidal an attack. The defenders were driven step by step down the back of the hill beneath by a sharp barrage of Japanese artillery fire. Any concentration of Japanese guns was unexpected at this stage of the war; our airmen, enjoying total superiority, claimed to have knocked out everything that did not move on two legs.

Frank and I found ourselves mixed up with a battered but determined platoon attempting to recapture the hill. Their intention was not immediately clear; all we could make out in the chaos of combat was that the commandos were about to advance. Their platoon commander had been killed leading an earlier assault. Dead lay all around the foot of the hill and among the trees and bushes that concealed the crest. One of the two General Grant tanks landed the previous day had been knocked out. It lost a track when an enemy soldier threw himself against the side turret with an explosive charge strapped to his chest. The man's helmeted head landed neatly nearby inside the field dressing station. Machine-gun fire poured down from above, whipping up the dust around us.

It wasn't long before I was telling myself this battle was hardly my personal concern. That was totally untrue. Our duties as naval cameramen naturally enjoined us to concentrate on the seaborne war. But being members of an inter-service organisation, our responsibilities could not cease at the beachhead and we were required to follow events ashore.

So now we were stumbling towards the lower slopes of the disputed hill and it was too late to turn back. Ahead lay the last few yards of open ground before we reached the hill. The firing grew heavier; the sergeant leading us went down with a bullet in his thigh, bleeding horribly, while the rest of us gratefully went to earth. Several sharp clicks came from somewhere up the hill. They were clearly audible through the din of battle. The Japanese were priming grenades by rapping them on their helmets. They sent them rolling them down the slope towards us. Fortunately the grenades went off before they could roll within range.

'Here they come!' Frank yelled and turned over on his back aiming his camera. I thought he meant the Japanese, doing another *banzai* from the hilltop, but it was a fresh squad of commandos charging across our cringing bodies.

I propped myself on one elbow and grabbed the only picture of close combat I ever managed to take. The light was not so good, clouds were piling up in the west, but I still managed a 250th at F-5.6. The result was disappointing, nothing like the immortal Capa shot of the Spanish Republican infantryman felled by a bullet. Nor did it match the drama of the moment. The shot showed a major with drawn revolver leading half a dozen men stiff-legged through clouds of dust. No way does it suggest these men were risking their lives in deadly combat. It's the kind of thing that's always liable to happen with still photographs: a lot of luck is required to capture mood and feeling no matter how many times you click the shutter. Stills lack the motion, the sound and the colour that injects reality into the stuff we see today on television. Frank's newsreel footage was monochrome and silent, yet the few minutes he managed to grab of startling footage were more convincing than anything caught by my camera.

The surviving tank roared past us. We crawled out of our sheltered position and followed, crouching behind its scarred steel bulk. The main gun banged and crashed, as I'd seen months before on the test range at Dehra Dun, except this time it was firing point-blank into an enemy platoon assembling for a flank attack from the back of the hill. Tracer poured from the tank's machine-guns. Thunderous rumblings came from the adjoining hills as dive-bombers went in with napalm and high explosives. Twenty-five pounder guns mounted on floats in the *chaung* brought the noise to a shattering crescendo, reminding me, for some odd reason, of my mother's sewing machine chattering away, greatly amplified, on a summer's afternoon in England. Fresh waves of commandos dashed past the tank to finish off the enemy.

They need not have bothered. No one was left alive. A trench at the bottom of the hill was filled to overflowing with obscenely tumbled bodies. One or two wounded men were finishing themselves off with grenades. There'd be that click again as they tapped them on their helmets, followed by the sharp crack of explosion as they held the grenades to their stomachs. An officer in steel-rimmed spectacles looked, at first sight, alive. He had slithered down into squatting position at the base of a banyan tree. His helmeted head lolled against the tree, both spectacle lenses shattered by bullets. A sergeant snatched the drawn sword from the dead man's stiffening fingers. A samurai sword was the ultimate souvenir in this ugly little war.

We followed a trail of corpses to the top of Hill 160. Enemy shells still crashed into the treetops, but they came too late to save the day. The crest was knee-deep in corpses. They were coated thickly with dust, looking doll-like and unreal. Automatic weapons, aimed low, repeatedly fired, had shot the dead so full of lead it took two men to lift them. Chunks had been sawn from the trees, close to the roots, as if a band of beavers had been gnawing them. The commandos cursed as they cleared foxholes of their weighty occupants. Defensive positions were more urgently required by the living in case of further attacks. A work detail hauled at the legs of one small khaki-clad figure, wearing a sergeant's collar tabs, slumped head down in a ruined slit trench. The body broke suddenly in two. I crept quietly away to be sick. All around lay the trash of battle. Perforated helmets, discarded rifles, water bottles, mess tins, packets of letters, even dog-eared family photographs infested the undergrowth. Looters had already been rummaging around for anything they could find. A medic swore ghouls had smashed the jaws of the enemy dead with boots and rifle butts in hopes of a harvest of gold teeth.

'Hey, you two!' It was the commando brigadier, a youngish man intoxicated with the hype of battle. 'Stop poncing around with those cameras and help carry in the casualties. Most of our stretcher-bearers have had it.'

No sense in arguing with a man in that state of excitement. Meekly we walked down to the field dressing station in search of a stretcher. Doctors were fighting to save the life of a Japanese soldier, knocked unconscious by an explosion before he could commit suicide, while outside enraged commandos clamoured to get their hands on him. Japanese prisoners were still a rare prize for our intelligence. A commando stood guard with rifle and fixed bayonet keeping his comrades at bay.

Lugging our stretcher the pair of us scrambled back up the hillside. A young lieutenant lay on his back among the bushes, wide blue eyes staring off into eternity. A single bullet had hit him in the forehead. We manhandled the heavy body on to the stretcher and carried it down to the doctors.

'Why bring us a mucking corpse?' a medic growled. 'Can't you find any wounded?'

We went back but found only dead. The young lieutenant Frank and I brought in won one of the two posthumous Victoria Crosses awarded for the Kangaw action. I persistently dreamed of him, especially when malaria came back to plague me years after the war.

All I can say today – and it hurts to do so – is that the Burma campaign, despite the casualties, the damage and the suffering, was an ultimate waste of time. The Japanese didn't want Burma. They should never have invaded the country. They made a major strategic error pushing up to the Indian border and over-extending their supply lines. The Americans didn't give a damn about the place. Their Limey-hating commander, 'Vinegar Joe' Stilwell, had not the slightest intention of spilling GI blood to salvage the

British Empire. His sole reason for being there at all was to open a back-door to China and in the mistaken belief that Chiang Kai-Shek's legions could be goosed into offensive action against Japan. He ended bitterly disillusioned.

The British ended up looking almost as foolish. We genuinely believed in the liberation of Burma. There was more incomprehension than surprise to find the Burmese didn't want to know us. Independent Burma quickly opted out of the Commonwealth. One of my favourite countries was left a legacy of racial conflict from ethnic minorities recruited, trained and armed to fight the Japanese; a conflict that haunts Burma to the present day.

Looking back on it all I am reminded of the perceptive punchline in Robert Southey's epic poem *The Battle of Blenheim*. The old man is telling an interested child about the slaughter that day upon the battlefield:

> *'And pray what good did all this do?' quoth little Peterkin.*
> The old man shakes his head in bewilderment.
> *'Ah that I cannot say,' said he. 'But 'twas a famous victory.'*

The Pirate had scarcely said 'Good morning' before he whipped out a Browning automatic and rammed it in the stomach of our assault-boat skipper.

'You'll do as I tell you,' he growled. His voice was chillingly low. 'You will take us another couple of miles inland or I'll blow you apart.'

The squirming lieutenant whined on about the dangers of rocks and tide so far behind the Japanese lines.

'I'll count from five,' said the Pirate. His moustache was bristling, his eyes flashed, a scarlet flush brought a dangerous glow to his waxen face. He looked, and, if legend was to be believed, he probably was, quite mad.

'Five, four, three – ' the lieutenant gave up. 'It's your bloody neck,' he groaned.

The Pirate chuckled, mollified. Minutes later we were back aboard the LCP, together with the group interpreter and the ten-man Gurkha bodyguard, tentatively picking our way through the maze of mangrove swamps. We disembarked at a small clearing where craft put about, racing seawards amid a shower of curses. The lieutenant stood in the stern shaking his fist at the Pirate. 'You're crazy,' he yelled. 'Stark bloody crazy!'

The man everyone called 'the Pirate' took not the slightest notice. He'd gotten exactly what he wanted. 'Saved us a day's march,' he shrugged. He turned a jaundiced eye on my pathetic little party. We stood out like pork sandwiches at a Jewish picnic. 'Who the hell are you?' he demanded. 'And who the hell are these?' He indicated my two US Army photographers. I hurriedly produced a sweat-stained authorisation permitting the three of us – all combat cameramen – to record for posterity the activities of 'V Force', a guerrilla group based way inside occupied Burma.

This force was 'an important and very valuable part of the intelligence framework', Field Marshal Slim wrote later in his memoirs. So valuable had it become that after a great deal of special pleading my public relations bosses in distant Delhi allowed me to attempt the assignment.

'It's top secret,' they warned. 'You might be wasting your time.' And your life, they could very well have added.

The idea came to me after the February landing on the northern end of Ramree Island. It was one of the last of the amphibious swoops that would carry us down to Rangoon. Apart from a short, half-hearted attack by Japanese fighters, the assault force ran in unopposed beneath the heaviest naval bombardment ever inflicted on the Burma coast. It was directed by the elderly battleship *Queen Elizabeth*, firing her 15-inch guns for the last time in anger. The huge shells roared overhead like express trains, throwing up fountains of dirt from the fallow rice-fields. They were completely wasted. There was nothing to hit. The only sign of hostility came close inshore when a landing-craft carrying the artillery headquarters group hit a moored mine. It blew up in a ball of fire. I was too far off to get a shot. Frank was luckier. He was on another landing craft. A gunboat blew up on another mine a few yards from him. He was knocked down by the blast but got amazing pictures when his camera, tied down on its tripod, kept operating. Of the Japanese there was no sign. They were trying to escape to the mainland. Their chances were slim: sharks and naval patrols were picking them off throughout the ten-mile swim.

Next day beside the half-built airstrip I fell in with an Anglo-American intelligence unit which specialised in activity behind enemy lines. The Americans claimed to be OSS. 'We're sorta super-commandos,' they declared with predictable modesty. They conducted periodic raids into enemy territory which often seemed to end in disaster. During their latest foray they had shot each other up in the dark and killed two of their own men.

The British were more low-key. Their job was to provide back-up for a mysterious outfit called V Force which had been operating behind Japanese lines on the Arakan for close on three years. It was from them I learned of the disintegration of the Japanese 54th Division. This once-formidable unit, victor of a dozen stiff encounters along this stretch of the Burma coast, had been assigned the hopeless task of covering the Japanese retreat from the Arakan. Now it was itself pulling back as fast as possible towards Taungup and the mountain escape-route into the Irrawaddy valley.

'You should be in at the kill,' one of the V Force officers told me. 'You ought to get in with the Pirate.' He chuckled at some private joke. 'Mind you he's an awkward old bugger. But he's never dull!'

We hitched a lift on the assault boat that made a fortnightly supply run at dead of night close to the Pirate's encampment. It was a remarkable piece of seamanship. Any skipper who could find a small guerrilla group in the pitch dark, some thirty miles down a hostile stretch of coast, deserved thanks, in my view, not threats of instant death. I would have felt happier with Frank Worth for company but he had gone back to Calcutta with equipment trouble. Two American cameramen attached to the OSS unit came along instead for the ride. It was their big chance to gain something they called 'combat credibility'. A case of K rations had cemented the deal.

It was obvious from the start that we weren't exactly welcome. The redoubtable Major 'Pirate' Edwards MC abhorred publicity. He bridled, too, at carrying sightseers. Still, there was nothing he could do about it. No way could he send us back for at least another two weeks. This forced him to accept our unannounced arrival with considerable ill grace.

'You march and you fight with the rest of us,' he said curtly. 'Fall out and you're dead. We stop for no one.'

That cheered me up no end. The affair at Kangaw had been terrifying enough. I began asking myself what mad impulse had dragged me on to this mission. The motivation was clear enough. I was victim of a macho mixture of ambition and curiosity. I wanted to get exclusive pictures of the collapse of enemy resistance. I was also anxious to learn more about this notorious guerrilla chief with the reputation of a Wyatt Earp and the build of an Arnold Schwarzenegger. Co-opted at last into his bandit band, I was not at all sure I liked what I saw. A former British Olympic swimmer, Edwards was indeed a mountain of a man. Dressed in tattered uniform shirt and ankle-length Burmese *lunghi*, he carried a Browning automatic hung on a string around his waist; slung across his back was a Burmese sword or *da* used mainly, he claimed, to hack back the undergrowth. Anti-malaria pills had turned his skin bright yellow, and for two years he had been ranging up and down the Arakan, playing hide and seek with the Japanese, virtually without a break. The strain plainly showed.

'You want to make films!' he exploded, on reading our orders. 'Where d'you think we are – Hollywood Boulevard?'

Well, not exactly. As far as I could make out we were holed up on the coastal plain not far from the township of Taungup. It was here that the Japanese were thought to be preparing their final stand. The town was reputedly a fortress barring further advance into Burma. The Pirate's group expected to pursue its cloak and dagger mission without undue interference from the enemy, since Japanese forces in the area were too busy fending off the advancing Indo-British armies to waste much time swatting away at us. It hadn't always been that way, though. Throughout the greater part of the war the Japanese had hunted our penetration groups, patiently and without mercy. There was no doubt the Japanese operated an intelligence-gathering network every bit as good as ours. A special reconnaissance unit, led by a one-eyed Japanese colonel, made sure the V Force reconnaissance groups were kept continually on the run. The

Pirate's immediate predecessor had been ambushed and killed by them further up the coast.

'The fool got careless,' the major said lightly. 'Round here you sleep with your eyes open.'

The Japanese special unit was still around, as we would soon discover, though its one-eyed commander was gone. He had made off into the jungle, villagers said, disguised as a Buddhist monk. The Pirate still hoped they would meet one day. Our group had lately switched from passive intelligence gathering to 'minor raiding operations' – here again I dip into the Slim memoirs – 'and frequently fought successful actions with Japanese patrols and detachments'.

Sometimes the confrontation grew brutal, if the legends are to be believed. A Japanese battalion commander is said to have demanded rice, girls and a barrel of local liquor from an Arakanese village. The headman told the local V Force commander, who put cyanide in the liquor. Several Japanese officers died. The survivors redoubled their efforts to wipe out V Force. There was a standing reward of several thousand rupees for the Pirate's head. There were other, equally nasty stories of booby traps and ambuscades with quarter neither asked nor given. Our Gurkha bodyguard produced several samurai swords acquired, I learned, in vicious night actions. The American cameramen shelled out bundles of dollars for these priceless souvenirs.

The morning we arrived the immediate threat came from our own side. We had scarcely disembarked before a Hawker Hurricane of the Indian Air Force closed in, searching for targets. Everyone dived for cover. Everyone, that is, except the Pirate who stayed deliberately in the open folding a ground-sheet into the shape of an Allied star. Things like recognition panels had not yet come into general use. The pilot hesitated, recognised a friendly unit deep in unfriendly territory and made off after circling our position, waggling his wings in salute.

'Imbecile!' growled the Pirate. 'Now the Japs know exactly where we are.'

Disorganised the enemy might be, but we were taking no chances. And as things turned out, that was just as well. Half marching, half running we headed inland, hacking our way through the undergrowth. Three breathless hours later, scratched and tired and streaming with sweat we burst upon a village. The women ran. The headman stood his ground looking scared. He was interrogated by the major's aide and interpreter, a cheeky young Burman educated at mission school.

'Headman says no Japs around here,' the interpreter reported.

Pirate Edwards looked up from the detailed maps he was unrolling on the ground. 'That man is lying!' he bellowed, groping for his automatic. 'I can see from the way he is curling his toes.'

The headman fell on his knees begging for mercy. Of course he'd lied; if he told the truth his village would be put to the torch. Yes, there were

Japanese troops in the neighbourhood. And they were looking for us. We must have brushed close past them without knowing it in the jungle. Later I asked the Pirate how he'd known the headman wasn't telling the truth.

'I didn't,' he said. 'I just had a hunch. You live or die by hunches in this game.'

The headman had given him one other important piece of information. The Japanese had a big gun dug in at the approaches to Taungup. Somehow or other we would have to destroy that gun.

'You want pictures,' the Pirate said. 'Now you'll get 'em.'

Major Edwards may not have welcomed our unexpected company but once it was accepted he did his damnedest to get us real-life combat footage. Half measures never suited him. The more we manoeuvred around enemy territory, however, the less enthusiastic I personally became; every clump of bushes seemed to conceal a patrol of sword-swinging samurai. Japanese resistance was supposed to be broken but I wasn't going to bet on it. The Pirate noted my nervousness with disdain. 'You'll get used to it,' he told me contemptuously. 'I'll blood you myself after our first shoot-out.'

Any day, he promised, we should see action. Our first target was the Taungup gun. It was dug into a hillside on the approaches to the town. Efforts to bomb the gun had failed and, short of attacking it ourselves hand to hand (I winced at the very thought), the most effective way of taking out the emplacement would be by accurate fire from our own long-range artillery. The plan was for our group to get the gun under observation at a distance of about half a mile and coolly zero our gunners in by radio.

'You can set up your cameras and get some good shots,' said the Pirate. Overnight he'd become another Cecil B. DeMille. 'But leave your tripods and run for it if we're spotted.'

Dawn next day saw us safely concealed in a small copse. The Japanese gun, deeply dug in and camouflaged, lay on the far side of some dried-out paddy-fields. The sun came up to reveal its crew lolling around the sandbagged hillside smoking, playing cards and hanging out a line of washing. These were the first live enemy soldiers I had ever seen and no amount of subsequent encounters ever diminished that initial excitement.

'There's a patrol around somewhere protecting these bastards,' the Major told my two American colleagues. 'Be prepared for trouble.'

I would have called the whole thing off, then and there, if I'd had any say in the matter, but I hadn't and that was the end of it. Live and let live has always been my motto. The Pirate was already providing our gunners with precise map references over the radio. The first shell came swooshing in five minutes later. It exploded harmlessly three hundred yards short of the target. The effect was nevertheless electric. The Japanese threw away their cigarettes, snatched down their washing and dived deep into the bunker. Our gunners inched closer under the Pirate's expert guidance until a round burst inside the emplacement, setting off a secondary explosion and hurling assorted debris high in the crisp morning air.

'Jesus!' exclaimed the American cine-cameraman, squinting through his viewfinder. It turned out later that his lens wasn't big enough to catch genuinely dramatic close-ups but the effect was still impressive. A minute later we were dashing across open ground towards the shelter of the jungle. Since we had crossed this terrain in the dark I hadn't noticed how exposed we were on our line of retreat. Another of those accursed Hawker Hurricanes of the Indian Air Force spotted us and came in for the kill. 'Run for your lives!' yelled the Pirate. The plane opened fire, missing us by a mile. Staggering under the weight of one of the American tripods I sweated and panted my way into the trees. One of the Americans had dashed ahead and unbeknown to me was filming our pell-mell retreat. A month later, when they screened the uncut film in Calcutta, a roar of laughter went up at my bedraggled and distressed appearance.

Our next trick was nearly our last. Aerial reconnaissance suggested that the Japanese were pulling out of Taungup; we were urgently required to confirm or deny. A two-day, circular march through the foothills of the Pegu Yomas, well clear of any possible contact with the enemy, brought us to the outskirts of the town. It did indeed appear deserted, not only of defending troops but of Burmese civilians as well. The one person we came across, an old Burmese puffing a cheroot beside an abandoned farmhouse, told us everyone was off hiding in the countryside. It was the bombing that scared them – the Allied advance was, to say the least, destructive. The old man was too frail to walk and had been left to take his chances with a few monks and chickens. The main Japanese force had gone, he felt quite sure, but there were bound to be a few enemy soldiers still around.

'They're a sneaky lot,' he told our interpreter.

Pirate Edwards decided, typically, to push straight on into Taungup and risk running into an ambush. Advancing into an enemy stronghold in broad daylight seemed suicidal and I didn't hesitate to say so.

'You want pictures, don't you?' the Pirate demanded sarcastically. 'How are you going to get them in the dark?'

I wished I'd never thought of filming V Force. Why volunteer for anything *this* crazy? The group split into two squads. We tiptoed in tandem down either side of the main street. Shops were shuttered and empty. Grass thrust knee-high through the asphalt. A cluster of Japanese landing-craft lay rusting inside a large attap shed. The place was littered with empty Japanese beer bottles and sardine cans. Of the enemy themselves, however, there was no sign.

The tension rose as we continued our advance. The guerrilla group in its oddly assorted uniforms pattering forward from doorway to doorway in sudden silent rushes, the pregnant pause, the oppressive silence liable to be broken any moment by a burst of gunfire, a blood-chilling *banzai* yell and still nothing but the barking of distant dogs, the nattering of insects and the nervous chatter of my teeth.

We halted at a pagoda beside the Taungup river. At this point it was no more than two hundred yards wide. A canoe was tied up on our side, complete with paddles. We were about to embark when a *punghi* (monk) came slithering out of hiding from somewhere inside the temple and warned us against going further. A Japanese patrol was watching and waiting on the opposite bank. Our precipitate retreat was conducted on all fours through overgrown vegetable gardens, night soil pits and decayed compost heaps. We reached the far side of town, puffed and pungent, and called down an air-strike on the enemy's approximate position. It hit the wrong side of the river, demolishing the pagoda, I later learned.

One Japanese patrol, undaunted by the air attack, followed us all the way back into the jungle. We spotted them tracking us through the outskirts of Taungup. It was our turn to mount an ambush. We set up the movie-camera alongside our Bren gun and prepared, once more, to grab some genuine action footage. Those drones back in Delhi would get the shock of their sweet lives, I told myself, seeing real live Japanese walking into our line of fire in something like mid-close up.

It didn't work out that way. Our pursuers tired of the chase. About half a mile from where we lay in hiding the Japanese sat down for a quick smoke before heading back to town. The place fell without a fight two weeks later. Our own effort was sadly wasted: censors seized our stills and movie film soon after the shipment reached India. They were consigned, under security seal, to vaults somewhere in New Delhi. They are there to this day, friends tell me, mouldering and forgotten.

The day we recaptured Rangoon was one of the busiest of my life. I rode around a jubilant city in a borrowed fire-engine, accompanied by an Anglican clergyman; together we robbed a bank, reopened the cathedral, drank tea at a thousand pounds (sterling) a cup and accepted the surrender of a battalion of supposedly hostile soldiers.

It all began well before dawn when I swung over the side of a landing-ship and joined troops of the 26th Indian Division for the assault up-river. My job was to take still pictures of the operation. It didn't sound too taxing because word had reached us that the enemy had gone.

The cheering news had been confirmed from various sources. Indian paratroops who dropped in two days previously, on 1 May 1945, to seize the entrance to the Rangoon river, quickly disposed of some thirty Japanese who put up the usual fanatical resistance. The *jawans* then found to their surprise that there was no one else left to shoot at.

The vast bulk of 14th Army was still fighting its way southwards down the Irrawaddy and Sittang valleys, hoping to be the first into Rangoon. They had done most of the fighting and deserved the victory. But they were beaten hands down by an RAF officer who crash-landed his

Mosquito aircraft on Mingaladon airfield and walked unchallenged to the city jail where he found dozens of Commonwealth PoWs waiting impatiently for release. Some had climbed on to the jailhouse roof and written JAPS GONE. EXTRACT DIGIT.

'The RAF slang was not only evidence of the genuineness of the message,' our commanding general, Bill Slim, later noted 'but a gentle hint to speed up operations'.

The assault-group padre, the Rev. P. C. (Pat) Magee, destined to be chaplain of King's College, Cambridge, joined me at the dockside in Rangoon. He spotted an elderly fire-engine, complete with driver, and commandeered it for the day; there was no other transport available. The fire-engine carried us through crowded streets, thronged with well-wishers, convincing us that after three years' hard slog, the Burma campaign had, in the end, been worth those oceans of blood and sweat and tears. Happy in our ignorance we clanged away on the bell.

Rangoon had been a colonial showpiece before the war. It was now apparent that the poor old place had seen better days. No one could have known at the time that the capital was in good condition compared with the mess it would find itself in forty years on in the future.

Pat Magee's first objective was the Anglican cathedral. I felt sorry for him when we found it: the nave was stripped of pews; many monuments had been defaced; the floor was ankle-deep in tomato ketchup – the building had been used as a pickle factory. A handful of the Burmese faithful timidly joined Pat as he waded through the ketchup and said a prayer before the place where the altar had once been. An old woman wondered when they would be reviving communion.

'Not here, not for quite some time,' Pat told her sadly.

We headed for Sule pagoda and the Strand Hotel. Smoke was pouring out of the National Bank of Burma. A mob of Burmans in vivid *lunghis* was scrambling to get inside the vault. Pat and I elbowed our way downstairs and stood gaping at what we saw. The red glow of the fire above our heads lit sweating, frantic men fighting to get through a hole cut into the vaults close to the ceiling. Some had hacked at each other with those long, sharp Burmese swords and blood-stained bodies lay trampled underfoot. Every few minutes someone threw a box of banknotes through the hole and the mob dived for it with a fiendish roar.

'I'm in hell,' Magee kept saying. 'I really am in hell.'

One large box landed on my head. I grabbed hold of it. The looters surged towards me, baying like hungry dogs, but held back when they saw our uniforms. I walked out carrying the box, leaving Pat to cover my back. The whole thing couldn't have taken more than a couple of minutes; to me, it seemed like years.

Using a wrench from the fire-engine's tool-kit we split open the box. It contained thousands and thousands of Japanese occupation rupees. As far as I could make out it was nothing but worthless paper. Who would ever want to kill to get their hands on this sort of stuff?

The young Indian who had volunteered to drive our fire-engine vehemently disagreed. British colonial currency had long since ceased circulating in Burma. Japanese occupation rupees were still legal tender ... almost certainly for the next few hours. Nodding and winking confidentially, the driver conducted us to the craft shops beneath the great Shwedagon pagoda which still sold ivory carvings of exquisite delicacy. Our funny money proved to be surprisingly acceptable, although at a ridiculously devalued rate. I bought the statuette of a beautiful little Burmese princess, which I still own, for the equivalent, at the official rate, of five thousand pounds (sterling). Pat Magee bought hand-carved dice and some small figurines.

We lunched at a nearby restaurant. That cost the equivalent of three thousand pounds because word was getting around that occupation currency would shortly be declared illegal. By afternoon a cup of tea cost a small pile of banknotes, valued officially at one thousand pounds; come dinner-time the Chinese restaurateurs refused to accept anything but genuine Indian rupees.

'Let's see the King Emperor's head,' they chanted. In those days Indian rupee notes had a crowned portrait of George VI printed across them.

Darkness was falling when the fire-engine ran out of gas. There was no more available. Petrol pumps at the only garage we found were rusted and empty. We had to walk back into Rangoon from the eastern end of town; the Indo-British forces had not yet penetrated this far. It was close to sunset. The thought began to occur to me that the pair of us were way out of touch with the liberating troops and very much on our own.

My hair stood on end when we turned a corner in the gathering dusk and came face to face with a large number of Japanese soldiers. But hold it! Doing a double-take, we saw the soldiers were not Japanese. They were Indians, dressed in Japanese uniforms, bearing Japanese arms; it dawned on me, with a nasty wrench to the stomach, that we had run into members of the JIFs, the Jap-Indian Forces – or as they called themselves, the Indian National Army. The INA had been recruited from the many Indian prisoners captured at Singapore. Its founder was a brilliant Bengali nationalist, one Subhas Chandra Bose, who had broken with Gandhi and defected to the Axis side as a means of speeding Indian independence. The Bose slogan *Delhi Chalao!* (Onward to Delhi!) had brought elements of the INA into action against our forces in Burma. Groups of them had infiltrated our positions on the Arakan coast and caused understandable confusion. But the Japanese collapse in Burma and elsewhere was known to have undermined INA morale. Large numbers had deserted in recent months. I hoped this lot was equally disenchanted. As it turned out there was no need to worry. The Sikh who came up to us wearing the collar tabs of a Japanese major was actually smiling.

The Japanese battleship Yamato

The Yamato *being blown up by US torpedoes south-west of Kyushu,*
April 1945

Royal Navy officers take surrender of a Japanese seaplane base in Penang. Russell took this picture before he and Frank went off to Malaya

Frank entering a liberated town in Burma

RIN LOG

MONTHLY MAGAZINE OF THE ROYAL INDIAN NAVY

HE PUTS YOU ON THE SCREEN

rescue party to a position off the Irrawaddy Delta, where the survivors of the crashed aircraft were located.

Within four hours of joining the R.I.N. as a Midshipman early in 1944, he was ordered to Chittagong for operational duties. As he was already wearing khaki shirt and shorts, he had only to buy a Naval cap—and that was all he had time for anyway.

"Frankie" has filmed the recent combined operations in Arakan from all angles. He has sailed in sloops, M. Ls. and landing craft, hitch-hiking to the assault beaches soon after H-hour to get shots on shore and flying over the ships in light aircraft for "bird's eye" views.

"FRANKIE" WORTH is a familiar figure in Arakan, where he has just completed shooting his 50,000th foot of film for the R. I. N.'s Operational Film Unit.

Many of his news shots have appeared in *Indian News Parade*, which is screened at hundreds of cinemas throughout India. Some of them have been seen in newsreels which have a world-wide distribution. *Universal News*, for instance, recently carried his picture-story of the rescue of eleven U. S. air men by two H. D. M. Ls. of the Royal Indian Navy. "Frankie" sailed with the

Back in Calcutta recently, he took his girl friend to the pictures one night. When *Indian News Parade* came on, he said to her, with justifiable pride, "Those are shots that I took". She refused to believe him. Then the Commentator unexpectedly came to "Frankie's" rescue by announcing: "These dramatic pictures were taken by Sub-Lieutenant Worth, of the Royal Indian Navy".

Frank makes it to the front page, May 1945

Japanese pilots plan their next attack

Frank (left) and Russell under escort of the Kempeitai, *the notoriously sadistic Japanese secret police*

The intrepid adventurers' glorious arrival in Kuala Lumpur on the way to Singapore. Note the Union Jack spread over the bonnet

On the road to Singapore. Russell took this picture of Frank negotiating the car across a bridge partially destroyed by guerrillas. Abdul has the tricky job of laying boards across the 30-foot drop into the river

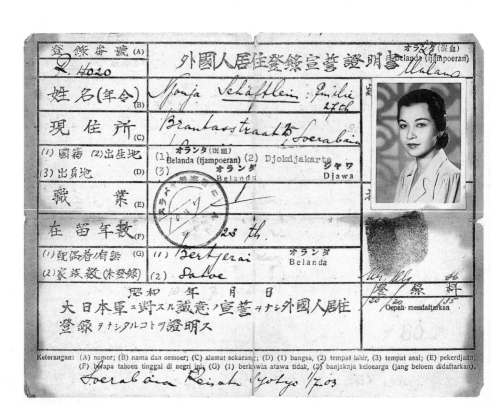

Millie Schaftlein's ID card

Russell's picture of Frank in front of Hiroshima station

Russell surveys the devastation caused by the atomic bomb dropped on Hiroshima. Frank took the photo

It wasn't all bombs and ships and Kamikazes ... as this picture of Frank and Russell in Bangkok shows, they also had time for other kinds of adventures!

Worth and Spurr, ever the exhibitionists. They didn't quite dress like the statue although – as they say – it pays to advertise!

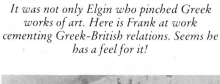

It was not only Elgin who pinched Greek works of art. Here is Frank at work cementing Greek-British relations. Seems he has a feel for it!

Not fame but sex is the Spurr! Russell with Greek nymph at the Acropolis

'Delightful to see you chaps,' he said. 'We couldn't wait to get this surrender business over.'

The men crowded around behind him murmured their cheerful approval. It was a massive relief.

'We're not in a position to accept your surrender,' I lamely explained. 'I am a cameraman. This man is a priest.'

'But we'll accept a drink,' Pat Magee chipped in.

'By jove, that's a jolly good idea,' said the Sikh major. 'We've still got some gin.'

He took us into the INA officers' mess. Subalterns crowded around to learn the latest news of India and the war. The Japanese had pulled out, leaving them to their own devices, and they were perfectly happy to opt out of further conflict.

'Pink gin suit you?' inquired the Sikh major. He handed us our glasses. Men who had lately been our enemies snapped to attention as the major called:

'Gentlemen. The King Emperor!'

PART FIVE

The craziest, most dangerous adventure of my life started in what we then called Ceylon. It ended, two months later, in what we now call Indonesia. During those two months I stole a car, posed as a personal envoy of the Supreme Commander, South-east Asia, Lord Louis Mountbatten, drove through Japanese-occupied Malaya to Singapore, 'liberated' several cities, including Kuala Lumpur, received (and rejected) the surrender of a Japanese cruiser, collided with the notorious Japanese secret police, the *Kempeitai*, drinking one of its officers under the table, helped a Dutch war prisoner find his wife and fell madly, if briefly, in love with a glorious Eurasian girl who claimed she'd had no sex for three and a half years. It all sounds, admittedly, like fantasy and you are at liberty to disbelieve. But I can assure you that every word is true.

Towards the last week of July 1945, Frank and I were assigned, as a combat camera team, to the Far Eastern Fleet in Trincomalee. Most of the ships in that fleet were British, not Indian. They were assembling for an amphibious assault on Malaya early in September. The thinly stretched resources of the various Indo-British public relations organisations, army, navy and air force, were to be pooled until that operation was over. The officer in charge of Far Eastern Fleet PR was a reserve commander in the Royal Navy. It was on his orders that the pair of us were assigned to the cruiser *Cleopatra* to cover the first of a series of softening-up strikes by carrier-borne aircraft against Japanese airfields in Sumatra.

That in itself was a put-down. You can't film air strikes from an escorting cruiser. The commander's own pet cameramen, sturdy Royal Navy types, had been installed in the carriers; Frank and I were relegated to picking up the crumbs in case some kamikaze pilot took a swipe at the escorts.

Late afternoon of 6 August 1945, a launch was taking us out to the cruiser. The great Ceylonese anchorage was jam-packed with warships. We passed the ageing battleship *Nelson*, all forecastle and triple turrets, and the more elegant French *Richelieu*, refitted in the United States after the British blew her stern off while in Dakar under Vichy command. There was an assortment of aircraft-carriers including the little flat-tops built on the hulls of merchant ships which we called 'Woolworth' carriers. The *Cleopatra* sat somewhere in the middle of this ménage looking ferociously businesslike.

'Guess what,' said the midshipman in charge of the launch as we manoeuvred alongside. 'The Yanks have dropped a new kind of bomb on Japan.'

BBC broadcasts transmitted over the Tannoy spoke of an atomic bomb dropped on a place called Hiroshima. I couldn't for the life of me imagine anyone constructing a bomb from anything as intangible as atomic particles, despite the efforts of some uniformed experts to offer a lucid explanation. It was months before I figured it out. The one aspect that impressed me at the time was the amount of damage the device appeared to have caused. A good-sized garrison town on the southern end of the Sea of Japan had been obliterated. I was able to verify this in person, six months later, when Frank and I found ourselves in occupied Japan.

The day after the bombing of Hiroshima, *Cleopatra* sailed with a dozen cruisers and destroyers escorting six of the Woolworth flat-tops. The war was still on, as far as we were concerned. Our attack on Sumatran airfields was scheduled for 11 August or thereabouts, after the newly-arrived aircrews had thoroughly exercised in the Bay of Bengal. The next two days were spent steaming into the wind as fighters and dive-bombers clambered off the carriers and landed back, awkwardly and delicately, on to the tiny decks. Pilots hated these cranky little ships; the rate of operational casualties among squadrons assigned to Woolworth carriers was scandalously high.

There would be plenty more fighting, we reckoned, before the Japanese called it quits. Eager for action our task-force took up position off northern Sumatra. No attack came. The force steamed around for hours without launching a single plane. According to below-decks scuttle-butt the admiral had been told to await further orders. It was some time before we learned that a few hours earlier a B-29 of the US Air Force, carrying the only other atomic bomb then in existence, had found its primary target, a city called Kokura, concealed by heavy cloud, and diverted to the historic port of Nagasaki.

News of the bombing spread like wildfire once the brief official announcement came over the Tannoy. Speculation began that an end to the war against Japan might actually be in sight. It was a novel thought. Pessimism was endemic to the Allied forces in Asia. The Japanese had fought fanatically in Burma, New Guinea and throughout the Pacific. Kamikazes had terrorised the US fleet. Universally it was assumed that a long hard slog lay ahead until the enemy had been virtually wiped out.

'The Golden Gate in '48,' chanted the GIs on Okinawa. 'The bread line in '49.' American troops took it for granted that the Depression would resume directly hostilities ended. The British, by contrast, expected miracles from their new Labour government, still blissfully unaware of Britain's bankruptcy.

The next few days we aimlessly circled the Nicobar Islands. Hopes rose with every dawn. Pilots flew less frequently off the minuscule carriers and landed ever more cautiously when they did. No one wanted to wipe himself out now that everything seemed over. The shrill, courtly tones of the Showa Emperor, calling on his subjects to surrender, squawked out of the radio as we returned to Trinco. The Japanese were being ordered to 'think the unthinkable'. But would they? Around the mess-decks the betting was ten to one against.

It was the evening of VJ Day before we dropped anchor. Ships around us were dressed overall with gaily coloured bunting. The signal 'Splice the Mainbrace', doubling the rum ration, flew from the flagship. Celebrations were already uproariously under way. The military liaison officer aboard *Cleopatra*, a one-armed colonel wearing the purple ribbon of the Victoria Cross, mixed a massive rum punch in a hip-bath in the ward-room. We toasted His Majesty seated, in the traditional fashion; after that, things became a trifle unclear. I have vague memories of cheering on an Australian destroyer shooting star shells directly at the flagship. Someone else was firing tracer across the harbour. Somebody shot back. A duel developed between landing-craft at the inner anchorage. Cannon shells flew hissing overhead. A midshipman urged me to get below because it was too dangerous topside but I curled up beside a life-raft to watch the fun.

The next thing I knew it was dawn. The hands were hosing down decks. The RN commander in charge of PR came out to visit us shortly after breakfast and ordered Frank and myself to stay aboard. *Cleopatra* was part of a force being sent to liberate Sumatra. The big show would be Penang, he told us; two landing-ships would shortly be leaving for the island off the Malayan coast, the first spot of Empire soil to be liberated, but 'more experienced personnel' would cover *that* story.

'We can't miss Penang!' Frank protested feebly. Who gave a damn about Sumatra? Our complaints were icily received. Naval commanders do not take kindly to junior officers questioning their orders. The poor chap was probably as hungover as we were.

'You will do as you are told,' was his parting shot.

'Bollocks to that,' said Frank. No sooner had the commander returned ashore than we scooped up our equipment and headed for the landing-ships. It was Penang or bust.

The Japanese surrender left half a million Allied war prisoners marooned in south-east Asia. Eighty-five thousand of them were in Malaya and Singapore alone. It seemed unlikely that every one of the hardy, stubborn, skilful fanatics who had consistently outfought us for the better part of three and a half years would meekly submit to the ultimate humiliation of laying down their arms on the strength of one broadcast by Emperor

Hirohito. Samurai tradition dictated otherwise. One clash was all that would be needed to touch off a bloodbath.

Strange reports were coming in of political unrest, particularly in the Dutch East Indies, but overall our intelligence was deplorable. We had next to no idea what was going on in Japan, let alone the scatterings of colonies swamped by the tidal wave of military conquest in the opening months of the war.

The British were anxious to demonstrate that the Japanese had been totally defeated. 'We did not want a repetition of the German First World War legend of an unconquered army,' General Slim wrote in his memoirs. 'With this in mind I was dismayed to be told that General MacArthur in his overall instruction for the surrender had decided that the "archaic" ceremony of the surrender of swords was not be enforced. I am afraid I disregarded his wishes.'

Experts on Slim's staff sided with the American supremo, complaining that the Japanese would lose face, lose control of their troops and commit suicide. Bill Slim replied that he was ready for any Japanese who cared to go on fighting. In a broadcast to the surrendered garrisons he promised that those Japanese officers who wished to commit suicide 'would be given every facility'.

The consummate British stroke against Japan, the invasion of Malaya, had been set for 9 September 1945. Somewhere in the course of that little lot, I gloomily reckoned, my luck would have to run out. The Japanese surrender on 14 August was so close to D-day, that it was decided the invasion would go ahead anyway. But Japanese reactions would first be tested by re-occupying Penang island on 3 September, followed by the liberation of Singapore two days later. It was the litmus-test landing at Penang that Frank and I were determined to cover.

We soon found it wasn't so simple. Comprehensive signals had gone out to all fleet units defining which cameramen and correspondents should be doing what ... and where. Two converted Dutch liners, *Queen Wilhelmina* and *Princess Beatrix*, fitted out as landing-ships, were to liberate Penang with a scratch force of 2,000 Royal Marines roped in from ships and shore establishments. Both ships carried a full complement of photographers and pressmen, some from Fleet Street, under the guidance of a crusty RNVR lieutenant-commander.

'Who the hell are you?' he demanded when we boarded the *Queen Wilhelmina*. We must have looked a scruffy pair; our threadbare jungle-green uniforms were sadly out of place alongside the Royal Navy's gleaming whites.

'Royal Indian Navy team to cover the landing,' we reported smartly. The lieutenant-commander – two and a half ringer – fished out a lengthy signal.

'Good try,' he smirked. 'You two are assigned to *Cleopatra*, the Dutch show. Away with you.'

He ordered a launch to take us back to the cruiser. On the way there I persuaded the coxswain to drop us off on *Princess Beatrix* for a quick chat with colleagues.

'Better be double quick, gentlemen,' the coxswain told us. 'These ships are due to sail in an hour.'

Everyone was too busy to notice us when we crept aboard the *Beatrix*. We kept out of sight on the boat-deck until Trincomalee was well astern. The two landing-ships were heading north-east towards the Andaman Islands ('until further orders') escorted by a few cruisers and destroyers. Satisfied that all was safe we checked in with the most senior PR person, a charming old actor famous for camp roles on the West End stage, now wearing the guise of a lieutenant, RNVR. We mumbled something about being unsure which ship we were supposed to be joining.

'Gracious me, darlings,' cried the PR lieutenant shuffling through a file of papers. 'The signal says you should be on the *Cleopatra*.'

'That's a cruiser, isn't it?' Frank was all bewildered innocence. 'We knew it had some woman's name.'

'Naughty, naughty,' chided the PRO. 'But being *Indian* Navy' – he sounded dreadfully racist – 'you wouldn't know a cruiser from a cargo ship.' He wrung his hands at the prospect of further paperwork. 'Well, since you're here, you'd better stay,' he conceded. 'Can't really expect you to swim back, can we?'

The marines sat on the cargo holds checking their weapons. They were a mixed bunch, unused to operating together, and understandably nervous about the reception awaiting them in Penang. Officers with maps and blackboards went over the operation until we knew it by heart. The assault craft now swinging from the ship's davits would head for the harbour in two waves. We hoped the Japanese would be waiting there to welcome us.

'We'll be so mucking lucky!' grumbled the pessimists. Odds had lengthened twenty to one in favour of a fight.

First objective on landing would be the government offices in Georgetown where the Union Jack would be raised. ('If we live that long,' moaned the marines.) On from there to the naval air station and Batu Feringhi beaches where the main Japanese strength was deployed. It was out under the palm trees that we expected suicide units to give us serious trouble. A chaplain said prayers over the Tannoy before we went over the side at dawn on 3 September. The assault craft, effortlessly lowered, were bumping gently against the ship's side in a pleasant swell. The heavily-laden marines crouched silently below the gunwales full of fear and foreboding. Dead on 0600 hours we headed for the lights of Georgetown. The black-out, we later learned, had only just been lifted. The dawn came up as we approached, rose-tinting a clock-tower, a small harbour and a boat bound for the mainland with glaring navigation lights. It was the regular ferry still running to the mainland port of Butterworth.

Frank and I were as heavily laden as the marines with our packs of spare film, bulky equipment and cases of canned rations. We were last on to the harbourside, scrambling with difficulty up some moss-grown steps, accompanied by our PR person, veteran of dramas on the West End stage.

'Watch it, darlings,' he warned, giving our bums a protective pat. 'And don't forget the Mosquito at 1600.'

A twin-engined RAF reconnaissance plane was due to take off from Penang airfield for Calcutta at 4 p.m. that day with film and news dispatches for a waiting world. If we missed that flight our liberation coverage would be wasted.

A dozen Japanese officers in neatly-pressed uniforms, with crumpled peak caps and highly-shone boots, were lined up on the quayside. They saluted the senior marine, handed over maps of minefields and military installations and invited us to headquarters for a drink.

'There is still some Scotch,' a smiling major told me. 'We captured so much in Singapore.'

I looked the man over curiously. He was the first Japanese officer I had ever seen, live and face to face. Only a couple of weeks ago he would have been hacking away at me with the sword that dangled from his belt. It seemed unreal consorting with an enemy who had, until now, been no more than a whiff of gunsmoke, a *Banzai!* in the jungle or a corpse crumpled in the dust. The major surveyed us with equal interest. We must have been the first British he had ever seen without their hands up. He remarked politely on our lack of weapons.

'Better to run than fight,' I joked. For a moment the major looked puzzled. It was our job to get pictures, not to indulge in mock heroics, Frank elaborated. The philosophy suited us both to perfection.

'Ah so!' the Japanese exclaimed, politely sucking in his breath. 'You must be *Ren Sendenbun* (military propaganda).' He wrote the two Kanji characters in my notebook. They would become our 'Open Sesame' in the days ahead.

A rumbling arose from Georgetown. It reached a joyful crescendo as crowds of cheering people broke through the Japanese cordons and rushed to greet us. I realise it's fashionable these days to decry British colonialism – no doubt it left much to be desired – but three and a half years of Japanese occupation had temporarily cured any gripes Penang might have had about their much-diminished white rulers. A largely Chinese mob, waving British flags, swept us into the city. The Japanese major disappeared in the mêlée and with him our chance of a drink in the headquarters mess. The marines had been striding purposefully through the streets, weapons at the ready, but found it impossible to look warlike as rice cakes, spring rolls and – unimaginable luxury – cold bottles of drinkable beer were forced upon them. There had been a near-total beer drought in wartime India. Supplies could no longer be imported; the output of India's nascent breweries was quite unspeakable. Most of us gagged down fiery Rosa XXX rum, the stuff the Gurkhas loved, and dreamed of beer, real beer, and, on second thoughts, women.

Lovely young Chinese girls were out in the streets greeting us like heroes. WELL COME, BLOKES read the sign outside a big colonial house, which turned out to be one of the more exclusive brothels. Girls on the balcony were proclaiming Happy Hour. But we had work to do. There was a frenetic flag-raising before the pair of us joined the marine company charged with taking over the naval air station.

The sight that greeted us was sobering to say the least. The air station was remarkably well-stocked. Planes of all shapes and sizes were lined up at the water's edge and on the runway. All had big, black bombs slung beneath them.

'Kamikaze?' I asked a Japanese sentry who stood guard in full equipment with rifle and wickedly-long bayonet.

'Yes please,' he grinned. 'They kill you!'

Frank Worth was ever the pictorial perfectionist, and was not above setting up the occasional shot. It's not the sort of thing you'd dare do nowadays but the hand-over, he declared, was an historic occasion, and his job was to make it look like one. The flag-raising hadn't looked like anything special. Here in the air station the Japanese were lined up on his orders while a bewildered Royal Navy lieutenant who happened to appear on the scene was sent walking up and down the ex-enemy ranks looking haughty and disapproving. Kitsch it might have been, but that scene told it all on the newsreels.

We next filmed the beach defences. They were competently manned by tough-looking troops who shouted their salutations and bowed deeply as we passed. How fortunate it was, I realised, that the Japanese had decided not to fight. The Penang garrison outnumbered us four to one and with their bomb-loaded planes and concrete redoubts would doubtless have cut our minuscule force to pieces.

The Eastern and Oriental Hotel had become the press centre. It was here we brought our film and dope sheets ready for the courier flight. For those who don't remember the pre-narcotics era, 'dope' in those days meant all possible information pertaining to the film it accompanied. Script and caption writers could not get on without it. The civilian correspondents had taken over the bar, and that triumphant afternoon the beer was flowing freely. So were the imbibers' imaginations.

'I fought my way through sullen hordes of pensioned-off kamikazes,' wrote a correspondent for one of the London tabloids. I looked over his shoulder while he typed, trying not to laugh. The man had hardly left the bar all day according to his colleagues.

Presiding over this hive of hyperbole was the Public Relations officer in charge, the crusty navy commander who'd directed us to cover Sumatra.

He had come ashore from our fellow transport the *Queen Wilhelmina*. Slamming down his glass he made for the pair of us, looking furious.

'I've been waiting for you two,' he snarled. 'I heard you'd pulled a fast one. Well, you're not going to get away with it. Disobeying a direct order, that's what you're being charged with. I'm going to get you court-martialled. Consider yourselves under open arrest.'

It was a sobering prospect. Frank and I sought fresh air in the hotel garden where ancient cannon scowl silently out to sea. Neither of us was particularly depressed: the adrenaline was running too high. But the thought of a hassle at this stage of the game set us thinking. Thoughtfully we watched the ferry chugging in from Butterworth. It was a car ferry, completely empty.

'Day and night it goes, *tuan*,' said the Malay waiter who replenished our glasses. 'Backwards and forwards, forwards and backwards. No one tell it to stop.'

Frank looked at me. I looked at Frank.

'Why not?' he mused. I nodded my assent.

'Let's take the ferry,' he said. 'Let's go liberate Malaya.'

It was 4.30 in the afternoon when the mad idea came to us. Somehow or other we would evade that angry commander, get on the ferry, bluff our way on to the Japanese-occupied mainland of Malaya and drive down to meet the British forces as they landed two days later in Singapore.

Three things made such insanity possible. First was the lack of established naval authority in the early hours of Penang's liberation. The commander's threats could for the moment be ignored. Second, we were beyond control of the Public Relations Directorate in Delhi. We had always had a considerable amount of latitude choosing our assignments, but direct links with our seniors had been broken in the chaos that followed VJ Day. Third was glorious coincidence: the continued operation of that ferry. It still strikes me as odd, even today, that no one should have seen fit to suspend the ferry service. There must have been some typically bureaucratic explanation. Whatever the reason, hours after the Royal Marines landed in Penang, the empty craft was still shuttling on schedule across the narrow strait to Butterworth, unnoticed in the first, heady hours of liberation.

Our immediate requirement was a car. No problem there; we were gathering our equipment outside the Eastern and Oriental Hotel when a Japanese colonel drove past in a 1938 Morris Oxford. The vehicle was in poor shape, its body was battered, its tyres dangerously worn. Still, we flagged it down and advised the colonel we would be needing his vehicle for an hour to rush a friend to hospital. 'You'll get it back,' I lied. Perhaps it would have been easier to haul the colonel out by the scruff of his neck. Our former enemies heavily out-numbered us at this stage, however, and we felt obliged to dissemble for the sake of peace. Besides, it would get us into practice for friendly encounters on the mainland. The colonel was left holding a receipt from 'Brigadier Oliphant, Grand Oriental Hotel' while we headed for the ferry. We had taken care to provide ourselves with a cover story. We had borrowed a correspondent's typewriter before leaving the hotel and faked a letter introducing ourselves as 'envoys of the Supreme Commander, South-east Asia, Lord Louis Mountbatten' and signed it with the same fictitious 'Brigadier Oliphant'.

A Chinese storekeeper in Armenian Street gave us a Union Jack, a white tea-towel, some string and a bamboo stick. We planned to fly the towel from the stick as a makeshift flag of truce and drape the Union Jack over the bonnet of the car. It might give the Japanese pause before they began taking pot-shots at us.

'Here we go!' Frank chortled as we drove on to the ferry pier. At that moment a dreadful thought struck me.

'I can't drive,' I confessed. It was true. My parents had never been able to afford a car. People of our class could afford a maid-servant in those days, but not a car. There'd been no chance to learn driving in the navy.

'How are we going to get to Singapore?' Frank wailed. 'I can't drive all the bloody way.'

A group of Malays in silk shirts and vivid sarongs were sunning themselves on the wharf. There were no guards around, as the liberating forces were spread too thin around the island.

'Can any of you drive?' we asked. One of the Malays, a small muscular man with gleaming, slicked-down hair ambled over to the car.

'I'm a truck driver,' he said.

'Want to go to Singapore?' Frank asked. The driver grinned. 'Nothing much else to do, *tuan*,' he said and hopped in the back.

Our arrival caused a sensation among the crew. The ferry captain, a bearded, grey-haired Malay, came down from the bridge to see what we were up to. The ferry had been doing its thing, quite empty, for the past week, he told us, and would continue to do so until he received contrary instructions. His actions, we assured him, were in the finest traditions of British colonial bureaucracy ... meanwhile, we interrupted, would he mind getting a move on since our mission was of the utmost importance. The captain looked shocked. 'I can't leave ahead of schedule, tuan,' he insisted. 'Timetable says 5.30 p.m. departure.' Any minute now some nosy parker from the liberation force would stop us or cancel the ferry service. Frank waved our fake accreditation letter under the skipper's nose.

'Blame it on Lord Mountbatten,' he said. 'And Brigadier Oliphant.'

'You know what you're getting yourselves into?' The captain tried one last shot. 'Plenty Japanese on mainland.' He drew a finger ghoulishly across his throat.

'That's our worry,' I said. 'Get this tub moving.' I had visions of the commander appearing on the wharf with a clutch of military policemen.

The captain shrugged, the engine-room telegraph loudly clanged, the hull shuddered and crewmen discarded the mooring lines. The ferry spun slowly round. Before long the lights of Georgetown were twinkling merrily astern in the sunset. As we headed into the narrow strait Abdul, the truck-driver, helped us fix the truce towel on to its bamboo stick and lash it to the offside front wing. The Union Jack was secured with string across the bonnet. Most of the camera gear was packed out of sight in the boot; we had no intention of provoking trouble by haphazardly taking pictures; certainly not until we had gauged the temper of the Japanese occupation forces.

Butterworth was almost blacked out. The only bright lights were on the quayside. They picked out the Japanese sentry with rifle and fixed bayonet at the top of the ferry pier. The sight of him sent shivers down my spine. We had no idea how our former foes would react to this intrusion. The pier loomed closer and closer overhead. The telegraph clanged again, the ferry slowed and the crew began loosening the rope ready to lower the ramp. Frank started the car and took over the wheel. The way we were facing he would have to reverse off the ferry. Frank gunned the engine and shot backwards up the ramp the moment it thudded down. The sentry leaped sideways to avoid us. We spun round on the wharf, tyres screeching, and caught a snapshot glimpse – will I ever forget it? – of four Japanese playing cards in a nearby guardhouse, gaping at us open-mouthed, half-risen from their seats. The sentry called on us to halt. We pretended we hadn't heard. Crouched low in the car we roared off into the night. No one took a shot at us. Clear of Butterworth, in the darkened countryside we began to breath a little easier.

The Japanese were actively patrolling the coastal area. Squads of men in camouflaged steel helmets showed up repeatedly in the headlights and each time a stab of fear shot through my gut. It seemed so unreal, driving cheerfully past the men we had been fighting these past three weary years. The men in question ignored us. Apart from them, the roads were deserted.

Tyre trouble stopped us in Taiping. The car was instantly mobbed by a cheering crowd. It was the first sizeable town we had reached, and we were the first British troops to get there. People crowded around demanding to know when the main forces would arrive.

'Soon,' we said vaguely, not having the foggiest idea.

Spare tubes, mechanics and even puncture solution appeared from nowhere and we were dragged into a Chinese restaurant and stuffed with fried rice and chow mein. A distinguished-looking Chinese in well-cut khaki drill introduced himself as area commandant of the Resistance Army. He claimed that his guerrillas, armed and equipped by Allied air-drops, had overrun much of the state. It would be extremely dangerous to drive southwards unannounced, he warned, because his men had cut the road between Taiping and Ipoh. If we would care to wait an hour he would pass word down to the road blocks and arrange for us to pass unmolested.

Five minutes later a worried young Indian arrived on a bicycle. He had a message for us from the Japanese *Kempeitai*, the fearsome combination of military police and Gestapo. Mere mention of their name obviously frightened our welcomers, some of whom slipped quietly off into the darkness. The message was that the Japanese knew of our presence 'and would be glad if we could come and see them'.

Filled with foreboding I made my way to the car down the poorly-lit street, dramatically proclaiming 'On to Singapore!' and promptly fell face-downwards in an open cesspool. The largely Chinese crowd fell about laughing. Oriental humour is shot through with *schadenfreude*.

'Hold it right there,' yelled Frank, as I spluttered around in the slime. 'I must get a picture.'

Abdul helped me out. He was laughing so much the tears were streaming down his face. My eyes were also streaming, but for different reasons. I was covered in what one might politely call night soil. The stench was unbelievable. A shopkeeper sponged me down but the Indian messenger kept nagging us to hurry up. Abdul spread newspaper on the back seat and drove into *Kempeitai* headquarters with me shivering and stinking.

A former colonial police post had been sheathed in sandbags, hedged in by double rows of barbed wire and floodlit on every side. Machine-guns peeped through slits in the bricked-up windows. Two young Japanese lieutenants bowed us into their office, wrinkling delicate noses at my smelly presence and offering cups of hot, green tea. They commiserated with me in my distress and sent a sergeant off searching for a change of uniform. I threw away my polluted jungle greens and gratefully changed into the clothes provided. It did not occur to me at the time, but I must have looked odd driving through Malaya in Japanese uniform!

The lieutenants listened gravely to our story. I must say, it sounded quite convincing. Lord Louis wanted us to make a quick, independent survey of road conditions in advance of the British arrival; though why it should be left to a couple of amateur sailors was never explained. Our hosts noted down the 'Oliphant' name in their log book and wrote us a permit to proceed. There had been trouble on the Ipoh road, they reported, but nothing to worry about. That showed how little *they* knew about the situation further south. Naturally we made no mention of the Resistance Army, having never even heard of it before, and hoped that the delays caused by my cesspool encounter would give the Chinese who called himself commandant time to call off his watchdogs.

It must have been midnight by the time we left Taiping. Abdul took the wheel. Forty miles from Ipoh the jungle closed in on the road and we began running into check-points. Sentries loomed out of the most unexpected places and our halts became longer and longer. We were finally detained at a large blockhouse where a *Kempeitai* platoon was brewing tea around a fire. The fire flung fantastic shadows on the road. It silhouetted the two tiny tanks parked on either side of the barbed-wire road-block. Japanese sentries closed in without a word, rifles at the ready. They examined our pass in silence. There was an awkward pause while an officer was called. It was at this point that I started to feel genuinely worried. The thrill of liberation was beginning to wear off. This absurd adventure had landed us deep in the Perak jungles with nothing but bluff and pleasantry to carry us through. Stupid over-confidence had manoeuvred us into a perfect spot for the Japanese to wreak private vengeance, if they felt so inclined; out here in the *oolu* (bush) no one would be any the wiser. The thought occurred that our so-called pass ordered the men at this particular road-block to take us off into the jungle and administer the samurai sword treatment. It was a cool night but I was sweating with fright.

An officer ran out of the blockhouse, buttoning his jacket and lugging a gigantic sword. I was reminded, momentarily, of the Lord High Executioner in *The Mikado*. He too examined our pass, grunted, and began writing in Roman capitals in my notebook. Written English came to him more easily than the spoken word. The lines of shaky capital letters declared we could proceed to Ipoh only under his escort. That was the last thing we wanted – the guerrillas could scarcely fail to attack a car under heavy Japanese guard – but again we kept quiet about the arrangements we hoped had been made by the Chinese commandant back in Taiping. It was useless to argue. 'Communist guerrillas' (the officer wrote 'gorillas') had cut the road ahead and we could not be permitted to go on alone. We bowed and smiled and pretended to look pleased and handed out some of our emergency supply of cigarettes. The Japanese offered us cigarettes in turn. Neither Frank nor I smoked but we lit up, coughing and choking and congratulating the Japanese on the quality of their tobacco. Anything to keep our guardians happy. The tobacco tasted like old socks.

The tanks started off, spitting out clouds of smoke. One drove ahead of us, the other behind, and behind that a truck with a machine-gun mounted on the roof and a dozen heavily armed soldiers inside. The Japanese officer joined me in the back of our car cradling a Thompson sub-machine-gun across his knees. The guerrillas were undoubtedly active in this part of Malaya. Rows of trees had been hacked down across the road which the Japanese had only just managed to clear. I sat with my hand on the door handle ready to dive out at the first sign of ambush. Surprisingly, nothing happened.

Dawn was breaking as we clanked into Ipoh. The population hardly had time to cheer before we were inside Japanese army headquarters, bowing, smiling and nodding our way through interminable speeches of welcome – 'Rord Rouis Mountbatten garrant helo (gallant hero)' – washed down with more, lots and lots more, hot green tea. It gurgled around our stomachs like the second rinse in the dishwasher. A nauseating experience: Frank and I were coffee-drinkers.

The Japanese had taken over a large British barracks. It was teeming with officers with shaven, shiny heads and polished, shiny boots. Telegraphs hummed and clacked. Dispatch riders hustled about the compound; the place fairly hummed with professional efficiency. A large picture in the entrance hall hung shrouded in canvas. Soldiers bowed when they passed it.

'That is Emperor's portrait,' a staff officer reverently explained, 'covered to conceal our disgrace.'

We were anxious to keep moving. It was now 4 September, and British troops would be landing in Singapore next morning. Another 175 miles of uncertain road had yet to be covered; the car was knocking badly and eating oil. The Japanese apologised profusely. An armoured car was essential for our continued escort.

'In your safety lies the honour of the Japanese army,' an elderly colonel explained. 'A little more time. So sorry, please.'

We set off finally at noon, the armoured car in the lead, rolling through overgrown rubber estates and hamlets of palm-leaf huts. The road was in good condition but the armoured car was not and there were further delays. Frank and Abdul, both exhausted, said I would have to drive but after a few minutes I hit a bend too fast and ran the car off the road. Frank went back, bleary-eyed, behind the wheel. Tea halts had been arranged at check-points along the road. Tea, tea and more tea. We were stiff with bowing, our faces ached with forced smiles and the cigarettes were beginning to run out. So was time. It was running out faster than the cigarettes. 'On to Singapore!' Frank kept chanting as he fought to stay awake. I wondered whether we would ever get there. We still had to pass through Kuala Lumpur and the guerrilla-infested rubber estates of Johore.

We rolled into Kuala Lumpur shortly before dusk, escorted by our dilapidated armoured car, and drove up to the front steps of the Majestic Hotel. A crowd began collecting at sight of the Union Jack on our car. Japanese troops filed into the streets and the crowd quickly melted away. The capital of the Malayan Federation had wilted under enemy occupation. Paintwork was peeling everywhere, windows were cracked and gardens were being replanted as allotments. Window boxes sprouted profusely as householders tried to grow more food. Public transport appeared to have broken down. Streets were rutted and littered with cannibalised cars. But that fantastic domed railway station looked as attractive as ever under a coat of dirt and streaky whitewash.

A reception committee of senior Japanese officers awaited us at the hotel. A major-general with a Hitlerian moustache read out a speech of welcome to the two representatives of the Supreme Commander, Southeast Asia, Lord Louis Mountbatten. After further injections of hot green tea we were provided with a comfortable room and bath.

No one needed the bath more than I did. The smell of the Taiping cesspool gave me a repulsive presence. Frank and Abdul claimed to have grown used to the stench but failed to hide their relief when I eventually emerged, soaked and bathed and fragrant as ersatz soap allowed. The three of us were asleep on our feet. We'd hardly nodded off since leaving liberated Penang the previous evening. So much had happened, driving down the Japanese-occupied Malay peninsula, that it seemed like we had been on the road for days. Longingly we looked at the comfortable hotel beds. A couple of hours' nap was all we needed, but too much distance remained to be covered if we were to beat the British troops landing at Singapore the following morning.

A British major accosted us in the foyer. He looked puzzled and annoyed. What the devil did we think we were doing? Perhaps he'd care to tell us what *he* was doing, we shot back. The major was in charge of a unit of Force 136, the clandestine force operating in the jungle with the self-styled Resistance Army. Only that morning he had emerged from the jungle under a safe-conduct from the Japanese. The enemy had been hunting him until a day ago, a hefty price upon his head. He listened impatiently to our unlikely story and departed with the reminder that in this area *he* was in command. I watched him stride off down the hotel steps, swagger-stick under one arm, ignoring the saluting Japanese. Strange people, the British. Here we were, ill-met among our enemies, and all this twerp could think about was who took orders from whom.

An eight-course English-style dinner comprising every type of colonial oddment had been prepared by the hotel staff. There were 'devils on horseback', crumbed chops, grilled fish and steamed ginger pudding. The Chinese cook came gleefully to tell us that these were the first Western dishes he had whipped up for three and a half years. We would have preferred sushi, to be quite honest, but ate our way dutifully through every course. The ingredients must have been hard to obtain because food was in desperately short supply. A submarine blockade of which we had never heard had curtailed and finally cut food shipments throughout the region since 1944. A campaign had been launched to grow more food locally, which had already consumed the golf course. The pitch in front of the Selangor Cricket Club (known to expatriates as 'The Spotted Dog') was sown with tapioca. There seemed no end to sacrilege.

Two Indian officers approached our table. They were prisoners of war from a holding camp in the Sanitary Board offices, a big barracks-like building across the road from the Majestic. Bugles were blowing familiar calls as we toured the place after dinner. Roomful after roomful of Indian prisoners clapped and cheered. Relief was in sight, we kept repeating; aircraft and fast ships were on their way to repatriate all Allied prisoners.

An old Indian *Jemadar* led us to a picture of George VI and Queen Elizabeth at the head of his room. He wept with joy when told he would soon be returning to India. Like many of the prisoners he had an unpleasant tale to tell. The Japanese had done their damnedest to force him to join the Indian National Army, and some of his comrades had died under torture. Five Gurkhas sprang to attention when we entered the next room. Their sergeant reported them the sole survivors of a battalion wiped out in battle on the River Perak.

'No one told us to retreat,' the sergeant said. 'The battalion went on fighting until almost everyone was dead.'

We parted sourly from our Japanese hosts. There was more bowing and hissing, but a lot less smiling. It wasn't difficult to imagine how these obsequious little bastards would have treated us a few weeks before. The same armoured car led us off down the Singapore road. It was dark again. Police posts now let us pass without question and we were making good time when our offside front tyre blew out. We mended it with difficulty. Then the armoured car broke down. An hour later our over-patched tyre blew again. We left the armoured car with steam pouring from its radiator and limped into Segamat for breakfast and repairs. No Japanese appeared to disperse the crowd this time and we sat at a roadside table eating before a huge audience.

This was the last lap of the race between ourselves and the British forces due to land in Singapore that morning. First troops would be off the troop-ships at 1030 hours. My watch warned that this would be in two and a half hours' time. It was a race we had little chance of winning. The fates conspired to delay us. An increasing number of wooden road bridges had been burned and torn apart by the guerrillas. Our car nearly fell through the middle of one bridge where the planking had been partially destroyed. Frank steered skilfully along lengths of wood Abdul and I laid over the gaping hole. Another tyre, badly retreaded, began to flap around the hub. We drove on, praying it would hold. There was no spare and small hope of help in the thinly inhabited reaches of northern Johore.

Rubber estates had appeared neglected north of Kuala Lumpur. Down here they were in better condition although some clearings had been hacked out for food cultivation. The clearings grew wider in the centre of the state where acres and acres of trees had been felled to make way for tapioca. The horrid root was rapidly replacing rice as the staple diet. The food campaign seemed badly organised, however; or else the Japanese were losing control of the countryside. Little work had been done on much of the reclaimed land and undergrowth tended to replace the trees. Signs showed many of the estates were under new management. It was obvious that most of the *zaibatsu* – the great trading houses like Mitsui and Mitsubishi – had profited handsomely from Japan's imperial conquests. Throughout the latter part of the journey we noted down the names, locations and condition of estates and passed on the information, innocently, when we reached Singapore.

Close to Johore Bahru the road grew choked with sullen Japanese pulling out of Singapore. They glared at us so angrily we began to regret the loss of our armoured car. Rows of trucks packed the roadside. Most of them were broken down, their frantic drivers juggling with the engines. All were piled high with baggage; some carried beds and furniture, one had a small car in the back. The Japanese were piled as high as their baggage, clinging on by every available means. Johore Bahru detained us a mere five minutes while I cut some of the surplus rubber from our flapping tyre with my last precious razor blade. Outside the Sultan's palace a small crowd cheered bravely, saw the Japanese closing in and changed their minds. From there on the streets were lined with fully-armed Japanese troops who scowled at our Union Jack. There were more scowls from the perspiring military policemen battling the chaos on the causeway. Breakdowns were causing mile-long tail-backs on either side. Empty trucks were trying to get back to Singapore while lines of laden trucks kept crawling into Johore. We threaded our way through the mêlée, hanging close behind a staff car full of high-ranking Japanese officers, gleaming with decorations and gold aiguillettes, which pulled out ahead of us and surged through the saluting sentries. We accelerated, acknowledged the bows and salutes of the astonished Japanese and raced on to the island. Our arrival came an hour too late, but amazingly we'd made it!

The liberation forces might have beaten us to Singapore but they had not advanced very far. Orders to proceed with the utmost caution were being religiously observed. We had driven all the way across the island deep into Singapore city before the first British troops appeared, in full battle order, creeping forward at the crouch from the direction of Collyer Quay. They looked a bit apprehensive – or so it seemed to us in our elated arrogance – rather as if the Japanese still had a suicidal trick or two up their collective sleeves. The Japanese were falling back, in fact, according to plan. They retreated as fast as the British advanced, leaving a half-mile vacuum in between. It was in the middle of this vacuum that the first advance patrols found us blithely looting supplies of petrol. We were not alone. The Japanese had dutifully assembled all commandeered cars and trucks and several fuel-tankers on the Maidan, the wide stretch of open park opposite City Hall. Once the foe was gone the Chinese poured in, helping themselves to cars and petrol. We joined the crowd around one of the tankers and were filling up our spare jerry cans when a plump, pink army lieutenant shouted: 'What d'you think you're doing?'

'Looting!' Frank laughed back over his shoulder. He handed a full jerrican to Abdul and started filling another.

'Stop or I'll fire!'

We looked round in amazement. The plump, pink lieutenant had us covered with his sten gun. He was hopping mad. His face was no longer pink but bright, beetroot red. Really it was too much. Surely we hadn't driven five hundred-odd miles through Japanese lines to be knocked off by one of our own troops?

'Relax!' I said. It dawned on me that the lieutenant was staring bug-eyed at my Japanese uniform. I could guess what he was thinking. All kinds of renegades could be at large.

'What's up?' demanded an officious-looking major. He too was kitted out in steel helmet, full pack, the works. He regarded me with considerable distaste.

'You been working for the Japanese?' he asked. His voice was menacingly low.

'We've just driven down from Penang,' I lamely explained. 'At Taiping I fell in a cesspit and the *Kempeitai* gave me a change of uniform ...' My voice trailed off. Even to my ears our story sounded a bit unreal.

'And how did you get down the peninsula?' the major asked. 'Malaya happens to be in enemy hands.'

'We pretended to be envoys of Lord Louis Mountbatten,' Frank chipped in. 'You see, we're combat cameramen. Royal Indian Navy ...'

It was no use. Military police hauled us off to a command post close by the plinth that should have carried the statue of Sir Stamford Raffles. The Japanese had removed it. Just as well, perhaps; the founder of Singapore would have considered our very presence a stain on the escutcheon of empire. Right now it was open season on memorials. A loud explosion shook the waterfront as we drove towards the command post. Sappers had blown up a monolith commemorating the foundation in Singapore of the Indian National Army.

An intelligence colonel listened to our story with decreasing disbelief once an aide had scrabbled through a bundle of those ubiquitous signals. The fact that we were missing, believed decamped to Malaya, had been advised by Penang. Shaking his head reprovingly the colonel told us to check in with the Public Relations unit already installed in the Cathay Building. The commanding officer of PRD, my outfit in Delhi, an Australian colonel called Jenkins, had parachuted into the island ahead of the liberation forces and told intelligence to look out for us.

'Two young fools,' was the way his advice was worded if memory serves me correctly. He put it more strongly when we met him. 'You pair of mucking idiots,' Colonel Jenkins growled when we checked into PR headquarters on the sixth floor of the Cathay Building. 'You might have caused an international incident. Still, you'd better make yourselves useful until I can ship you back to India.'

The Cathay was in those days the tallest building in Singapore and the most fashionable address. Its owner, the millionaire businessman Lok Wan To, arrived in rags a couple of nights later. He had been hiding from the Japanese in up-country Johore. His appearance was so shabby that the Indian watchmen would not allow him into his own premises. His first night of freedom in Singapore was spent sleeping on the steps.

Beer fumes filled the Cathay press room. You might have been in one of those sordid pubs on the fringes of Fleet Street. Someone had liberated a truckload of lager from the Tiger brewery. It tasted, believe me, like nectar of the gods. Everyone was gulping it down, hunched over their typewriters as correspondents and PR-types blearily created deathless prose. Among them was a chap from the London *Daily Herald*. We had last seen him filing his story from the hotel bar in Penang.

'Glad you made it!' he cried, waving a cheery hand. 'We heard you'd done a bunk. Can't think why the Japs didn't shoot you.' He emptied his beer glass. 'Come to think of it, that would have made quite a story.' The fact that we had survived did not make news. Man has to take a mighty great bite out of dog to get much attention these days.

The only correspondent who showed the slightest interest was Arthur Helliwell of the London *Sunday People*. He took down the fullest details of our dash from Penang. We both felt highly flattered. Sam Goldwyn always said 'there's no such thing as *bad* publicity'. As it turned out, Helliwell did not file a word. He made careful note of the condition of certain rubber estates we had identified in Johore and cabled a buying order to his stockbroker. 'Thanks boys,' he said a few days afterwards. 'You made me a nice little bundle on that one.' It never even earned us an expense-account lunch; understandably, perhaps, because there wasn't much to eat apart from army rations.

Our first job was to visit the Singapore naval base. After all, we were naval cameramen. Conditions had not been conducive to much photography during our drive through Malaya. We had thought it wise to stick to our Mountbatten fairy-tale and leave the cameras locked up, out of sight. The time had come to justify our existence and produce something to send back to Delhi. Tired as we were, that first day the excitement kept us going. A courier plane was departing shortly before nightfall. We had to get a shipment ready before it left. Our driver was outside keeping an eye on the car. We had left it parked in front of the Cathay Building. The white flag and Union Jack were gone. Most of the travel stains had been washed off. Abdul had even taken the trouble to trade one of our fuel jerricans for two fresh front tyres. The tyres were not brand new but they weren't as worn as the old ones. Our silk-shirted Malay friend was showing admirable initiative. We were not to know he planned to steal the car himself directly we left town.

The Japanese were still in charge of the naval base when we drove in. An armed sentry on the gates saluted smartly. A handful of sailors toiling on the wharf in khaki fatigues threw us a curious glance. The select group of RN officers and engineers who were due to take over the place was still several hours away. We stopped the car beside the vast dry dock built in the 1930s for the fleet Britain could never afford. After the First World War British strategic planners had tried to develop Singapore into a bulwark of naval power in the south Pacific, but by then it was too late. Britannia was too broke to rule the Asian waves. Dissipation of wealth, unending economic decline and that symbol of fiscal defeat, the Geddes axe, had reduced the post-war Grand Fleet to an outmoded skeleton; there were neither the funds, nor the will, to create the kind of force that would establish a credible British naval presence east of Suez. The Americans and Japanese were pouring money into ship construction Britain could no longer match. British politicians were forced to fight for treaties of limitation. Singapore was born (and died) a toothless tiger. The Japanese killed it off with contemptuous ease.

The dockyard had taken a pasting from the air. Its long concrete wharves lay shattered by penetration bombs. Most of the shoreside workshops had lost their roofs. Rain had poured into foundries, machine shops and store-rooms, coating their contents with mould and rust. At least a dozen wrecks dotted the harbour. A light cruiser lay, decks awash, inside a sunken floating dock. Thickets of masts, spars, funnels and rusting upperworks protruded from the outer anchorage. A weed-grown neglect blighted once-smart lawns and ornamental gardens. Windows were broken and unmended in headquarters offices left gloomy by lack of electric power.

Stacked in neat rows in one corner of the yard, now smothered in grass and creeper, were spare barrels for the naval guns that were supposed to protect Singapore from the sea. It has since been argued that a few of these great guns did cover the land approaches to the island – not all were pointing vainly out across the Macassar Strait – but we believed then, and I still believe today, that their primary, mistaken purpose was to prevent seaborne invasion. The planners who failed to provide a fleet for Singapore failed equally to understand that an assault could come from the rear, from the nearby Malayan peninsula. But it wasn't merely myopic planners, wrongly sited guns and unbegotten battleships that provoked the most disgraceful British defeat since Yorktown. It was an inability to recognise the potential of awakening Japan; a blindness born of arrogance that prevented Westerners from appreciating the impact of their own culture and technology on peoples they despised ... a fatal miscalculation that later cost so many lives in Korea and Vietnam and other pressure-points in the post-war Asian world.

'Gentlemen, I salute you.'

The speaker was stiffly formal. He wore the peaked soft cap and neat drill tunic of an officer of the Imperial Navy.

'Commander Nakajima at your service.'

We returned his salute with some embarrassment. Our job was to grab as many pictures as possible and head back to town to catch that courier. There wasn't time to get involved in ritual encounters.

'I am the Executive Officer of the cruiser *Takao*,' the commander went on. 'It is my duty to conduct you to our ship.'

He nodded towards a small island at the far end of the anchorage. Moored beneath mountainous camouflage netting was a large Japanese warship. It was the most unexpected sight. The Imperial Navy had been virtually wiped out, according to our uncertain knowledge. Only later did we learn that the *Takao* had limped, damaged, into Singapore from the massacre in Leyte Gulf. She had been lucky to survive the battle in the Philippines, late in October 1944, when the Japanese made their last hapless attempt to alter the course of the Pacific war. Shortly after the cruiser reached Singapore, midget submarines were sent in to sink her. The heroic raid failed to eliminate her although it managed to compound the damage to her stern.

Commander Nakajima took over the front seat of our car and gave orders to Abdul in Japanese. Our driver appeared to understand every word. We took a circuitous route through a cluster of anti-aircraft guns set up on the adjacent shore. The cruiser towered above us as we made our way to the companionway ladder across a creaky wooden catwalk. There was a squeal of bosuns' calls when we mounted the ladder and saluted the double rank of officers and sailors lined up to greet us. It was an awkward moment.

'We have been expecting you,' the commander said, introducing us to the acting captain.

'Acting?'

'Our commanding officer, Captain Fushida, ended his life the day His Imperial Majesty ordered us to cease fighting. You may inspect his cabin. It has been scrubbed clean.' The commander's face tightened perceptibly. 'Captain Fushida chose to use a hand grenade.'

I felt impelled to apologise to the assembled officers. The Japanese thought we had come to take surrender of the ship. We were in no position to do any such thing, much as we would have liked to walk away with a clutch of souvenir swords. Frank and I were *Ren Sendenbun*, military propaganda, and all we asked right now was permission to take a few pictures. The commander shrugged.

'We are at your disposal,' he said resignedly.

The *Takao*, an ugly looking brute but frighteningly formidable, was an extraordinary vessel. Three 8-inch gun-turrets were grouped together on the foredeck, the third turret pointing oddly towards the stern, and there were two more turrets aft. Jam-packed between them was an assortment of secondary armament and eight 21-inch torpedo tubes. These fired the oxygen-driven 'Long Lance' torpedoes that caused us such grievous losses early in the war. Two funnels, one of them trunked, and a tall, bulky bridge gave the mistaken impression of top-heaviness. The upperworks were coated with a thin clinker to deflect radar signals. That was a surprise. The Japanese were not supposed to be into radar. Yet the bridge, we found, was topped by a big 'bedstead' antenna. We had always understood the Japanese electronics industry was so underdeveloped that it couldn't develop anything in the radar field. Our visit was indeed an eye-opener.

The Japanese gave little thought, we found, to the warship's crew. Envious British sailors used to say that the Americans allocated accommodation in their warships before adding the guns. British designers, on the other hand, installed the guns, then looked around for somewhere to put the crew. Aboard the *Takao* comfort was totally sacrificed to compartmentation, armour and fire-power. The captain's cabin was little bigger than a closet. Someone had placed a spray of white lilies on his pitted steel desk. Everyone else seemed to share quarters. Some were squeezed into the most inadequate space. Others lived close to their battle stations. The torpedomen slept on the steel deck on straw mats rolled out beneath the tubes. The main radio room was strung with hammocks and the operators' laundry. The officers' ward-room seated thirty at a pinch. The other officers – some seventy out of a complement of 692 – must have taken meals with their men.

The acting captain and his immediate staff ushered us into the bare, grey-painted room, bowing as they entered to a large, leather box on the forward bulkhead. It encased the Emperor's portrait, shielded, they told us, from their current shame. The only junior officer present explained (through the commander's translation) that his job was to salvage the portrait and transfer it to another ship if the *Takao* was in danger of sinking.

'What if no other ship was around?' Frank asked.

'The lieutenant would remain with the portrait when the ship sank,' the commander replied. 'It would be a matter of honour.'

The way he spoke you'd have thought it the most natural thing in the world. Stewards passed round shallow wooden boxes of cold sake. There was salt on the rim of each box. The acting captain licked the salt and proposed the health of King George VIII. We felt unable to correct him, time was pressing, and I toasted, in turn, the Emperor of Japan. The officers turned as one man towards the portrait, bowed, and drained their sake boxes to the last drop.

'A pity you could not stay,' the commander said as they piped us over the side. 'Some of us are in the mood for drinking.'

It was two o'clock, four hours to go before the courier, and we had one more call to make. The liberation of Rangoon had been hectic enough. This day was positively frantic. Both of us were dizzy from lack of sleep but there was still so much to do ...

A mob of ragged prisoners met us outside Changi Jail. They looked horribly emaciated. All told shocking stories of maltreatment and starvation, though conditions were nothing like as bad, survivors assured us, as on a railway the Japanese had been trying to build between Thailand and Burma. The Burma Railway? We'd never heard of it. Prisoners spoke with awe about a place called the River Kwai, where thousands had died. The men of Changi bitterly demanded revenge. Some told equally shocking stories about the fall of Singapore. Certain soldiers and civil servants had deserted their posts, their colleagues and, in some cases, their wives and children, to escape the Japanese. There was discernible tension when several of these escapees returned with high army-rank and jobs in the military administration. Those who had been in what they called 'the bag' fumed with impotent rage.

Most of the expatriate journalists working in Singapore when the Japanese attacked had been recruited into the local defence force. Few had managed to get away. One man had bravely shipped out his wife and returned to the fray, spending the rest of the war in Changi. The day after the Japanese surrender this same man came on the radio with a message for his wife. Word had reached him that she had reached the safety of Delhi. Being a persistent soul he wangled a seat on an RAF transport for India as soon as Singapore airport reopened, rushed round to his wife and found she had borne two illegitimate children to an artillery major. Stories like that were commonplace. Many of the British troops who arrived in Singapore were veterans of the Burma campaign, and most had served at least five years overseas. 'Dear John' letters were raining in from wives back in Britain who had found solace with the Americans. Much of the drinking and mutinous behaviour that soon plagued the British liberation forces could be blamed on the plummeting morale that correspondence inspired.

An elderly man pushed his way through the mob of prisoners. He looked thin but tough as nails. He would have to be: few of the old ones survived the horrors of captivity.

'You boys goin' into town?' he asked. The accent was Scottish. The name: Robbie Burns. The man eased himself gratefully into our car and swigged the last of our whisky. 'Where you going?' he asked. We had thought of commandeering a room at the famous Raffles Hotel. 'Why not?' said Robbie. 'I own a controlling interest.'

Robbie Burns listened respectfully to the tale of our exploits in occupied Malaya as we drove back into town. All around us Singapore was exploding into riotous celebration. Chinese brass bands were parading the streets in fanciful costumes blaring the most unlikely music. A white-clad ensemble from a funeral home was playing, of all things, 'Ain't it Grand to be Bloomin' Well Dead!'

Staff fawned around us when we checked into the Raffles. Half the hotel register had been torn out, the pages presumably containing the names of Japanese and other guests tainted by the occupation. Our names were the first under the new régime. Large suites were put at our disposal, boasting super-sized beds with heavy mosquito nets, overhead fans and (unbelievable luxury!) marble-floored private bathrooms.

Frank and I were wrapping up our film shipments when Mr Burns dropped in on us. 'When you've finished at the Cathay come back here and pick me up,' he said. 'I'll take you to the *Straits Times*. I own that too.'

Expatriate staff members of the leading Singapore English-language newspaper, straight out of prison-camp or internment, were working flat out under the direction of Fleet Street veteran Frank Owen (promoted a colonel in public relations) to get the liberation issue on to the streets. It would be the first version of the paper to appear since the surrender. The *Straits Times* had been turned into the *Shonan Shimbun* (still in English) during the Japanese occupation. After three years under enemy management things were in bad shape. The presses were in urgent need of repair, valuable files had been destroyed, and there were no wire services. Apart from the communiqués put out by the British military government there was little concrete news. The expedition Frank Worth and I had mounted all the way down from Penang offered the first glimpse into conditions on the still-occupied Malayan peninsula; the news editor, half-starved and dressed in ragged khaki, gratefully accepted the account I wrote of the journey. It made the back page of the (one sheet) 6 September edition.

Three years of Japanese occupation had left the Singapore Chinese in a state of shock. They had resisted the enemy as best they could and paid a most fearful price. A beach on one of the offshore islands was said to be alive with sharks attracted by the constant dumping of slaughtered prisoners. Everyone had some tale to tell about the secret police, the dreaded *Kempeitai*. The building that has since become the Singapore National Museum, not far from Orchard Circle, had been the *Kempeitai* headquarters. Two or three days after the liberation we were summoned to a news conference in the basement where a Chinese woman described her torture and interrogation at the hands of the Japanese. It hardly endeared Frank and myself to the personable young officers who had acted the solicitous hosts in up-country Malaya. The woman and her husband were both awarded the George Cross. It was and still is Britain's highest civilian award for gallantry.

Shortly after eight o'clock on the morning of 12 September 1945, I took up position on the steps of City Hall. My job was to provide exterior stills of the formal Japanese surrender. It meant missing the ceremonies inside where General Itagaki used his personal seal to sign away the Lion City. General Slim, sitting alongside Lord Louis Mountbatten, noted 'a spasm of rage and despair' twisting the general's face. 'I looked at the impassive masks that were the faces of the Japanese generals and admirals seated opposite,' Slim wrote. 'Their plight moved me not at all.'

Frank caught that look on Itagaki's face. He was inside City Hall, camera on tripod, long lens aimed directly at the Japanese. A British admiral sat down in front of the camera completely blocking the view. Such an act would be unthinkable in this televisual age but back in those days the 'Silent Service' was notoriously contemptuous of publicity. Frank politely asked the man to move.

'I'm here to see this ceremony,' the admiral snarled.

'With respect sir,' Frank politely replied, 'I'm here so the whole world can see.'

There was an altercation. The admiral eventually moved. But not before he had identified this impertinent sub-Lieutenant.

'You and that fellow Spurr ... you're the ones who deliberately disobeyed orders ... drove through Malaya ... nearly caused a diplomatic incident,' the admiral stuttered. 'I'm hauling you both before a court of inquiry.'

Fortunately we had friends in high places. Both of us had from time to time filmed the Commander-in-Chief, India, Sir Claude Auckinleck. He sent us personal letters of congratulations for '... your drive from Penang to Singapore through country, at that time, not yet occupied by our troops.'

The Auck's secretary added, 'He has asked me to send his personal congratulations on your courage and enterprise.'

Frank's letter had the words 'well done' added in the C-in-C's handwriting. There was no more talk of a court of inquiry.

The British were determined to exorcise their shame. They had gone to great lengths to invite members of the Asian community to witness the enemy's abasement. The same flag had gone up over City Hall that the Japanese hauled down in 1942. Outside on the steps stood a platoon of communist guerrillas invited by Mountbatten to form a guard of honour. Their commander, Chin Peng, stood close to me. He looked smart in his khaki shorts and puttees, crowned by a strangely peaked red-starred cap, and sporting, if I remember rightly, a British decoration, the Order of the British Empire, no less, in recognition of his jungle struggle against the Japanese. The lean, athletic young Malayan Chinese and his not-so-merry – indeed, distinctly surly – band of men posed for me a trifle self-consciously as the theatrical but thoroughly professional Supreme Commander delivered a brief speech to the populace packed in across the *padang*. Immediately afterwards Chin Peng strode off with his men at the head of an all-services parade through the crowded streets. The communist platoon drew far louder applause from the mainly Chinese spectators than the British and Indian troops who marched behind them – so much so that they must have already believed that the Malay peninsula and all its rich resources was theirs for the taking.

The military administration soon threw press and PROs out of the Cathay Building. It was far too good for riff-raff like us. Somebody had been seen throwing beer bottles out of the upstairs windows. The whole lot of us were transferred, grumbling, to three staff houses on an estate owned by Fraser Neave, the soft-drink bottlers. The houses had survived the occupation in mint condition. There were delicate Chinese prints on the walls and an upright piano in the main dining-room. Within two or three days the gentlemen of the press had reduced everything to wreckage. A band of drunks threw the piano out into the garden the night of our house-warming party, chopped it up with samurai swords and danced naked round the blazing wreckage.

Something told me it was time to move on. Frank and I began studying maps of neighbouring Sumatra. It was the place we had been supposed to go to in the first place. The Dutch-owned island had not in fact been reached so far by liberating troops. Indo-British forces were not due to go in for another month, though thousands of Allied prisoners were known to be held there. The biggest camps were outside the oil-town of Pakenbaru. It sounded like a great story.

'Why not?' I asked Frank Worth, tapping the map on the press room wall. 'Maybe we should liberate the Dutch East Indies.'

It would be no more, we believed, than a repetition of our Malayan exploit: another fabulous stunt for two energetic young men in a world without restraint. But this time we were wrong. We hadn't reckoned on running into a revolution.

Droves of Allied war prisoners were dying in camps all over south-east Asia by the time the Japanese surrendered. And there wasn't much any of us could do about it. For three seemingly endless years the prisoners had been starved and maltreated by an enemy who had, until lately, regarded capitulation as the ultimate degradation. Lord Mountbatten sought to avoid further, unnecessary deaths by flying in medical rescue teams the moment Emperor Hirohito's broadcast ended hostilities on 16 August 1945. He requested the go-ahead from the Joint Chiefs of Staff, arguing that many lives could yet be saved. His plan, unfortunately, was vetoed. The American Supremo, General Douglas MacArthur, with his own highly-developed sense of theatre, forbade forays into Japanese-held territory until he had personally received the formal surrender of the Japanese Empire. The ceremony was fixed originally for 31 August in Tokyo and thus for twelve days – which turned into two weeks after postponement to 2 September – the main rescue teams were kept fuming at their bases in India.

Mountbatten managed to infiltrate a few doctors, posing as 'plenipotentiaries', who gamely parachuted into the bigger camps. One group reached Bangkok on 3 September (the day Frank and I went ashore at Penang) and by 11 September doctors and headquarters staff of the 20th Indian Division were in Saigon. Little could be done for the large PoW camps in Sumatra. Officers of the clandestine Force 136 came out of the jungle to shoo away the Japanese camp guards but Liberator bombers based in what was then Ceylon dropped in only three doctors with minimal medical supplies. Once Singapore was secured the plan was to launch a full-scale airborne rescue into Sumatra. The camps at Pakenbaru in the northern part of the island held some 22,000 Allied prisoners, Commonwealth and Dutch, in miserable conditions. Six Dakota transports loaded up with doctors, supplies and Lady Louis Mountbatten in her capacity as head of the British Red Cross, left Singapore for Sumatra early on the morning of 13 September.

Reporters were barred. The official excuse was that every inch of space would be taken up by supplies and essential personnel; the truth was that relations with the Japanese were still so tenuous, and the political situation in the Indies grown so fraught, that the British authorities baulked at a wild bunch of newsmen clumping around the place stirring up further trouble. Frank and I refused to be deterred. We were determined to repeat the coup we had just pulled off in Malaya. Before dawn on the day of Lady Louis's departure, we went to Kallang airfield determined to thumb a ride.

'It's more than my job's worth!' groaned the squadron leader, a man from Melbourne who was in charge of the airlift. Something about the way he spoke convinced us he didn't mean it. Australians, when you get to know them, are always ready to bend the rules.

'You'll be demobbed soon, anyway,' Frank said soothingly.

'And think of the publicity,' I added. 'Fancy a mercy mission like this going unnoticed – you'll be front page in the Melbourne *Age*,' I wheedled.

The squadron leader glanced around nervously. 'Put on some flight overalls and hide in the back,' he whispered hastily. 'And see you spell my bloody name right.'

We loaded our few bits of baggage, mostly film and equipment, into one of the waiting Dakotas, assumed aircraftsmen's overalls and concealed ourselves behind cases of blood plasma. A note had been left in the typewriter of our acting boss, the choleric Colonel Jenkins, in the certain knowledge that he wouldn't find it for hours. We advised him that film and copy would be carried back ('pigeoned') by the squadron leader to tell all to a waiting world.

Permit me to insert an historical note. Many people may not remember but there used to be a popular cinema newsreel called *Movietone News*. It was the key eye-witness of events long before satellite television blanketed the world. Some of Frank's footage occasionally made the programme. The newsreel opened with a montage of car crashes and general mayhem, surmounted by a town crier tolling a soundless bell. The signature tune (ta, tiddle umpetty umpetty ah) had become something of a joke between the pair of us. Whenever we started some particularly novel adventure Frank would strike up the tune. He did so now as we headed at first light across the Malacca Straits (ta, tiddle umpetty umpetty ah), the beach-girdled Sumatran coast sliding swiftly beneath us (tum tee um tum tum ta tiddley um), while directly below lay a large airfield dotted with camouflaged Japanese bombers. 'Kamikazes,' grinned the flight-sergeant, pointing through the open cargo door. There was a shade of contempt in his voice, but I doubt if he would have been grinning so broadly if Hirohito hadn't done his Imperial thing. The parked bombers took me back eighteen months – was that *all* it was? – to that scary morning in the Bay of Bengal.

The big, camouflaged planes hounding our ships as we fled north ... the sticks of bombs teetering down, the water fountaining up as one after the other the damned things burst.

Frank and I leaped out while our plane was still rolling to grab footage of Lady Louis and her entourage submerged in a bowing, hissing group of starched, pressed and polished Japanese. They included one uneasy-looking individual afterwards identified as the commander of the three PoW camps in Pakenbaru.

'You there!' called Lady Louis, gesturing in our direction. The aristocratic accents parodied Lady Bracknell and every other crusty dowager caricatured by Oscar Wilde. 'You there! I thought no coverage was allowed?'

'Royal Indian Navy camera team,' Frank yelled, coming in for close-up, as if that explained everything.

'Just spell my name right,' growled the squadron leader, beaming uneasily over milady's shoulder.

Her ladyship accepted our presence with what I suppose you'd call *noblesse oblige*. She stopped on the right marks once our cameras started rolling, talked to the right people with exactly the right expression; it was, overall, a thoroughly professional performance. Her husband couldn't have handled it better. But nothing could conceal the fact that what milady saw and heard was terribly disturbing.

The camps were pure horror. The perimeter guards had been withdrawn, especially the hated Koreans who had proved more sadistic in some cases than their Japanese masters. Several had been drowned in the lavatory pits, we later learned. The first shock was the smell. It was the smell of inadequate sanitation, of unwashed bodies, suppurating sores and the sour-sweet stench of death. Burial parties were disposing of last night's quota of corpses in a newly-dug mass grave when we picked our way towards them through a forest of crosses and headstones.

'Ashes to ashes, dust to dust ... ' a half-starved padre intoned.

A doctor approached us angrily.

'You could have come sooner,' he shouted.

Anyone would have thought it was *our* fault. The doctor had been air-dropped five days before; since then he had hardly slept. He took us to a long *basha* (palm-leaf) hut where dozens of skeletal objects sat propped against the wall, soaking up the sun.

'This is the death house,' the doctor told us bitterly. 'There's nothing we can do for any of these poor buggers. They'll be gone by tomorrow. A week ago we might have had some chance of saving them.'

Ragged Indian prisoners asked me to take a picture of their platoon *havildar* (sergeant). Four of them carried him out of the hut in a crudely-made bamboo chair. The poor man might have been straight from Belsen. The skin had shrunken back across his cheekbones, the rib-cage protruded through his scrawny carcass. Only the eyes moved, flickering querulously over the well-fed interloper aligning him in the viewfinder. Slowly the inert face came into focus. The eyes stared at me, briefly, through the ground glass of my Rolliecord. I snapped the shutter. The man looked strangely satisfied. One hundredth of a second at F-11 according to my calculations. Maybe half a stop extra to allow for the man's dark complexion. The note on the dope sheet intended to inform some caption-writing fat cat in distant New Delhi stated baldly:

'Shot Number Six: Unnamed *havildar* of the Punjab Regiment. Dying of starvation in PoW camp. Pakanbaru, Sumatra. Sept 13/45.'

It was a picture, I knew, that would never be used. I went on with my work, wracked by that helplessness reporters and cameramen so often feel as the privileged voyeurs of tragedy.

'But you must see our tomatoes!'

The speaker was a tall, gangling wing commander complete with bristling moustache. The paper-thin RAF uniform was bleached white, patched and repatched until little of the original remained. The third most senior officer in Number Two camp conducted us proudly to the vegetable patch. 'Picked the seeds out of our own, er, night soil,' he explained delicately. 'Grew all these crops here.' A dozen green, unripe tomatoes dangled from the plants. 'Helped out with the rations. Good-oh. Eh. What?' He looked the pair of us up and down. A shadow crossed his face. 'Either of you got a gun?' he whispered. 'Old scores to settle, you know. Some of the guards are getting away scot-free.'

The doctor came bustling up. 'My dear Wing Commander, time for your rest.' He put an arm around the tall man's bony shoulders. 'Back to the sick bay for your injection.' He might have been talking to a child. The doctor glared back at us with real loathing. 'Can't you leave 'em in peace?' he spat over his shoulder. It seemed we were intruding on a terrible, private grief. Quietly we crept away to hand our film to the man from Melbourne.

The Japanese courteously installed Lady Louis and her party (which grudgingly included Frank and myself) in an old Dutch guest-house next door to their main officers' mess. The Supreme Commander's wife had decided to stay overnight, sending her Dakotas back to Singapore (loaded with stretcher cases) to bring in fresh supplies. The Japanese danced attendance, over-eager to please. Their sentries were everywhere, mounting guard with fixed bayonets and bowing and shouting every time we passed. Officers clattered around in full clobber with pistols and samurai swords at their belts.

The only operational Allied troops who had preceded us into the area were air-dropped guerrillas from Force 136. Led by a captain, they had been maintaining a furtive existence in the nearby hills until Emperor Hirohito called a halt to hostilities. Some of them joined us in the guest-house for a frugal lunch; there was scarcely any food. It was hard to eat, anyway, after the things we'd seen that morning. The meal was a depressing affair.

'What you chaps need,' said an affable member of Lady Louis' entourage, 'is a good stiff drink.'

The source of solace was an Indian prince, a cousin of the Maharajah of Jodhpur. He invited three British NCOs from the Force-136 group, as well as Frank and myself up to his room. From his rucksack he pulled out an unlabelled bottle of clear, slightly perfumed liquid. We drank. The taste was, to put it mildly, peculiar. The effect, though, was electrifying. I didn't know it at the time but we were guzzling *arsha*. No other drink has ever gotten me into so much trouble in my life (and that includes the cognac that induced me to hurl a chair through the plate-glass window of the *Time* magazine correspondent's house in Hong Kong). It's possible you may never have heard of *arsha*? Let's assume that is just as well. You can't buy it in any known bar. *Arsha* is made in Rajasthan, where for centuries it has inspired the warriors of north-eastern India to feats of valour on the battlefield and acrobatics in the boudoir. The base-liquor, as I understand it, is raw alcohol. But the maharajahs who once monopolised its manufacture are said to have thrown game fowl and venison into the vats during maturation. I have only drunk the stuff once and I assure you the story I am about to tell is true. As true, admittedly, as I can remember.

The *arsha* was going down without touching the sides. We sat sipping it upstairs in the guest-house room while platoons of Japanese troops drilled in the grounds below. Each sip left me with the distinct feeling that the top of my skull was lifting off. Right off. I was floating. I was laughing. I was raging. Those bloody Japs ... the things they'd done!

Retribution was required, urgently. The whole crowd of us went mad – and I mean really mad. The NCOs began firing sten guns out of the window. We then tumbled downstairs, waving various weaponry, invaded the Japanese officers' mess and held the occupants at gunpoint. There were several thousand Japanese troops in Pakanbaru, all armed to the teeth. It says something for our madness and a lot more for their self-restraint that the denizens of the headquarters mess allowed us to walk away with armfuls of their personal belongings, including their swords, cameras and remaining supplies of Scotch whisky – anything, in fact, that we could lay our hands on.

Back in the guest-house we were just finishing off the Scotch when the Force 136 captain burst in.

'Lunatics!' he screamed. 'Do you want to get us all killed?' He scooped up swords and cameras and, aiming an accusing finger at me, the seniormost gangster present, declared: 'You'll hear more of this.'

Chastened and hungover, Frank and I joined Lady Louis Mountbatten and her party for dinner. It consisted mostly of the emergency rations we had brought from Singapore. Halfway through the meal a Japanese colonel arrived. He was visibly distressed. He had been planning, he said, to present her ladyship with a bottle of Scotch but unfortunately it had been stolen by two of her officers. Lady Louis was indignant. Her officers would never do such a thing, she declared.

'Oh yes they would,' said the colonel. 'And those are the very officers over there.'

He pointed to Frank and myself. Lady Louis laughed about the incident when I reminded her of it many years later, but she didn't think it so damn funny at the time.

Something extremely odd was happening in Sumatra. Frank and I noticed it the moment we had recovered from the shock of filming the prison camps. The Sumatrans, we found, were nowhere near as welcoming as the lately liberated peoples of Malaya and Singapore. The folk we met seemed hesitant to talk and even slower to smile whenever the pair of us glad-handed our way through the surrounding kampongs. The Japanese, still militarily in charge, advised us against moving about the countryside unescorted. We couldn't for the life of us think why. The propaganda line fed us throughout the war depicted the Dutch as model colonialists; the great, sprawling archipelago they called the Dutch East Indies a paradise for its native inhabitants. The kind of hectoring nationalism young Britons like myself had encountered first-hand in India simply did not exist. Or so we were led to believe.

So what were these strange flags? They certainly weren't Dutch. The flags we saw flying from every building were red and white divided in two horizontal halves. We asked a Dutch officer what they represented. The officer shrugged nervously. 'Could be political,' he mumbled. 'This war has changed many things.'

The officer was a colonial army major called Palmers. His home was in Surabaya, eastern Java, where he had managed a swimming pool-cum-health spa. Called up into the reserve forces when the Japanese attacked, captured without firing a shot, he had spent the past three years in one of the now notorious Pakenbaru camps. Politics did not interest him, he assured us. His overriding ambition was to find his wife. The last he had heard she was interned somewhere in Java.

'We're going that way,' Frank volunteered. 'You might as well join us.'

Frank was talking, as usual, straight off the top of his head. Neither of us had yet decided what trick to pull next. The expedition from Penang, through Malaya and Singapore had, after all, been across British territory. Here we were on somebody else's soil. We knew little about the geography and absolutely nothing about the crisis soon to engulf the Indies – had we known what was coming we might very well have joined Lady Louis's flight back to Singapore.

'You're going to need plenty of help from the Japanese to get across this country,' Palmers said when we told him our plan. 'The first thing is to throw your weight around, then the Pakenbaru garrison will probably get you to army headquarters. You can put your ideas to the general.'

The Japanese military headquarters in Sumatra was tucked away in a hill resort called Fort De Kock, today known as Bukitinggi. The place lay a day's drive from Pakenbaru. The only available transportation we could rustle up was a battered Japanese army truck with two armchairs in the back. The pair of us struck up the *Movietone News* theme as the truck pulled out before dawn 16 September 1945 and headed into the mountains. Palmers rode in the cab, acting as interpreter for our Japanese driver. Our new-found adviser spoke reasonable Japanese, fluent English, the local lingua franca, Bahasa, and (naturally) Dutch; with his aid we hoped to repeat our death-defying stunt in occupied Malaya.

I am still astounded decades later at the confidence, even the arrogance, of our behaviour. The British have been so subdued by the collapse of empire that today I would never presume to bluff my way through the ranks of a recently defeated enemy. Our experience since landing at Penang had convinced us that the Japanese were harmless, but it was an in-built belief in British inviolability that swept us forwards. Back in the mid-1940s we sincerely believed that Britannia ruled enough of the world to overawe any number of Asian revolutionaries. On this occasion, of course, we could scarcely pretend to be envoys of Lord Louis Mountbatten. Remembering how the *Kempeitai* officers had spoken of *Ren Sendenbun* (military propaganda) we decided to claim to be gathering advance news coverage for the Indian armed forces. There was a smidgen of truth in that lie, even if we *were* joy-riding, mindlessly, across what proved to be a powder keg.

The Japanese commander in Sumatra, Major-General Ito, was installed in a clump of handsome buildings that once housed a Dutch boarding school. Sentries with rifles and fixed bayonets shouted and bowed – almost making me jump out of my skin – as we walked up the steps into the main building. A tall, grim-faced colonel with a mouthful of gold teeth introduced himself, in English, as the military chief-of-staff.

'The general trusts you will be our guests,' smirked Gold Teeth. 'Our staff has the best quarters in town.' Guests of the Japanese army? The idea sounded more bizarre then than it does today. A month before we had been doing our utmost to kill each other.

Major-General Ito received us behind a carved oak desk in what might have been the principal's office. He was squat, bald and bespectacled; remarkably like those Hollywood caricatures of your typical Japanese officer in the late-night movies. The general remained bland and blank, sipping that wretched tea, while we lamely justified our presence. Our request for travel permission to Java evoked a frown.

'The situation in Sumatra is relatively peaceful,' the general assured us. 'The same cannot be said for the rest of Indonesia.'

Indo-*what*?

'Indonesia,' the general repeated with a flicker of a smile. 'Haven't you heard? The Republic of Indonesia declared independence from colonial rule about a month ago.'

Gold Teeth was positively beaming at our discomfiture. 'You might think you won this war,' he seemed to be saying. 'But in fact, you lost.' He went on dutifully translating for the general.

'I am sure the Indonesian authorities will be glad,' General Ito was saying, 'to welcome two distinguished officers from India.' He had a point there. A Labour government had been installed in London. Talk of Indian independence was very much in the air. Playing the India card might ingratiate us with the Indonesians and dissuade them from cutting our throats.

Dinner that night in the headquarters mess was an arduous ritual. The general occupied the top table with six gold-braided officers, Gold Teeth among them. All sported short-sleeved green uniforms with white shirts peeping out at the neck, highly polished knee-boots and shaven, equally well-polished heads. Throughout most of the meal a field-rank officer stood at a lectern reading from a military treatise in a low-pitched growl. The diners listened in respectful silence. Frank and I tried to act as unobtrusively as possible, although the pair of us were immediately in trouble. The only eating utensils provided were chopsticks. Neither of us had ever used them. Some of the younger officers sniggered as we vainly tried to pick up bits of salt fish and pickled turnip.

Gold Teeth apologised afterwards for the meagre fare. 'Your sub-marine blockade has been all too successful,' he hissed testily. 'Sumatra is on the verge of starvation.'

'Especially the prison camps,' Frank snapped back.

A pained look came over the colonel's face. It was a tender subject. Three years later our genial host, the major-general, would himself be hauled before a war crimes court in Manila charged with ill-treatment of Allied prisoners. He was hanged by the neck until he was dead.

Curiosity impelled me to ask the colonel why he had so cheerfully accepted surrender. What would he have done a month ago had we met face to face? Gold Teeth smiled his narrowest smile. 'I would have been delighted' – he fairly spat out the words – 'I would have been delighted to have met you on the field of battle.' Damn right he would: cold shudders slid down my spine.

Most of that night Frank and I sat up practising the use of chopsticks with pairs of pencils. We made mighty face next morning by downing our rice and pickle breakfast with nary a fumble. I've been adept with the eating sticks, come to think of it, ever since ...

The general provided us with a jeep and letters of safe conduct to Batavia. The long-time capital of the Dutch East Indies is better known today as Jakarta. Our plan was to drive south through Padang and Palembang, get a lift across the Sunda Straits aboard a Japanese patrol boat and pick up fresh transportation in Java. The short, final leg to Batavia was not expected to present any particular problems. It says a good deal for our ignorance and stupidity that we took this ambitious itinerary completely for granted. Palmers expressed faint surprise but reckoned we could do it. We could go on from Batavia, he further advised, and end up in Surabaya. It was there, naturally, that he hoped to be reunited with his wife.

But first we had to conclude a piece of unfinished business. The rumour buzzing round Singapore was that a man considered a renegade by the British, an Indian army officer called Mohan Singh, was living in a village a few kilometres outside the Sumatran port of Padang. It was no more than a night-stop on our way to Java. Mohan Singh had been one of the first and brightest Indians to graduate from the Indian Military Academy at Dehra Dun. He was commissioned into the 1/14th Punjab Regiment in 1934, captured in Singapore, went over to the enemy and recruited fellow prisoners into a force which proclaimed itself the Indian National Army. It was one of their detachments I had run into in Rangoon. Mohan Singh soon quarrelled with the Japanese, finding them as overbearing as the British. The rest of the war he spent under house-arrest in Sumatra. Frank and I had scant hope of unearthing the missing man, but we did hope that if we put the word around Padang, Mohan Singh would try to find us. We were, after all, fellow officers in the Indian armed forces; the prospect of hearing the latest gossip from the fading Raj should prove strong enough, we reckoned, to lure the elusive collaborator into breaking cover.

The port of Padang appeared to be operating normally. An elderly Dutch coastal steamer lay moored alongside the quay. Closer inspection showed it was a burned-out hulk. The tall, single funnel and elegant upperworks were blackened by fire and riddled with bullet holes. A few Indian stores remained open in the town. Their owners had little to sell but were eager for foreign currency. Most looked askance when we mentioned Mohan Singh. Only one man said openly that the person we were seeking lived in a *kampong* further up the coast.

We had been driving for half an hour along the coastal road when Palmers noticed we were being followed. A big black sedan had been behind us since we left Padang.

'God help us,' said Palmers, crossing himself. 'It's got to be the bloody *Kempeitai*.'

The Japanese were held responsible for law and order in Sumatra pending the arrival of the Allied forces. Their secret police presumably played an essential role. The village we sought straggled along a beach of black volcanic sand. Surf thundered in with a boom like ancient cannon. Fishermen sat mending their nets among the high-prowed boats drawn up in rows along the beach. Palmers drifted off to chat to the fishermen while we parked in the main street outside a two-storey Chinese restaurant. The black sedan pulled into the curb further down the street. A young Japanese officer got out and walked up to our jeep, pistol on belt, sword clanking at his side. He saluted and explained in fractured English that 'Imperial authorities worried about your safety'. Red and white flags flew over every home. 'People not friendly,' the young officer warned.

Palmers came back a moment later, warily eyeing the Japanese but confirming what he had said. An armed rebel unit was operating in the vicinity. By 'rebel', he meant forces of what we were beginning to call the Indonesian nationalist movement.

'Time for drink,' said the Japanese. 'No trouble when *Kempeitai* around.'

The main rooms of the restaurant were on the upper floor atop a flight of steep steps. The *Kempeitai* officer proceeded to ply us with some noxious local brew and ask us what we were up to. 'Sightseeing,' said Frank. We thought it best not to mention Mohan Singh.

'A toast!' cried the Japanese. 'To General Churchill!' We all stood up. Before we could sit down again I toasted Emperor Hirohito and one or two others. A fair quantity of liquor slid down the hatch.

'Let's get out of here,' said Palmers. He was distinctly nervous.

'King George VIII!' cried the Japanese. He was swaying slightly.

'Admiral Yamamoto!' I countered. The architect of the Pearl Harbor attack was long dead.

'Roosevelt!' said the Japanese, not to be outdone. 'He dead too.'

Our companion from the *Kempeitai* had turned bright red. He spoke with difficulty, slurring his words. 'England and Japan small islands,' he babbled. 'England and Japan good friends. I toast your national hero' – he groped for the name – 'yes, I have it, Admiral Trafalgar!'

On the way out he fell heavily down the stairs and had to be carried to his car. The driver laid the officer on the back seat and drove off without a word. We followed, feeling ill. The search was off as far as we were concerned; it would be tough enough getting to Batavia without risking a brush with the Indonesians or a hangover at the hands of the *Kempeitai*. Mohan Singh was nowhere near Padang, we later learned. He gave himself up to Indian troops elsewhere in Sumatra after they landed on the island three weeks later.

It had begun to dawn on us that there was trouble all over the Dutch East Indies. The Japanese invasion had sparked off a revolution. The Dutch complained that throughout the past three and a half years of occupation the Japanese had waged a blatantly racial campaign against white colonialism. And on this point at least the Dutch were not far wrong. Japanese propaganda hacks in Batavia, 'the *Ren Sendenbun* boys', showed us newsreels they had made featuring nationalist leaders we had never heard of – including an engaging demagogue called Sukarno – which ended with shots of that strange red and white flag everyone seemed to be flying. Credits came up on the reel with an urgent voice calling out the increasingly familiar name: INDONESIA!

'The Dutch are only getting what they deserve,' shrugged the head of the Japanese film unit. 'They treated the natives like cattle.'

Here was the first Japanese who addressed us without obsequious apologies. He was a small, testy man, uncharacteristically assertive, an avowed racist who patronised the Javanese with the amused contempt of old-time white colonials.

'Japan has smashed European colonialism,' he said with fanatic certainty. 'It was Japan's historic mission.'

Outside in the capital's sun-baked streets the protest banners limply defied the midday breeze. Most of the inscriptions featured the word 'Freedom'. Or '*Merdeka*' as we were beginning to call it in Bahasa. Scrawled across walls were quotations from the American Declaration of Independence. The revolutionaries were proving unexpectedly savvy. They'd already found where the power lay in the post-war world. A tramcar clanked past, a slogan painted on its side: VAN MOOK (it jeered) WHAT YER DOIN' HERE?

The jibe was directed at the embattled Lieutenant-Governor of the Dutch East Indies, a certain Doctor Van Mook. The poor man had flown in to take peaceful possession of a compliant empire, only to be met by clamorous confrontation. His frustrated colonial officials, guarded, ironically, by Japanese troops, were weakly claiming a spontaneous nationalist movement did not exist on any scale anywhere in the Indies. The challenging flags and banners belonged to 'a Japanese puppet government of totalitarian character'. The Dutch had refused from the start to recognise the Indonesian republican government proclaimed by Ahmed Sukarno on 17 August 1945. The new régime was written off by The Hague as a hotchpotch of collaborators thrown hastily together in the wake of the Japanese surrender. There was no evidence, in the Dutch view, of any widespread popular support. From what we'd seen, Meinheer was in for a nasty shock.

Frank and I discovered Sukarno – bursting, literally, upon his presence – in a modest brick bungalow on the outskirts of Batavia. A mast bearing the republican flag sprouted from the flowerbeds in the well-tended front garden. Nothing else showed that the most important person in Indonesia was in residence. The household atmosphere struck me as remarkably laid-back. There were a few guards around wearing red and white armbands but none of the bustling staff, the secretaries, telephonists and messengers one would normally expect to find around a revolutionary headquarters. The date was 20 September which meant that theoretically the President had been a whole month in power. Perhaps the plan was to play things cool and see what happened.

Sukarno was stretched out on a chaise-longue beneath a slow-turning verandah fan reading a paperback novel. The man did not then strike me as particularly dynamic. I couldn't have been more wrong; first impressions can be extremely misleading. The pair of us were received with gentle courtesy, despite the reproachful hint that we had interrupted the presidential siesta. We introduced ourselves as *Ren Sendenbun* in search of news coverage for the Indian armed forces. Sure enough the magic word 'India' became our Open Sesame. Frank and I came as officers, almost as emissaries, from the jewel of another empire on the brink of dissolution. Neither of us felt the slightest commitment to the Indian Raj – and no sympathy whatsoever for the Dutch – and soon we found ourselves acting as go-betweens, introducing Sukarno and his friends to the bewildered foreign correspondents now trickling into Batavia. Frank helped organise an introductory news conference and filmed it for the Indian and world newsreels. I feared it would never be shown. But the British had lately lifted political censorship. Frank had the pleasure of later seeing his own film in a Calcutta cinema being wildly applauded by the nationalistic Indian audience. Censorship was immediately reimposed. The historic piece of film probably still moulders in some vault in Delhi, unknown even to archivists. Frank still treasures a document from Sukarno appointing him 'propagandist to the Indonesian republic'.

Sukarno had been trained as an engineer; he also happened to be an art collector and a gifted amateur artist in his own right. There were moments when I wondered whether art interested him a great deal more than the nitty-gritty of politics. The bungalow he occupied was filled with canvases. There were neo-impressionist scenes of the volcanic country around Bandung and lots of lovely, langorous nudes. The women in these paintings were absolutely stunning. Some of them looked like members of his household. Sukarno obviously loved every one of the girls who brought us snacks and iced tea. He patted and stroked his female staff whenever they came within reach. He was one of those peculiarly tactile people who seem to commune by touch. Whenever possible he kicked off his shoes – going barefoot, he told us, maintained communication with the spirits of the earth. It was strange hearing a Muslim talk this way; Islam had obviously absorbed some weird influences in Java.

But at this point my attention was diverted from the Indonesians and their revolution. The person to blame, I suppose, was Palmers. The Dutch captain had been with us all the way from Pakenbaru and was touchingly determined to find his wife, last seen in the Javanese port of Surabaya. The Dutchman was only too glad to accompany us, acting as interpreter and general factotum, as long as we kept heading in the right direction. Thanks largely to his tact and understanding we had inveigled our way a thousand kilometres from northern Sumatra across the Japanese-occupied Indies into the heart of Batavia.

The journey was not quite as simple as it sounds. The Japanese were concerned for our safety at the hands of the rebellious Indonesians. They insisted on providing *Kempeitai* escorts in town and country. We grew accustomed to travelling among assorted thugs bristling with weaponry.

The *laissez-passer* from the Japanese military commander in Sumatra did not always guarantee instant movement, as most military vehicles were on their last legs. The Imperial Navy had trouble finding a vessel to carry us across to Java; Allied submarines had lately sunk everything in sight. The best the Japanese could muster to cross the Sunda Strait was an ocean-going tug which originally belonged to the Dutch. Its crew was terrified to leave Telukbutang harbour. Look-outs kept jittery watch for tell-tale torpedo wakes as we plodded towards Java. It set me wondering whether some adventurous submariner might even now be tempted to forget the cease-fire and blow our beckoning target out of the water.

A big Buick staff car awaited us at the small Javanese port of Serang. It was parked outside the very Dutch-looking offices built to house the harbour master. A delegation of Japanese officers was standing round the car along with a group of young Indonesians wearing bicolour armbands; the two parties did not seem to be on speaking terms. The Japanese warned us of dangers on the road ahead. They kept glancing irritably at the young men with the armbands. The Indonesians introduced themselves as representatives of the provisional republican administration of west Java, making it clear that without their say-so we would never reach Batavia – or Jakarta, as they insisted on calling it. British forces were due to land in Java towards the end of the month, they told us, and it was assumed there would be no attempt to restore Dutch rule.

There was a hint of menace in their voices. The British had only to pull a fast one, the Indonesians seemed to be saying, and there would be hell to pay. Neither of us was in any position to offer optimistic assurances but we gave them anyway. A kind word and a friendly smile, we were beginning to learn, averted no end of wrath. By the time the British came blundering in we expected to be safely back in Singapore. The Indies appeared set for an explosion; this once we had no intention of getting involved.

'There are thousands of Dutch civilians still interned in Java,' the Indonesian spokesman told us. 'We wouldn't want them caught in any hostilities.'

The warning came through loud and clear. The civilians were hostage to political fortune. There were eight thousand Dutch women in Batavia alone, detained in a suburb the Japanese had wired off as an all-female internment camp. Palmers hoped to find his wife there, and kept nagging us to visit the place. We drove finally through the gates, innocent and unsuspecting.

I blush to describe what followed. The most delicate way I can put it is that years without male companionship had stimulated the appetites of the interned women beyond the bounds of social propriety. Frank and I were in no better shape. The deprivations of war had left the pair of us lustful and rapacious. It was the stuff of fantasy. No sooner had we left the car than two Dutch matrons dragged – yes, literally dragged – Palmers off to their quarters. Feebly and ever more weakly he kept inquiring about his wife. 'Surabaya,' I could hear him mumbling. 'I believe she's in Surabaya.'

A beautiful brunette who turned out to be Belgian was fumbling with Frank's uniform buttons. In full public view. 'Hey wait a minute – ' he gasped.

Diving off to grab my camera I collided with a tall blonde teenager. The blonde was bursting out of her dress, which was entirely understandable – she had been wearing nothing else since the Japanese interned her. During that time she had grown from a skinny thirteen-year-old to a magnificent woman which three years of short rations had entirely failed to deflate. Hugging me urgently tight to her pneumatic bosom she whispered suggestions that your even more liberated, latter-day feminists would nowadays hesitate to formulate. This once I was lost for words. Years of promiscuous dreaming were rushing, as it were, to fruition. All I could stammer out was: 'Can you wait until we get to the hotel?'

The Americans used to sing a song during the Second World War to celebrate their effortless seduction of British womanhood. It began with the words 'I don't want to join the army, I don't want to go to war', and went on to advocate loitering in the vicinity of the Piccadilly underground station, fornicating until death. Those were exactly my sentiments in what we then called Batavia during the last week of September 1945. There I was, a lusty twenty-three-year-old, immersed – yes, almost literally immersed – in raunchy Dutch women.

Five weeks after the Japanese surrender it had been my pleasurable duty to drive into the wired-off suburb where eight thousand of these sex-starved women were interned. The idea was to offer physical proof that the Second World War was over. Maybe it was, but plenty of problems remained. Allied troops had yet to land in the East Indies. It would be eight more days before the first contingents reached the nearby port of Tanjong Priok. Meanwhile the Japanese who had overrun the Indies three years before were stuck with the delicate task of maintaining law and order. A nationwide nationalist upsurge, instigated, obliquely perhaps, by the Japanese, was making our surrendered enemy's position increasingly difficult. The situation had lately grown so serious that they felt it their duty to escort Frank and myself wherever we travelled round the city. The pair of us had insinuated ourselves illegally into the Indies on the excuse of obtaining propaganda film for the British-India Command in distant New Delhi. The Japanese took our story seriously. They nearly had a fit when we proposed travelling on some six hundred kilometres across the length of Java to the eastern seaport of Surabaya.

'The countryside is in rebellion,' protested the Japanese garrison commander in Batavia/Jakarta. 'Any European is liable to be lynched.' The harassed officer looked at us appealingly. 'Even Japanese aren't too safe,' he said, 'once they get outside the city limits.'

The truth was that I had no desire to leave Batavia. Like the Americans in blacked-out Britain I did not want to go to war. Or revolution. Or anything remotely resembling it. I was perfectly prepared, like the GIs in the song, to romp around with these insatiable women, making up for their years of sexual deprivation and truncating my life in the process. It was a measure of Palmers' determination that he persuaded me to button up and move on. Our Dutch friend had also tasted the temptations of the Batavian Love Camp. He remained determined to find his wife, however, last heard of in Surabaya. There was a tenacity, a touching loyalty about his quest; persistently he interrupted our bedroom antics with tempting talk about the wonders (and the women) on the other side of Java. Ultimately he appealed to the same misguided sense of adventure that set Frank and me on to our indulgent odyssey from liberated Penang. Three weeks later we still believed it possible to bluff our way through Japanese-occupied territories. Granted the Dutch colonies were in open revolt, but we kidded ourselves that the bluff would continue to work. The danger lay in growing over-confident.

'We can easily get to Surabaya by train,' Frank Worth told the Japanese. He had been fed this line by Palmers.

'The trains are running,' the garrison commander conceded. 'But I can't guarantee that they'll keep running. Or that you'll reach your destination alive.'

'This whole business is a Dutch problem,' I said carelessly. 'We're not Dutch. The Indonesians won't bother *us*.'

The Japanese colonel smiled politely. He clearly thought us out of our tiny minds. Perhaps he'd heard Noël Coward holding forth about mad dogs and Englishmen. Nevertheless, his caution was catching. I thought it best to check things out with Palmers.

'Everything will be all right,' our Dutch friend assured me. 'You mustn't take this revolution too seriously.' It was the routine Dutch colonial line at the time. Nothing could have been more incorrect.

Two *Kempeitai* guards turned up at the station to escort us. They did not look at all happy. The much-dreaded gendarmes would have had the locals bowing and scraping a month ago. Not any more. Our odd couple tried to appear deferential. Silently they took over the far end of our empty, open-plan compartment and sat smoking pungent Javanese cigarettes, staring gloomily out of the window. Passengers who might have travelled with us took one look and found seats elsewhere on the train. Nobody seemed to relish our company. Fortunately there wasn't much crush. Few people were travelling.

It grew dark shortly after we left. Slowly we chugged through terraces of rice-fields, past clumps of vivid green foliage, stands of high bamboo and drooping palms, to emerge next morning, after a fitful night, beside a sea shimmering on our left in the bronze light of dawn. Frank had stretched out on a seat, his head on his camera box. Palmers slept upright, open-mouthed. The Japanese nodded in their seats, rifles beyond reach in an overhead luggage rack.

The revolutionaries burst in at Cheribon. A curious crowd pressed around the compartment windows directly we pulled into the station. People stood and stared without responding to our nervous nods and gestures. Hubbub further down the platform announced the arrival of a band of youths with red and white armbands. They carried Thompson sub-machine-guns and looked determined to use them. Our guards promptly threw up their hands and pointed meekly towards the luggage rack. The kamikaze spirit had died with the Imperial surrender. One of the youths grabbed the rifles and shoved the Japanese out on to the platform. The leading youth swaggered up to us speaking Dutch. Palmers turned pale. I motioned him to keep quiet.

'We are *British*!' I stoutly declared.

A declaration like that would nowadays send people into stitches. But these were still the mid-1940s. We had yet to accept the collapse of Empire. My indignant affirmation way off in revolutionary Java stopped the youths in their tracks. Their leader examined us warily. A companion who spoke English demanded to know our business. He looked incredulous when we told him. After a lengthy exchange (in which we passed Palmers off as an Australian) the journey continued under Indonesian escort.

'What about the Japanese?' I asked.

'They won't be harmed,' said the interpreter. 'But they can't go any further. This train only goes as far as Semarang. You'll have to night-stop there.'

Palmers sat very still looking out of the window. He had long ago removed his rank badges. There was no way the Indonesians could tell he was Dutch. Unfortunately, he understood everything our new escorts were saying. 'They're taking us for interrogation at Semarang,' he whispered. The town was about three hours from Surabaya on the coastal line.

'What was all that about when they entered the compartment?' I asked quietly.

'They were going to shoot us,' the Dutchman told me. 'I'm afraid I've got you into a lot of trouble.'

It could have been a lot worse. The interrogators listened gravely at Semarang station while I made a short speech about India's historic links with this new place known as Indonesia. It must have sounded strange, coming from a British colonial, but the nationalists were looking for all the overseas support they could get. They were particularly anxious to establish good relations with India. That's where we came from, according to our identification, and when Frank produced his camera to shoot some footage of the Semarang patriots, they fell over each other to oblige.

We reached Surabaya late the next afternoon. I still have visions of a well-ordered town, wide streets with occasional canals, mostly wooden houses, a largely Chinese business centre close to the docks and a clean, airy hotel, the Oranje, with high, shuttered rooms, overhead fans and mosquito nets. Somerset Maugham might recently have been in residence. The Dutch manager was fresh from internment. He had good news for Palmers about his wife. The last he had heard she was in a hostel filled with women internees a kilometre or two down the road.

We set off to walk there through the tropical dusk, stopped by occasional patrols of Japanese troops. The Japanese were exceptionally jumpy. There was a crackling tension in the air, rather as if a thunderstorm was brewing and, as we neared the hostel, forked lightning stabbed at the rusting rooftops. Palmers broke into a run. We came panting after him. The Dutchman ran around the compound calling frantically for his wife. Sitting with her back to the doorway in one of the outer buildings a woman was quietly knitting. It was Mrs Palmers. She was safe and well and naturally delighted and surprised. There haven't been that many happy endings in my life but this was one of them.

Women came crowding round to meet the two gallant officers who had engineered this unlikely reunion. One of them was a marvellous olive-skinned Eurasian. Her name was Millie Schaftlein. She walked straight up to me and said: 'It's been so long since anyone made love to me.' The pleasure would be mine, I hastily assured her, to be of service. Indeed it was, despite the gymnastics in Batavia. This was one of the most beautiful girls I had ever seen.

'I know where we can get a drink,' Millie said.

We took a cycle rickshaw to a small night-club. The mostly male clientèle was dancing to the rhythms of a perspiring band. Its most-repeated tune, which struck a responsive chord in both of us, was 'In the Mood'. No one could have put it better. We danced close, breathing heavily. For once I had a partner who didn't mind my treading on her toes. But even here tension persisted. The dancers weren't as carefree as they should have been. Their movements were taut and nervous. Faces looked alert and strained. Everyone seemed to be waiting for a brawl to break out at any moment. Millie sensed the brooding atmosphere and shivered.

'Let's get out of here,' she said. 'I'm scared.'

Lightning flashed through the night-club windows. A thunder clap drowned out the band. The dancers winced but went on dancing. Most of them, I realised, were heavily armed. Some of the men jived with Lugers in their belts.

'Something's going to happen,' Millie said. 'Something awful. We'd be safer back at your hotel.'

We hurried back to what was going to be our prison.

I had more than the storm to keep me awake: Millie made sure of that. Like all the women interned in Java, my new-found girlfriend was clamant for coition. She'd been tormented, she said, by the years of enforced celibacy. 'I'd never have made a nun,' she moaned. She had a point there: the girl lacked vocation; that was undeniable. Outside the thunder crashed, lightning blinked boldly through the bedroom shutters, the rain drummed steadily down. But we ignored the elements, insulated by togetherness.

The turmoil died away shortly before dawn. A Javanese waiter in neatly pressed uniform brought coffee (giving me a cheeky wink on the way out) and by seven o'clock we were seated on the front verandah consuming an enormous Dutch breakfast of eggs, cheese, cold ham, sausage and chocolate cookies. There was no shortage of food in the Hotel Oranje. It was sheer pleasure sitting there watching the world go by. The street outside was packed with people. The waiters were swift, unobtrusive and efficient. 'The old standards are being rapidly restored,' the Dutch manager told us smugly.

Frank stopped by our table, announcing his departure for Bali. I wished him godspeed. We hadn't split up so far but nothing at this magic moment was going to drag me away from Surabaya. It was true that in those days Balinese women went about bare-breasted. Revolutionary prudery had not yet reached the island; Frank reckoned it would make great footage. Besides, the Japanese commander there had reputedly refused to surrender and was holed up with a few fanatical supporters someplace inland.

'You can go if you want to,' Millie whispered, melting me with her dark doe-eyes. Frank looked us both over and chuckled.

'See you back here in a couple of days,' he said. He wasn't to know it would be weeks before we met again. And it would not be in Indonesia.

A British major arrived in crisply starched khaki. His uniform creaked and crackled as he walked. He introduced himself as another of those guerrilla agents dropped into the country by Force 136.

'Be careful,' the major warned, setting about his own breakfast. 'Things are getting nasty here.'

Millie nodded. She knew Surabaya better than I did. But obtuse as ever, I tended to scoff. What tension was the man talking about? The overnight storm had blown itself out. There was a new-scrubbed look about the sky. The day felt far less oppressive. 'I think we should stay in the hotel,' Millie advised. She nodded coyly in the direction of the bedroom. It was a tempting thought, but there was time enough for dalliance during the afternoon siesta. My plan was to spend the morning in the docks. Warships were moored there, the major had told us, and I was keen to inspect them.

Millie and I crossed the city in a rickshaw while she told me about her father, a German engineer called Schaftlein, and her Javanese mother. Both parents had died, I think, before the Japanese invasion. The girl herself went free in the early days of the occupation, thanks to her German ancestry, but two years before the end of the war she too had been interned.

'I never thought I'd meet someone like you,' she said. Me neither. For the umpteenth time I'd fallen madly in love.

That morning the Japanese were out in force. They were manning road-blocks all over the city. Their street patrols, each at company strength, wore pudding-basin steel helmets instead of the casual peaked forage caps. Most of the soldiers' uniforms were old and threadbare. Baggy breeches ended at the knee in tight-wound puttees and split-toed rubber shoes. It looked like they were wearing their oldest gear in anticipation of trouble. Only the officers were sharply turned-out, clean-shaven and decidedly over-dressed.

A handful of warships sheltered in the Surabaya docks. There was an exceptionally large Japanese submarine coated with the radar-deflecting clinker we had seen on the cruiser in Singapore. Moored nearby were three rusting patrol-craft half the size of destroyers. Little had survived of the proud fleet that blew the British, Dutch and Americans out of the Java Sea. The most curious exhibit was a German U-boat, camouflaged green and brown, moored alongside the main jetty, its crew on deck stringing washing from the conning tower. The German commander came ashore to introduce himself. He was tall and blond, the archetypical Aryan superman. His English was fluent, with a decided stutter.

'W-w-welcome to this h-h-hellhole,' he greeted me cheerfully. I was reminded of my old skipper back in the 55th ML Flotilla. It soon became apparent that the commander was not as cheerful as he sounded. He was a youngish man, no more than thirty at my guess, and he had done more than his stint with the Atlantic wolf-packs. He had survived eighteen months – 'd-d-double the average' – and had plainly had as much as he could stand. His hands trembled as he lit a cigarette. His U-boat had been sent off on a world voyage when morale was near breaking-point. It must have been a kind of consolation prize. The mission was to carry lens-grinding equipment to Japan. One of Hitler's last gestures to his distant Oriental allies was to help the Japanese set up a high-quality optical industry. German camera-makers would lose a lot of business, as a result, in the post-war world.

On the way back to Germany the boat put into Surabaya for minor repairs. The engineers were still tinkering around when the European war ended. Uncertain what to do next, and restrained to an extent by the Japanese, the crew were content to forswear further hostilities and spin out their days fraternising with the Javanese women. The German commander eyed Millie approvingly. They spoke together briefly in German. Talking his own language the commander no longer stuttered.

'He said he was ready to surrender to me any time,' Millie sniggered as we walked off around the docks. She clutched my arm nervously as a squad of Japanese marines loped past with rifles at the ready. A riot was raging around the dock gates. An Indonesian mob was trying to storm past the Japanese guards. The Japanese didn't want a fight – they were keeping control on British orders until Allied forces arrived – and in less than five minutes the feebly protesting soldiery were swept aside. No shots were fired. Young men wearing nationalist armbands snatched the soldiers' rifles and fanned out through the dockyard yelling incomprehensible slogans. Millie and I ducked out through a side gate and started back on foot to the hotel. The streets were milling with people. The Japanese and their road-blocks had disappeared. A number of buildings were being occupied and ransacked. Freshly-scrawled posters proclaimed the hour of revolution was at hand.

History records that on 25 September 1945 the Surabayan nationalists decided to assert themselves. They had declared their independence of Holland; now they intended to seize control of the city from the Japanese. British-Indian forces were due to land within a week or two and it was rightly suspected that the British would attempt to restore the discredited Dutch. The nationalist leadership in Surabaya was determined to demonstrate its power. The plan was to face the British with a *fait accompli*; to threaten a bloody fight if anyone tried to put the clock back.

The coup led, inevitably, to attacks on foreigners. But not that first day. The citizens of Surabaya were too busy taking over police stations and government offices to bother about the handful of idiots – people like Millie and myself – who ventured out into the streets. Demonstrators swirled around us brandishing captured Japanese weapons. Once or twice they stopped us, yelling '*Merdeka!*' (freedom), and ordered us to join in. Millie yelled something similar (but ruder) in French which passed unnoticed.

Our Dutch friend Palmers was peeping out of the hostel where his wife had been interned. The internees were scared and Palmers was a deeply worried man. 'I've led you into trouble,' he mumbled yet again. He reminded me that the one Bahasa expression commonly used in English was the word 'amok'.

'The Javanese are a quiet people,' he observed as a truckload of screaming demonstrators sped past. 'But every generation or so they explode. I'm afraid this is what's now happening.'

The Oranje Hotel was eerily quiet. The servants had fled. The Dutch manager came out to apologise as we sat watching the street demonstrations from the front verandah. The British major, the German U-boat commander and some of his officers were getting together for a drink. It was strange to see the Europeans, such recent enemies, drawn together in this threatening Asian environment. The Germans had rustled up beer and a couple of bottles of Geneva gin. It tasted like castor oil but I felt badly in need of a drink.

I was sipping my gin, whispering sweet nothings to Millie, when a couple of Japanese armoured cars drew up opposite the verandah. Their gun turrets swung towards us. Everyone froze. The U-boat commander threw himself to the floor. Millie cringed and cried. The rest of us sat rigid with fright, expecting the worst. A squad of Indonesians emerged from behind the armoured cars aiming their rifles and automatic weapons. They lined us up against the verandah wall. The squad leader shouted things in Dutch. The British major answered fluently and indignantly. We were foreign nationals, he protested (as I later learned); in no way were we connected with the colonial power. The Indonesians looked doubtful. They ordered us to our rooms 'pending investigation'. I was slinking off with Millie when one of the revolutionaries grabbed her by the wrist.

'She's with me,' I said in English. The man eyed us both and laughed.

For the next two days we stayed confined to the bedroom. Sparse meals were left at the door. Most of the time we made love beneath the mosquito net. Life looked so tenuous we decided to enjoy it to the full. The sense of imminent danger seemed only to whet our appetites. I was in a decidedly weakened state when a delegation of Indonesian nationalists released us on the third day. Perhaps we hadn't had enough to eat. Millie stayed behind in the hotel, now under Indonesian occupation, while a group of officers conducted me to the newly-appointed Governor of Surabaya, a lieutenant-general called Sudirman.

The Governor was a scholarly, kindly man who regretted the indignities I had suffered at the hands of 'our over-zealous elements'. Anyone from India was more than welcome in Indonesia, he declared, and the text of his somewhat fulsome speech was reproduced next day in the nationalist newspaper. There was also a front-page picture of myself, looking somewhat wan, scribbling attentively in my notebook.

The formalities over, Governor Sudirman got down to business. His staff left the room. We were talking, he emphasised, in strict privacy. The American expression 'off the record' was not yet widely used. The Governor's problem was that a lunatic fringe, possibly communists, was eager to resort to violence. He wanted me to make my way back to Singapore without delay and advise the British High Command of the critical situation in Surabaya. It was no good trying to explain things in Batavia – correction, Jakarta – because the Dutch would refuse to believe it. The British major had already been asked to take on the job but Force 136 had ordered him to stay put until the Allied relief forces arrived. The radio link to his headquarters in Colombo was (typically) out of order.

The Governor gave me a run-down of his force strengths in the Surabaya region. The Allied landing could meet fierce opposition, he warned, unless the Allies handled it carefully. The whole thing might have been a clever deception, it occurred to me afterwards, although I did not think so at the time. I now feel sure it wasn't, in view of what happened later. A train was leaving for Jakarta within an hour and I would be escorted back to the capital. There might not be another train and I had better catch this one. Surely they did not expect me to leave Millie?

'I can only guarantee your safety,' Sudirman said. 'The Red Cross is arriving here tomorrow to organise the evacuation of civilian internees. The girl will be perfectly safe.'

There was time for just the briefest of goodbyes. My escort was anxious to leave. The three uniformed army officers who would ride with me all the way back to the capital gathered my belongings from the hotel and waited tactfully outside the room while the pair of us pledged eternal troth.

'I've got a bad feeling about this,' Millie wept. And of course she was right. We never saw each other again.

I hated being hustled out of Surabaya. It meant passing up a good story. Besides, it severed contact with Frank Worth. Most distressing of all my hasty departure snatched me from the ardent arms of my new-found girlfriend, Millie Schaftlein, now back in the unguarded internees' hostel awaiting evacuation by the International Red Cross. Everyone in that hostel, everyone identified, in fact, with the colonial régime, was liable to attack by increasingly racist demonstrators. The Indonesians ignored my pleas to take her with me, they couldn't guarantee getting me back to Batavia in one piece, the last train was waiting in the station. Three soldiers with sub-machine-guns welcomed me into my reserved compartment. The luggage racks were strung with little notices – 'Freedom, Man's Birthright' and 'Welcome friends from India' – obviously, the propaganda department was working overtime. The official reason for my peremptory exit was the need to protect an officer of the Indian armed forces. The truth, as I well knew, was that the self-appointed Governor of Surabaya, General Sudirman, and other Indonesian moderates, wanted me to warn the British that extremists were preparing to give incoming Allied relief troops a hostile reception.

It was apparent to me from the start that the general grossly exaggerated the influence of a humble lieutenant, RINVR. Already I was in a questionable position. I was absent without leave on a crazy jaunt through Japanese-occupied South-east Asia. But it wasn't General Sudirman's fault. Frank and I had bluffed our way so far during the past three weeks that we were beginning to believe our own bluster. A military committee came to see me off. They must have wanted to make sure I left. A twitchy youth wearing Dutch colonel's insignia delivered an impassioned speech supporting Mahatma Gandhi and the Indian drive against imperialism. I felt it politic to applaud. I had little time for the British Raj though it was uncomfortably obvious (to me at least) that I was ethnically, if not ideologically, one of the hated imperialists. The anomaly never occurred to the Indonesians, thank goodness, or I might have ended on the wrong end of a bayonet.

The train took the longer, central route through Jogjakarta and Bandung. It started off briskly in an afternoon rain storm that left the flooded countryside a burnished checkerboard. Half an hour out of Surabaya it was halted by youthful militia who insisted on searching for 'enemies of the revolution'. They glared at me hungrily until my escort ordered them out of the compartment. Three or four other passengers were hauled onto the platform and forced to grovel on hands and knees. One was a young, dark-haired Dutchman. His face was frozen in a smile, stiff with fear. The train moved off as a shouting mob began beating their prisoners.

'Can't we do anything?' I asked the sergeant in charge of my escort. 'It is fate,' he mumbled helplessly.

This particular incident did not end too badly. A Dutch newspaper correspondent turned up nine years later in Hanoi. He looked remarkably like the young man I had last seen being beaten by irate Javanese. Yes, he had been interned in east Java. And the Indonesians *had* dragged him off a train around the time I must have been travelling. It was towards the end of September, 1945. Some soldiers had saved him from the mob and he'd been released after several months' imprisonment. It turned out to be the same man.

Vigilantes kept stopping and searching the train throughout the night. None of us got much sleep. Representatives of so-called revolutionary committees claimed the right to direct rail traffic through the areas they controlled; from time to time I was invited – no, ordered – out on to the platform to hear speeches addressed to 'the freedom-fighter from India'. Time and again I acknowledged the misguided acclaim, told the revolutionaries they were doing a great job and shouted the now obligatory '*Merdeka!*'

But at last I was beginning to wilt. Weeks of over-excitement were catching up on me. Recent bouts in the boudoir had taken their toll. Another attack of the recurrent malaria I had contracted in Burma set me shivering and sweating as we rolled into Jogjakarta. My escort was alarmed. The soldiers had orders to deliver me alive to whoever was running the show in Batavia – correction, Jakarta – and the train was held up while a doctor was found to check me over. He recommended removing me to hospital but my escort wisely refused. They promised to nurse me through with aspirins and cool towels. Privately I cursed myself for throwing away my anti-malarial tablets. The wretched things were supposed to reduce your potency. It didn't much matter in Burma. Here it was different with such friendly females around.

The sergeant propped me up by the window and wiped me down with the towels. Each stop he went off in search of ice. The stops became increasingly frequent. The confrontations with the revolutionaries grew louder and more contentious. The flame of active insurrection first lit, it appeared, in the port of Surabaya, was spreading ahead of us faster than the train could travel. Peering out with aching eyes I could see buildings burning in some towns. And everywhere huge mobs rampaging across tracks and platforms as if our progress contradicted and somehow offended the overall disorder.

'They keep threatening to suspend all train services,' whispered the sergeant after he'd beaten off a group intent on interviewing me. 'We'll be lucky to complete this journey.'

Complete it we did, although my memories of the final stages tend to be woolly. My ever-solicitous escort found an RAF advance party at Batavia airport. A friendly medic shovelled me on to the first available flight to Singapore. It turned out to be a twin-engined Mosquito fighter-bomber and I crouched miserably at the feet of the navigator while the pilot roared flat-out across the city rooftops. Pilots had orders to 'shoot up' the place to impress 'the natives'. The man at the stick of my Mosquito took his orders much too seriously, concluding his particular display of suicidal acrobatics by diving between – and I mean between – the spires of Batavia cathedral.

I fought off the fever in the Singapore press billets, which were now decidedly the worse for wear, and checked in as soon as possible at army headquarters. The onset of peace had left the place lively as a dormant beehive. The social round interrupted so rudely by the invading Japanese was rapidly being revived; the afternoon tea dance (officers only) was back in full swing at the Raffles Hotel. A resurrected Tanglin Club (Europeans only) had just reopened its doors. The languid intelligence colonel who granted me brief audience in one of the highly-polished staff offices was unimpressed by my travel-worn appearance. The jungle green uniform I had filched from the stores in Singapore was falling apart. The G-2 took perfunctory note of my observations before sending me on my way.

'We are perfectly capable of dealing with a handful of Javanese,' he told me. 'The Dutch are keeping us fully appraised of the situation.'

I ventured to suggest that the Dutch might have political reasons for playing down the extent of the Indonesian revolution. The colonel bridled at the lately-coined word 'Indonesian'. It was a word only used, as yet, by rebels.

'It is our opinion that agitation in the Indies is confined to a handful of hooligans,' he admonished. Strange how those stock phrases still surface, decades later, among those who insist on fooling themselves. The last time I heard it was after the massacre in Tienanmen Square. The colonel sighed, swung round dismissively in his chair, opening a fresh file. He glanced up, surprised to find me still standing hesitantly before him.

'Let me tell you, young man.' He spoke slowly in the patronising tones Englishmen use to address idiots and the lower orders. 'There is no widespread disloyalty in the Dutch East Indies. The bulk of the citizens of these colonies remain loyal to the House of Orange.'

The colonel smiled the smile of the self-satisfied smart aleck privy to knowledge denied the hoi polloi. Nasser smiled at me that way on the eve of the Six Day war. So did the French commander at Dienbienphu three weeks before the jungle fortress fell to the Viet Minh.

'The 25th Indian Division is going into Surabaya,' the colonel called after me as I neared the door. 'They'll be well able to cope with a bunch of agitators.'

I had a special affection for the 25th Division. I had covered some of their landings on the Burma coast. But I felt I had gained useful insights into the nature of the Indonesian revolution. It was no comfort later when, despite my warnings, the division suffered heavy casualties in Surabaya. One of its brigadiers was killed. British warships retaliated by bombarding the city. Mobs attacked Dutch internees as they were being evacuated by the Red Cross. One truck convoy filled with women and children was ambushed and machine-gunned close to the Surabaya docks. Word reached me that Millie Schaftlein was among the dozens killed. It wasn't until years afterwards that I heard she was safe and happily married in Holland. Palmers, the ultimate survivor, had also escaped with his wife.

Frank Worth never reached Bali, which was just as well because the recalcitrant Japanese garrison commander had already committed suicide. But on the way an even bigger story blew up in Frank's face – or rather his camera. The Japanese commander of the huge Batoporan Naval Arsenal destroyed the place to prevent its contents falling into Indonesian nationalist hands. Frank's footage was spectacular. Flames shot five hundred feet into the air. The commander and his second-in-command then committed *seppuku* (hara-kiri) by holding hand-grenades to their stomachs and blowing themselves up. The nationalists went beserk. Chaos reigned. Japanese tanks and armoured cars seized by the Indonesians careered through the streets, firing indiscriminately.

Frank had to get his dramatic footage out to the world somehow – and fast. Batavia was the only link. Returning by train had become even more perilous since my departure. He was lucky to get as far as Bandung. Rail communication was finally cut. Struggling out to the airport, he found it in the hands of an hysterical mob. Two Dutch planes were ablaze. A third, a Mitchell bomber of the Royal Netherlands Air Force, had its markings crossed out and the words 'Property of the Indonesian Republic' scrawled along its fuselage. A mob armed with knives was slashing the pilots' parachutes. A flight engineer who protested was kidnapped. The mood was viciously anti-white.

Frank found himself confronted by an armed and hostile crowd. He demanded to know who, if anyone, was in charge. A surly young man emerged to examine Frank's papers. They included a *laissez passer* from the Indonesian Foreign Minister. On seeing this, the young man's face lit up.

'Why, that's my father!' he exclaimed. He went on to explain that a Japanese bomber-cum-transport had just landed. His men were at this moment interning the crew.

Frank did a quick double-take. Looking at his watch he begged the nationalists not to touch that plane. It had been sent to rush him back to Lord Louis Mountbatten with on-the-spot reports of the situation in central and western Java. The plane's engines were still ticking over. Congratulating the mystified pilot for arriving so promptly, Frank climbed aboard. The now-friendly mob cheered as the plane lumbered off down the runway. It was airborne before the pilot, greatly relieved, asked 'Where to?'

'Batavia!' Frank replied, as if instructing a taxi driver. He returned to Singapore a few days later and, like me, was ordered on to India. The pair of us were in deep trouble. Our antics had offended a lot of influential people. We had flagrantly disobeyed orders, engaged in the most reprehensible activities, endangered the armistice and laid ourselves open to court martial.

'You're for the high jump,' an Indian colonel told me with considerable relish when I checked into our New Delhi headquarters. There was no mistaking the note of sadistic satisfaction. He produced a photostat of our fake orders signed by the mythical Brigadier Oliphant.

'Who,' the colonel demanded, 'is this fellow Oily Pants?'

Fortunately our overall commander, the head of Indian Interservices Public Relations, was a brigadier called Desmond Young. The old boy had been captured by Rommel in the Western Desert and managed to escape. A year after the end of the war he came out with a best-selling biography of the late Afrika Corps commander. It was the first sympathetic study of a German general published in the West. The book was made into a movie, *Rommel – Desert Fox*, in which Desmond Young played himself.

'You lads have been taking liberties,' Desmond Young scolded. We stood solemnly to attention in his office in South Block. 'But,' the brigadier added, 'I'm damn sure I'd have done the same in your place.' With a forgiving wink he threw our files into the Out tray. The parting shot reached us as we made for the door.

'You know,' he said, 'you lads have had a pretty enjoyable war. It's supposed to be hell!'

PART SIX

The end of the war, the advent of a Labour government in Britain, renewed nationalist agitation in India, an upsurge of demand, in fact, for speedy constitutional change, had together brought India to a fever pitch of hysteria. Sympathetic as I was to nationalist aspirations, the excitement left me largely unmoved. India had been an educational experience for a youthful nobody from suburban England. My stint as combat cameraman had provided valuable new insights into the business of journalism. I now needed to get on with earning a living. It was important to hustle back and carve a niche in an overloaded labour market and the depression years had left me pessimistic about my prospects.

The chance of one final adventure persuaded me to linger a few more months in the Royal Indian Navy. The need for propaganda had not ended on VJ-Day, but had actually increased. Efforts to convince the Indian public of their armed forces' true worth were admittedly ineffectual. Frank Worth's films in Malaya and Indonesia had been well received, on the other hand, in military camps across the country. They demonstrated the vital role Indian troops were playing in the historic events unravelling in Asia. Boosting the *jawans'* (soldiers') morale was vital. The Indian army was all that stood between a peaceful, and by this time inevitable, hand-over of power, and outright anarchy.

There would be more film to come, Frank told our old friend, Brigadier Desmond Young, if he would only permit us to publicise the single sloop India was sending to Japan. The head of Interservices Public Relations listened impassively. He had one of those wry, quizzical faces that watches the world with a certain wary caution. At last he nodded.

'All right boys,' he said. 'Something tells me I'm wrong but I think I'll humour you ... only this time forget the fun and games.' He signed our movement order and slid it across the desk. 'Forget the games, anyway,' he added. 'You're heading back into foreign territory, so for God's sake behave yourselves. I can't face any more whingeing complaints.'

The snow came rustling in so thick and fast we could scarcely see the forecastle. The forward guns blurred to an indefinite smudge; beyond them, up in the bows, the anchor party had completely disappeared and snatches of the sailors' chatter were all that reached us on the bridge. The snow-muted sound seemed oddly distorted. Sirens moaned faintly from invisible ships that might have been miles away – judged purely by ear there was no way of telling. Our own engines were almost inaudible, rumbling gently, Slow Ahead, deep down beneath us. Everyone jumped when the Tannoy squealed into life, ordering 'Hands to Tiffin'.

'I'm bloody starving,' grumbled the navigating officer bending irritably back to his charts. He and the radar-operator had been on duty since well before dawn, groping blindly through the unfamiliar reaches of the Inland Sea of Japan. A Goanese steward appeared with a tray of *samozas* and mugs of strong, sweet Darjeeling tea.

'Bearing two-eight-oh,' the radar-operator reported.

I peered over the man's shoulder trying to grasp what he was on about. What object in heaven's name was bearing 280 degrees? Certainly nothing visible. I hoped this strange equipment knew what it was doing. It was the first time I'd seen radar in action; our little launches in Burma never ran to anything so sophisticated. Sonar was our most advanced gear and that never seemed to work when we wanted it. The navigating officer, munching thoughtfully, drew fresh pencil lines across his chart. 'Steer one-seven-oh,' he ordered.

The quartermaster, an experienced Muslim from Ratnagiri, blue with cold despite his brand-new duffel coat, acknowledged the order. He eased the helm until the required bearing appeared in the monitor strip above his head. 'One-seven-oh it is, sir,' he confirmed in his shrill, lilting drawl.

The new course was as meaningless to me as the old one. Nothing could be seen beyond the wheelhouse windows, only a powdery void. But the ship crawled on into the murk, threading her way through alien waters aided solely by a file of navigational notes – wreck warnings, that sort of thing – and this extraordinary piece of electronic gadgetry. Without radar, the navigating officer had told us, we would be forced to anchor until visibility improved. Any other time, perhaps, we might have done so. This morning, of course, we were duty-bound to stage a virtuoso performance: preparations were in hand for our entry on to the international scene.

I peeped back into the cubbyhole that housed the radar. It looked positively unreal. A revolving streak of light resembling the beam of an old-fashioned lighthouse seemed to be piercing the storm in an unearthly sort of way, creating a map of our surroundings on the radar scope. Pale spidery shapes revealed that land we couldn't see was slipping past on either beam, while directly ahead through the mushy clutter on the scope lay the entrance to Kure harbour. A scattering of blips across its wide waters suggested the presence of myriad small islands.

The latest course alteration took us past a projection – a peninsula, perhaps? – hard on our port beam. 'Wouldn't want to hit *that*,' the navigating officer said mysteriously. He tapped the navigational notes. Hit what? I wondered.

'Oh certainly, not *that*,' the commanding officer agreed.

What were the two of them talking about? They might have been conversing in code. The navigating officer waltzed his dividers across the chart. 'Won't be long now,' he said.

The CO nodded approvingly. 'Good work,' he commented. 'I think we're going to surprise the lot of them. How many minutes to harbour stations?'

'Reckon about twenty, sir,' said the navigating officer.

'Right on the ruddy dot.' He had every right, I suppose, to look pleased with himself. Our estimated time of arrival at Kure was 1400 hours Japanese Standard Time. It would be quite a coup making the deadline in spite of the weather.

The CO turned to Frank Worth. My fellow cameraman was crouched inside the wheelhouse shielding his lens from the snow. 'Wrong sort of day for pretty pictures, eh?' the CO jeered. There were the usual sycophantic titters. Commander K. R. U. Todd RINR plainly disliked Frank. He disliked me as well, probably with more reason. He had taken the pair of us reluctantly aboard in Hong Kong for the last leg of the voyage to Japan. The atmosphere was tense enough without two unorthodox passengers who refused to be awed by big ship routine.

HMIS *Sutlej* would not have been considered big in anyone else's navy. But early in 1946 these British-built, Improved Swan class sloops (1,375 tons, six 4-inch AA) were the biggest ships in the RIN. And as such they conducted themselves with the ritual formality – or as Frank and I preferred to put it, the mind-numbing bullshit – of a full-grown British battleship. Everything was tortuously immaculate: decks were holystoned, brass buffed, paint refreshed, bottle-screws greased and guard-rails brushed as if our destination was the Spithead Royal Review. Given enough polish I swear the crew would have Simonised the hull. The result was, in RN parlance, an extremely tiddly ship.

The atmosphere aboard was tense because a week or two before, in February 1946, much of the Royal Indian Navy had mutinied. Ships in the main Indian ports, chiefly Bombay and Karachi, had been seized by sailors demanding independence for India. Their actions were thoughtless and premature. The Raj still ruled, albeit weakly, and when the Indian Army showed no signs of disaffection, RAF bombers were paraded overhead, threatening to blow the mutineers out of the water.

The *Sutlej* received reports of the mutiny while steaming up the Indochina coast. The sloop had been assigned to represent India in the Commonwealth occupation of Japan. Her destination was the great imperial naval base of Kure in south-western Honshu. The question her officers nervously began asking themselves was whether they would ever get there. Some feared hotheads would seize the ship and sail off to the nearest neutral port. There was indeed cause for worry. One morning, a couple of days south of Hong Kong, the green, white and saffron flag of the Indian National Congress was found flying in the bow. Whoever put it there had done the job with commendable stealth. The look-outs claimed to have seen nothing.

The most senior Indian officer aboard was the ship's doctor. It was typical of the insensitivity of the Raj that the token Indian contribution to the Japanese occupation should be officered largely by Britons. There was an ample pool of senior Indians who could have taken effective charge. But the subtleties of political point-making were beyond the harassed desk-wallahs in New Delhi. The doctor was an aristocratic Punjabi who'd done his medical training in Britain. He spoke mellifluous Oxbridge English. He later went on to a top rank in the navy of independent India. It was his idea to address the crew over the Tannoy system.

'My fellow countrymen,' he said in Urdu. 'We all look forward to independence. There is every indication we shall soon get it. It is up to us, meanwhile, to maintain discipline and show the world that Indian sailors are a match for anyone. Ill-considered acts will get us nowhere. I appeal to you to do nothing that would mar our future reputation.'

There was no further trouble. Active debate continued, of course, throughout the ship. We settled ourselves aboard the *Sutlej*, drinking pink gins in the wardroom and talking politics. There wasn't much else to talk about; people in India could think of nothing else. Talk among the younger Indian officers fairly reeked of what we would once have termed sedition. 'It really is time you buggers quit,' said the assistant gunnery officer, a smart, loquacious Bengali.

It was an indication, if ever there was one, of the fast-changing political climate. I made the mistake of agreeing. The Number One (second-in-command) was sitting nearby and took me aside. 'You're obviously not up on shipboard etiquette,' he said severely. 'Aboard this ship, officers – er, British officers – don't talk politics. Especially these days.'

'But Lieutenant Dutt – ' I began.

'Lieutenant Dutt's always looking for an argument,' the Number One cut in. '*British* officers are not expected to give him the opportunity.' The tone smacked of Lady Bracknell.

Word reached the CO. He buttonholed me the following day. 'Politician are you?' he growled. Commander Todd had been an officer in my father's shipping line, the P&O. It explained why the ship was run so formally. The P&O had a snobbish reputation, and its officers could be every bit as stuffy as the stuffiest members of the regular RN. 'Around here politics is a touchy subject,' the CO continued. 'You'd better learn to keep your mouth shut.' He seemed to be echoing Lord Rowallan's advice without his additional reference to the bowels. The commander stood back a pace, looking me up and down. Unlike his ships' officers, smartly kitted out in new blue winter uniform, I was wearing a blue serge battledress. It looked, and was, unorthodox. Commander Todd found the sight offensive. 'Never seen such a rig-out,' he snarled. 'Call yourself a sailor?' This once I kept quiet and refrained from a cutting riposte. The commander looked me coldly in the eyes. 'I knew your father,' he added unpleasantly. 'A right hard case. You'd better watch it.'

The snow suddenly lifted. One moment we were eyeless in the whispering storm, and a moment later we were inside an enormous anchorage steaming gently through a slate-grey sea. Surrounding hillsides glowed frosted white. Full along our port beam stretched mile upon bombed-out mile of cranes, workshops and rusting wreckage. Scattered offshore were the carcasses of sunken ships – the blips that looked like islands on the radar scope – some small, some barely visible, some monstrously large, all rising battered and forsaken from the oily waters.

Close astern lay an elderly cruiser with three squat funnels, the *Kitakami*, burned out and beached. This was the projection – the peninsula – we had just avoided by radar. The navigating officer must have known it was there, warned by those voluminous notes. Out to starboard lay the aircraft carrier *Amagi*, half-submerged on her side. Streaks of rust ran down her buckled flight-deck. Workers with oxy-acetylene torches clambered about like steeplejacks high above the water dismembering sections of the upperworks. Moored alongside the capsized carrier was a destroyer whose bow had been blown off. The remainder of the hull was at least afloat. The masts and funnels of less fortunate craft protruded from every corner of the anchorage. It was a marine graveyard. The biggest and most spectacular wreck turned out to be the battleship *Ise*, driven aground and listing heavily, covered by the same sad rust. The complex stages of her towering 'pagoda' bridge, tipped over towards the water, were red with it, dappled in turn by the droppings of nesting seagulls. The long slim barrels of her fourteen-inch guns splayed from their turrets, aiming forlornly at the sky. The after-guns had been removed to make way for a miniature flight-deck when the Imperial Navy tried tardily to boost its air power. The men who gave the world Pearl Harbor had learned their own lessons a touch too late.

Most of these wrecks dated from the dying days of the war. On 24 July 1945, three weeks before the Japanese surrender, the full strength of US Task-force 38, the most powerful carrier attack group ever assembled, was thrown against the Kure anchorage. Some 1,747 sorties were launched in one of the heaviest carrier assaults of the Pacific war. All that was left of the Imperial Japanese Navy – which wasn't much by this time – was sunk or irreparably damaged at its moorings. The British Pacific Fleet, steaming in the vicinity, was specifically excluded from the operation. The American fleet commander, Admiral 'Bull' Halsey, declared he would never countenance any post-war British claim to have delivered 'even a part of the final blow that demolished the Japanese'.

HMIS *Sutlej* was an impressive sight sidling up to anchor. Recorded music (a brass band version of Walton's *Crown Imperial*) boomed from the deck speakers, pennants fluttered brightly at the yard, while the crew lined up neatly topside in their newly supplied blue uniforms. Most of them (like me) had never worn winter rig. Many looked distinctly unhappy. They were shivering with cold. The sailors gawked and gasped (as I did) at the unfamiliar, snow-bound landscape, and at the wreckage around us. Pipes shrilled as we passed an Australian cruiser moored off the naval base. Dead on time the Royal Indian Navy had made its first (and probably last) official entry on to the world stage.

The Australians watched us, I later learned, with considerable curiosity. 'Should we shoot 'em or salute 'em?' one officer is reputed to have inquired. The arrival of 'the mutineers' (or Gandhi's navy, as some called us) had been awaited with mild trepidation by the Commonwealth fleet in Kure. There was admiration, as well as relief, at the way we had arrived smartly on schedule despite the wintriest storm in years. The Americans had handed Kure to the Commonwealth forces a few months previously. The half-dozen or so warships now moored there all wore the white ensign. The Australian cruiser flashed us a generous welcome: NICE WORK IN THIS WEATHER came the message. *Sutlej* laconically flashed back A PIECE OF CAKE. It was a moment of minor triumph. The CO positively purred with pride. Our stylish entry had won the RIN much-needed face. Self-congratulation was the order of the day. The pink gins would really flow down in the wardroom. That is, unless the Australians invited us over – the word was they had real beer aboard. Frank and I excused ourselves. We were anxious to get ashore. There was plenty of work to be done.

A slow drizzle had set in by the time we got ashore. The snow had turned to slush, the frozen earth to mud, and the ice was thawing off the stagnant pools that filled the bomb craters. There were so many craters that in some places the dockyard might have been worked over by a gigantic mattock. Little of anything had survived intact. The rain dribbled off the warped skeletons of giant hoists, burned-out barrack buildings that trailed off as far as the eye could see and vast, roofless workshops where dozens upon dozens of enormous lathes, metal presses and milling machines lay exposed to the destructive weather. The base that once serviced a mighty fleet seemed wrecked beyond repair. But, as we soon found, that wasn't entirely true. Despite the most appalling damage Kure had carried on to the last.

Shortage of steel halted the construction of surface ships towards the end of 1944. The little steel that was left went into midget submarines. The dockyard was packed with them. They were stacked up, rusting, on the wharves. A particularly large dry-dock, the largest I had ever seen, was filled so tight with these odd little craft that they looked like sardines in one enormous can. Kure had produced them frantically during the last months of the war. The submarines came in two sizes. One model was 80 feet long, weighing 87 tons. It was of modest range, electrically propelled and operated by a crew of three. The smaller model, at 41 feet, with a two-man crew, was equally short-ranged and all-electric. Both types were built to carry two 18-inch torpedoes. They were the best the Imperial Japanese Navy could muster as a last line of defence against an impending US invasion. Given the dedication of the submarine crews, resigned to sacrificing their lives, plus the suicidal enthusiasm of the Kamikaze pilots, the desperate warlords of Japan hoped to inflict unacceptable casualties on the Americans before the nation went down in an orgy of self-destruction. Thanks largely to Emperor Hirohito, the suicide finale was averted.

By now it was late afternoon. The wind was rising from the north. We clutched our greatcoats about us as Frank finished shooting *Sutlej* at anchor. A blood red sun sank symbolically behind the sloop. We had no colour film in those days but the sunset made great pictures. The waters gleamed briefly between the outcrops of angular wreckage before the night came hustling in and the rain resumed in earnest.

The Kure dockyard was still at work. The Japanese were no longer building submarines: they were scrapping them. Flashes of blue light spluttered from their cutting torches. From time to time there was a metallic clunk as chunks of shorn metal fell to the ground. A squad of men in ragged clothes ran up and down the wharves, heaving the metal on to small hand-carts and trundling it off to a waiting train. The swords of the samurai were being broken up for ploughshares.

'Want to look inside one these things?' The voice was American, the speaker Japanese. He was a young man about our age wearing the shabby, badgeless jacket of an Imperial Navy officer. 'Call me Joe,' he said, shaking our surprised hands. 'Born in LA, would you believe, for all the good it did me.' Bitterly he told us of his childhood in California, of his orthodox Nisei father who sent him back home to study; the war had caught him in high school in Osaka whence he was conscripted into the navy and employed, thanks to his fluent English, as an intelligence officer monitoring US communications at sea.

'At least I knew what was going to hit me when our, I mean, the American planes, closed in,' he chuckled grimly. 'I'm lucky to be alive. Poor old dad died in camp.' He was one of the thousands of Japanese Americans rounded up and thrown into detention camps at the outbreak of the Pacific war. 'Now I'm stuck in this God-forsaken country,' Joe sighed. 'My American citizenship was cancelled directly the navy grabbed me.' He hesitated to make the inevitable request. 'Got a cigarette?' he finally begged. Non-smokers like us were incapable of understanding what it meant to be deprived of tobacco but we had brought cartons of Camels to use as currency. Joe snatched a cigarette and lit up. He drew so hard and deep I wondered when the smoke would reach the soles of his feet. 'Hubba hubba!' he breathed luxuriously. He was using the new-minted jargon of occupation which gave us words like 'Mama-san', still used in Asia for the woman in charge of anything from a disco to a brothel, and 'honcho', which denotes a leader, an enthusiast or achiever. 'Hubba hubba' expressed admiration, usually for a beautiful girl.

'You haven't any food as well?' the young man inquired. The small wistful face looked pinched and hungry in the fading light. Frank fished out a chocolate bar which Joe wolfed hungrily. 'Come into this sub,' he said, indicating one of the larger midget models. 'I was supposed to command one of these junk heaps in the last days. You know, faithful unto death ... all that garbage.' He grinned ruefully.

'Would you have done it?' I asked. The thought of coolly killing yourself, as the Japanese had done, continued to intrigue me.

'Guess I would,' Joe replied. 'It was easy to get carried away by all that Sun-god hype.'

He had held the rank of ensign until the IJN was abolished after the surrender. His last ship had been sunk off Okinawa in April, 1945. Since no other surface vessels were available he was given a brief course in midget submarine warfare right here in Kure harbour. 'It was pretty basic,' he said, climbing up the hull. 'More people died in training than in operating these things.'

Joe lit the way down the conning-tower with my flashlight. I followed reluctantly, feeling increasingly entombed. The interior was suffocatingly small. Twin steering wheels which might have belonged to a small car controlled depth and direction. The commander sat behind, as the former ensign demonstrated, conning the boat through a primitive periscope. At his right hand was the button that fired the torpedoes and another that set off scuttling charges. There was no time-delay on the charges that would allow the crew to escape.

'You mean you'd sink the boat with yourselves in it?' Frank asked. Both of us were growing claustrophobic in these confined quarters.

Joe shrugged. 'Those were the orders. I'm not sure whether I would have carried them out. But I know plenty of people who would. Care to meet a Kamikaze pilot?'

There was an ominous ticking. 'Christ!' yelled Frank. 'A bomb. The bloody thing's booby-trapped!' He struggled to climb out of the conning-tower, myself close behind him. We jammed together in a flurry of arms and legs.

'Hey! Hold it, you guys!' Joe was laughing his head off. 'That's no bomb!' He indicated an unlit hurricane lamp swinging against the bulkhead. Lamp striking bulkhead produced the ticking sound. He leaned over and stopped the lamp swinging. 'One of us must of touched it,' he choked. 'Haven't had a laugh like that for months.'

'About that Kamikaze pilot,' I said when we had regained our composure in the open air. The chance of meeting one of these mystic figures sworn to death-dive straight into our ships – as recently as seven months ago – was something I'd been waiting for. I was curious to find out, if possible, exactly what went on in the Kamikaze's mind.

'But no fakes,' I warned Joe as we agreed to meet later. I had been forewarned of a racket. Men were often presented as Kamikazes to cadge food and smokes from the victorious *gaijin* (foreigners). Some but by no means all of those claiming to be pilots were not the genuine article.

'No fakes,' Joe promised.

He changed some of our Australian pounds into black market yen. The occupation authorities had not yet gotten around to printing their own scrip. Forces in Kure used Australian currency because the base was under Australian administrative control.

This much was certain: the occupation of Japan was proving astonishingly peaceful. The disciplined good manners of a nation so recently determined to fight unto death were downright astounding. The Japanese were so exceptionally law-abiding. There was little of the robbery our forces faced in Italy, for instance, where you could come back from lunch to find your parked jeep minus its wheels. An element of thievery would have been nearly forgivable though, in that first winter of defeat. The Japanese were glum, dejected and spiritually drained. Many were homeless. Every article of everyday life was in crucially short supply. Food rations were minimal. So little food was available to the civilian population that the occupation forces were forbidden to dine in what were quaintly designated 'native' restaurants.

The orders, like those forbidding fraternisation with the defeated foe, were already being largely ignored. It was impossible to avoid such a friendly enemy. Occupation troops were treated with obsequious respect. Small boys fought to clean our boots. People from once-proud families clamoured to groom our barracks, take in the laundry and staff the service clubs. Some extraordinary people obtained employment. A former naval captain served in our cookhouse at Kure. The widow of an admiral took in our mending. Few knew it but the bartender in the Commonwealth camp in Tokyo had been a uncommonly sadistic sergeant-interrogator in the dreaded *Kempeitai*.

Women were everywhere available. Mobs of them milled around the conquerors vying to sell their favours. Families were fed by daughters-turned-prostitutes in what was then the one growth industry. Black marketeers were everywhere, seeking to corner the most commonplace goods, proffering anything from illegal yen to exquisite heirlooms. Small shops appeared selling nothing but the treasured possessions of the hungry upper class. Lacquered screens, beautifully embroidered silk robes, fans, ceramics and statuettes fell cheaply into the hands of the foreigner with food to trade. Samurai swords were still the most prized souvenirs. Magnificent swords made centuries before by master craftsmen, part of a family's heritage, were purchased for a case or two of canned meat.

Frank and I checked in at a restored building close to the main gate. It housed the shore-based staff of the Commonwealth naval forces. A talkative Australian petty officer showed us into a comfortable, almost empty dormitory and a bath-house the size of an indoor swimming pool. A handful of beefy men had cleaned themselves under the shower, Japanese-style, and were now turning lobster red in the deep, hot communal bath.

'Oh yes, Russell, I like the Jap baths,' said the petty officer. He had immediately latched on to my first name. 'But there's nothing else I like about these gook bastards. I loathe the little monkeys. Lost a brother on the Burma railway.' We told him of our pending date later that evening. 'You must have met Joe Suzuki,' said the PO. 'Always trying to cadge food and cigarettes. Personally I hate the creep. Traitor I call him. Did he offer to meet you at the dance hall?' Yes, we said, strictly for a meal. 'Well, be careful, it's liable to be raided. Too much black marketing goes on there. And besides, you're not supposed to eat gook. You're not supposed to fraternise either,' the petty officer grinned indelicately. 'Except sly-like, with the sheilas. Hubba hubba. Wait and see what the little beauts get up to!'

The moon had risen when we left the base. Its cold bright light revealed a wasteland. The city of Kure had been erased. A forest of 30-foot brick chimneys was all that remained of thousands of shops and houses. The B-29s had done the job with frightening efficiency. Sent in at low-level from March to July 1945, stripped of armaments and packed with incendiaries, the big bombers had torched millions of civilian homes in what can only be described as terror raids. M-47 incendiary canisters spewed clusters of napalm sticks two feet long on to their hapless targets.

Fire had always been a hazard in a land where urban construction was largely of wood. Conflagrations were so frequent in old-time Tokyo that citizens referred to the flames as 'the flowers of Edo'. Throughout the last months of the war city after city was reduced to ashes. Fire services were simply overwhelmed: the Japanese had neither the men, the equipment, nor more particularly the water to deal with meticulously planned mass arson. The first incendiary raid on Tokyo set off a fire-storm that wiped out six square miles of the city and killed 130,000 people. But there was more, much more, to follow. All the major cities of Japan had been burned down by the time the weird, piping voice of the Emperor ordered his nation to surrender. Allied intelligence did not know it but the combination of B-29s and the blockading American submarines had hamstrung the empire months before Hiroshima and Nagasaki were bombed. The A-bombs did no more than provide a face-saving excuse, albeit a vital one, for the Japanese militarists to obey the Emperor's order to surrender.

Two new buildings had arisen thus far from the ruins of Kure. One was a brothel, the other a dance-hall. The staff were interchangeable. Hungry girls would forsake their shared beds in the brothel to practise next day on the nearby dance-floor. Business must have been slack the night we called. Pairs of novice dancers were still shuffling through the quickstep with looks of grave concentration. The Japanese have a knack of learning to do whatever they have to as perfectly as possible. It is one of their national strengths. The girls' lips moved, counting the beat, while a portable gramophone ground out *Bye Bye Blackbird*. More contemporary records were not yet available. I couldn't help wondering what would happen when jive hit the scene.

'You come meet Suzuki-san?' inquired a dignified old woman in a plain black kimono. The Mama-san conducted us upstairs to a back room. The place was impeccably Japanese, with *tatami* mat flooring and sliding wall panels of opaque paper. A roaring party was going on nearby. Australian officers, aided by hostesses, were performing what I came to recognise as the coal miners' song. Tumpty tee tum tum ... well-lubricated diners were supposed to stomp around pushing the coal wagons down the mine; over in the adjacent room there were hoots of laughter as someone tripped and fell heavily on the matting.

The ensign and another young man silently awaited us, puffing away at black market cigarettes. The room was blue with smoke. Two girls in brilliant orange kimonos removed our shoes, clucking politely, and shepherded us to the squat central table opposite our guests. I had no doubt who would be paying. The Mama-san grovelled in the doorway and moved across the *tatami* on her knees. With metal chopsticks she enlivened the small stone *hibachi* (brazier) that smouldered listlessly in the corner. The warmth the coals threw out fought vainly against the icy draughts seeping around the paper screens. A meagre meal of fish, seaweed and rice arrived, washed down by bottle after bottle of *sake*. The hot rice wine brought a flush to our faces. We toasted the usual things that young men toast, and talked, tongues loosened, about the war.

The Kamikaze seated beside Joe Suzuki was genuine, I felt sure. His story was too artless to be contrived. His name was Hara. He spoke in halting English, helped periodically by the ensign, recalling how he had been pulled out of the Etajima Naval Academy at nineteen years of age to train as a suicide pilot. 'We weren't learning much anyway,' he apologised. 'Etajima, Class of '45, was known as "the tunnellers". We spent almost our entire time digging out the hillsides to shelter factory equipment from the bombers. Round here there are tunnels as much as two kilometres long.' He was a small delicate youth, unnaturally thin, with hands that shook so much he had difficulty swallowing his sake.

The nearby party burst into song. 'Waltzing Matilda, waltzing Matilda, I'll go a-waltzing Matilda with you ...' Hara listened for a moment, smiled, and resumed.

'The situation was growing graver every day,' he said quietly. 'Defeat became a possibility. It was not the samurai tradition to accept defeat. So I volunteered for *Tokko* (suicide) operations. I felt there was no other course. The whole nation had to go down fighting.'

It was a dreadful prospect. I remembered the stories I had read of Japanese civilians, mostly women and children, throwing themselves off the cliffs of Okinawa in the ultimate stages of the American invasion. I declared the idea quite abhorrent. The young man threw me a self-deprecating smile. 'It sounds shocking today. It was not so shocking yesterday.' He fixed me with a curious stare. 'Didn't you expect to lay down your life for your country?'

I replied that 'expect' might not have been the exact word. Anyone who joined the armed forces in wartime was liable to get killed but I did not necessarily *expect* it. (My God I didn't, though once or twice, coward as I was, it had been a close-run thing.)

'We were imbued with the fighting spirit of the Yamato people,' young Hara said. 'It is difficult to describe what that means – or meant at that particular time ...'

We were becoming embroiled in incomprehensible beliefs. There was no way I would ever understand them. I'm not even sure the Japanese understood these things themselves. It was peer-pressure as much as belief, I suggested, that recruited the Kamikaze. Conformity cements Japanese society. At least one young suicide pilot, to my knowledge, had been a Christian. He left a farewell note claiming he died 'in the bosom of Jesus Christ'. Joe listened to my views with particular interest. 'Remember what I said about the hype,' he suggested.

The Australians burst into *The Road to Gundagai*. There were cheers and the sound of rhythmic clapping.

'I did some flying training at Iwakune,' the young man went on. The large Japanese air-base not far from Kure had lately passed into Commonwealth hands. 'I learned the rudiments of flying. I was not very skilled but it should have been enough to get me close to an American carrier. After that it was a matter of awaiting the summons. I never knew how it was decided. Names were picked, I think, at random. My friends were called, one by one. They took off and never came back. We drank their health as their planes rolled down the runway. They inflicted heavy damage on the enemy – or so we were led to believe.'

The Kamikazes did nowhere as much damage, official reports later revealed, as the single typhoon that hit Task-force 38 earlier that year. But there's no doubt the Americans were impressed. The sheer bravery of the attackers convinced the US that nothing less than atomic bombing would cow Japan.

Squeals came from the hostesses with the Australian party. Loud male laughter followed.

Hara proposed a toast to absent friends. His hands shook so much he spilled the *sake*. I thought fleetingly of the dusty Commando dead, laid out below Hill 136. Our Japanese guests looked equally thoughtful for as long as it took to down the wine.

'One day we heard the Emperor over the radio telling us to lay down our arms.' Hara said quietly. His face grew taut as he remembered the morning of 15 August 1945. 'Our squadron was lined up in parade order before the loudspeakers. Most of us burst out crying. We prayed it could not be true. One or two of our senior officers took off on their own to attack the Americans. We never heard what became of them.'

The Australians were into *We'll Meet Again*. It was a sad song made famous by Vera Lynn.

'I was ill for a long time after the surrender,' said Hara. 'I was partially paralysed. It was difficult to use my hands.' He held them out, still shaking. 'The doctors said it was psychological. A sort of nervous breakdown. I'm better now.'

I asked him whether he would again offer to die if the Emperor demanded it. He stared thoughtfully at the table. 'It's not like it was,' his voice dropped to a whisper. 'Things have changed. I tell myself today that I must work for the future of Japan.'

It did not appear to have much future at that particular point in time but the phrase was to resurface often in later years. We all now know that the Japanese turned their warlike energies to rebuilding their country by pacific means. Young Hara hoped to get into university. It would have rounded off my story neatly if he had said he was going into electronics but no, he intended to graduate in chemistry.

Screams and yells broke out downstairs. Mama-san poked her head round the door panel shouting in Japanese. Joe Suzuki leaped to his feet. 'It's the MPs again. Another raid. Grab your shoes and follow me out back.' Feet thumped as the Australians stampeded ahead of us to the exit.

We halted breathlessly at last beside the dockyard gate. Sailors were running past buttoning their clothes. They had been rousted out of the brothel in their underwear. The former Kamikaze was gone. 'Want to know more about suicide operations?' panted Joe Suzuki. 'Meet me tomorrow beside the graving dock ... the big one full of those submarines. I'll tell you the rest of the story.'

Commander Todd caught up with us beside the graving dock. 'Don't lose touch now,' he said. 'We're due to sink some of these things' – he indicated the jam-packed mass of midget submarines – 'you'll have to take pictures of that.' He intended to make his mark on posterity.

'Aye aye sir,' said Frank. Whenever he sounded that nautical I knew he had something on his mind. As soon as we could make it, I guessed we would be off on another swan: this time around Japan.

Joe Suzuki strolled up. This morning he cadged a whole carton of Camels. A carton of cigarettes was worth a great deal this early in the occupation. 'It'd better be good,' I warned him. Looking back I fear I was hard on the lad.

Joe nodded gravely. 'I'm going to tell you,' he said 'how the biggest battleship ever built committed suicide.' He paused for dramatic effect, peering over into the dock. It was a spiel he must have made dozens of times. Way below us scores of workmen were scurrying about feeding wire strops around the submarines before hauling them up on to the wharf. 'This,' Joe went on, seeing us all agog, 'this is where they built the *Yamato*.'

The what? The name meant nothing. Isolated in our vicious little sideshow in Burma, we knew precious little about the Imperial Japanese Navy or the war it had waged in the Pacific.

The Japanese had long been preparing, Joe explained, for a showdown with the United States. The British were discounted as a declining power. It was the US Japan knew it would have to fight for command of the Pacific. Plans were therefore drawn up for a class of super-battleships capable of outfighting anything afloat. The US Navy would never be able to build such massive ships, the Japanese reckoned, because anything that big would be unable to pass through the Panama Canal. It was felt unlikely that the United States would ever get around to building separate fleets for the Pacific and the Atlantic. The US was a sleeping giant – an isolationist giant at that – with no intention of becoming a superpower.

The first of the new battleships was secretly laid down in Kure in 1937. She would weigh 71,659 tons fully loaded with a crew of more than three thousand. Her primary armament consisted of nine 18.1-inch guns in three triple turrets. Each of these turrets weighed 2,730 tons, as much as a heavy destroyer. The guns could fire a 1.5-ton shell twenty-two-and-a-half miles. The hull was massively armoured, divided into 1,147 watertight compartments. According to the designers, these made the ship virtually unsinkable.

It was an amazing piece of shipbuilding, completed at great cost to a depression-hit economy. But it was one of the several mistakes that cost Japan the war. Most Japanese admirals, like their counterparts in Britain and the United States, were still fighting the Battle of Jutland. They expected sea battles to be decided, as they had been for centuries, by duels between battleships. Foolishly overlooked was the progress Japan (and the US) had made in naval aviation.

The new supership was named *Yamato*. It was the ancient, mystic name for the homeland of the Japanese people. The ship was commissioned about the same time as the Japanese carriers attacked Pearl Harbor. She was rendered obsolete, in other words, when scarcely out of the shipyard. Acting as flagship at the battle of Midway, six months later, the *Yamato* could only watch helplessly as the Americans sank the entire Japanese carrier force. From then on aircraft carriers dominated the Pacific; only once was the great ship brought to battle, in the disastrous 1944 action in

Leyte Gulf off the Philippines. For the first and last time her mighty guns opened fire upon enemy warships. They missed. The battle left *Yamato* the IJN's remaining major asset. Everything else had either been sunk or damaged.

The American invasion of Okinawa in April 1945 roused pleas for help from the army. The naval high command came under extreme pressure to commit the ship no matter how hopelessly. It was decided to despatch her with a six-strong escort to burst into the midst of the US invasion fleet, sink everything within sight and beach on the beleaguered island so that her sailors could stream ashore and join the defending forces. The plan was plain lunacy.

'It was really a death sentence,' Joe said. 'We all knew it.' He stood staring moodily into the vast graving dock where the *Yamato* had been built. 'I was aboard the destroyer *Isokaze*. When we learned we could expect no air cover on the run down to Okinawa we knew we were as good as dead. There was no way we could survive all the way to Okinawa without escorting fighters. Fighters were no longer available. Everything that flew was being used for Kamikaze attacks. So the night before we sailed we celebrated our own funerals down on the mess-decks. Farewell toasts. Patriotic songs. Last letters home. My friends mailed parings from their nails and locks of hair to their families. I didn't.' He gave the rueful shrug that accompanied almost everything he said. 'Where could I send them to? California? The censors would've had a fit.'

A rainsquall swept in from the anchorage forcing us to shelter in the lee of a dockyard crane. Joe got stuck into the cigarettes. 'Just to show they meant business,' he went on, 'they filled *Yamato* with only enough oil for a one-way trip and cut off the pipe manifolds to make sure the ship would never be refuelled again.'

The small attack force left Kure on 6 April 1945. The super-battleship towered over her minuscule escorts – a light cruiser and five destroyers – as Joe remarked: 'A regular whale among minnows.' The departure of the force was detected by a US submarine. Reconnaissance planes from the waiting US carriers picked it up next morning while still within sight of Japan. Another twelve hours' steaming lay ahead. The Americans launched more aircraft against the battleship and her escorts than the Japanese had thrown against Pearl Harbor. Within three hours it was all over.

'I didn't see much at first,' Joe said. 'I was down in the radio room. But I could tell from the chatter of the pilots and the sound of explosions that our force was under heavy attack. *Isokaze* shuddered and bucked as we dashed about at top speed. Without air cover we were helpless. I heard one of the pilots saying "get that little bastard over there". I was certain he meant us. We were trying to get alongside the light cruiser which was sinking. There was a series of tremendous crashes. The engines stopped. The power cut out. The radio room filled with smoke.

'I was driven up on deck, coughing and gasping, and found the upper part of our ship was on fire and pounded to pieces. Funnels, bridge and gun positions were torn up like paper. Bodies lay everywhere. The decks were slippery with blood. You'd have thought we were in an abattoir. Several of the other escorts had vanished. The *Yamato* was listing heavily, pouring smoke, and circling under hard left rudder. We were dead in the water and soon lost sight of her. She capsized, I was told, some half an hour later. The watertight compartments in the hull weren't designed to take sixteen torpedoes. Only about three hundred of her crew were saved.' Another of those rueful shrugs. 'Three destroyers survived. One of them took us off before sinking *Isokaze* by gunfire. No wounded men were rescued. The skipper of the destroyer that rescued us was half crazy. He still wanted to go on to Okinawa. He would only take fit men able to help crew his ship. Fleet headquarters ordered us back, thank God, and kept us in quarantine so the news wouldn't leak out. Rumours spread all the same. I believe some Tokyo newspapermen picked up the news from American broadcasts on a radio hidden in the office lavatory.'

I checked Joe's story. It was substantially correct. Thirty-three years later I wrote the saga of the *Yamato* and her suicide mission. The tip-off cost me one carton of duty-free cigarettes. It was the best investment I ever made.

The waif offered us two tiny skulls. They'd been 'burned small', the pimp told us by the, er, *thing*. He cast his eyes piously skywards. The waif did the same. She pulled open her ragged shirt to show the burns. 'This girl lucky,' said the pimp. 'Many burns kill.' He shooed the child away. 'Don't mind her. I get you better souvenir in city.' He pointed outside the station. There was no city, only an undulating stretch of fire-blackened rubble, punctuated by the inevitable chimneys, stretching away as far as the eye could see. It was a familiar enough sight by this time. Kure, Iwakuni, Tokoyama and other adjoining cities were every bit as desolate. The difference was that this was Hiroshima. The desolation was the work of a single bomb.

We had guessed what we were in for as the train puffed out of Kure along the shores of the Inland Sea. The journey took little over half an hour, winding through picture-book country. Great gnarled pines leaned out over glassy water. Women in straw hats laboured among regiments of oyster beds. Successive vistas composed like woodblock prints gave the running, erroneous impression of a series of delightful lakes. Farmhouses and the occasional temple slid gently by, nestling in woods and hillside clefts; a huge red *torii* rose from the shallows on the further shore offering symbolic entrance to the venerable *Kompira* shrine. Its deity guards sailors and anyone with business on the ocean.

A party from HMIS *Sutlej* travelled with us. They were to feature in our next film report. An uneasy gloom descended as Hiroshima drew nearer. The first signs of the holocaust became evident fifteen miles from the city. At first it was no more than a few farmhouses missing a roofing tile or windowpane. But as we grew closer whole roofs were stripped and windows smashed until we were passing complete houses squashed awkwardly sideways. It was as if they'd been struck by a particularly powerful typhoon. By the time we reached the rail yards two miles out, there was nothing but unending rubble.

Souvenir sellers, pimps and beggars posing as guides were waiting at the roofless station eager to show us round. The currency, as usual, was candy bars and cigarettes. Even in adversity the Japanese had not overlooked the possibilities of tourism. We filmed the sailors staring unbelievingly at the damage.

Frank's shot-list went something like this: Close-up, Indian sailor, staring; Mid-shot, group of Indian sailors, all staring; Long shot, Indian sailors picking their way through the rubble; Mid-shot, booted feet treading cautiously through rubble past shattered child's doll; Close-up, doll; Extreme close-up (which meant an awkward change of lenses), shattered doll's face. It was a pity we had no sound, otherwise the techniques were much the same as they are today. The professionals call it 'cutting in the camera'.

The pimp showed us a Shinto shrine, or what was left of it. (Long shot, shrine; Mid-shot, large rock.) The rock marked the spot where the main hall of the shrine had stood. An old man was limping round the rock fingering his rosary. 'Must go around hundred times,' the pimp told us. 'Get rid of his sins.' He led us to a small shrine facing the street. Women were placing pebbles before a bald figure indistinguishable, as far as I could see, from the Amitaba Buddha. It was in fact *Jizo*, the patron saint of children.

(Long shot, women; Mid-shot, sailors watching women; Close-up, hands placing pebbles).

Cadging an additional carton of Camels, our impromptu guide explained that according to Japanese belief the spirits of dead children were detained on the banks of a river rather like the Styx by a she-hag *Shozuka-na-Baba*, and forced to build towers of stone that would elevate the children to paradise. But every night the hag tore the towers down, condemning the dead children to perpetual limbo. Each pebble the women placed before the saint helped rebuild the towers and thwart the wicked witch.

'So many children,' a woman said to us in English. Her name was Mrs Sato and she taught English at one of the high schools. 'All of us have lost children. I lost four.' She was a faded, fortyish matron, scarred across the face, with greying hair and a fixed unsmiling smile. I recognised her strange expression. A stoic self-control is required of adult Japanese. Grief has to be covered by a kind of smile. So undemonstrative are the Japanese expected to be that when baseball was first introduced the crowds sat completely silent, as if attending a funeral.

'My children were in primary school,' said Mrs Sato. 'I was at home sick that day. I had just heard my husband had been killed in China. Suddenly our house collapsed. I dug myself out of the wreckage. I went searching for my children but the school was – ' she made helpless little gestures with her hands ' – the school was knocked flat.' She spoke slowly and painfully still wearing that disturbing smile. 'I could hear the children crying inside but the school was on fire. I burned my face trying to get near. Many people tried but it was too hot. Like a furnace.'

'I was catching a train that morning,' another woman volunteered. She too was smiling. Mrs Sato provided a skilful running translation. Our Bengali friend, Lieutenant Dutt, translated into Urdu for the benefit of the sailors. They listened horror-struck.

(Long shot, woman talking to sailors; Mid-shot, sailors listening; close-up, woman talking – where oh where was the sound? – close up, lieutenant translating.)

'The air-raid sounded as I boarded the train,' the woman said. 'Nothing happened. It seemed like a false alarm. The train was about to start when there was this flash. I threw myself on to the carriage floor. The other passengers piled on top of me. I felt hot, suffocated, and must have fainted. When I recovered everything was burning. The people on top of me were dead.'

The atomic bomb, nicknamed Fat Boy – or *genchi bagudon*, 'first child bomb', by the Japanese – was aimed at the domed Museum of Science and Industry not far from the River Hiroshima. The ruined museum with its skeletal dome has been preserved in what's now known as the Peace Park. The bomb parachuted slightly off target and burst on the morning of 6 August 1945, above the *torii* of the Gokoku Shrine alongside the garrison parade ground. The parade ground was packed with soldiers. Hiroshima was the main military centre of south Japan. The moment the bomb burst a Korean prince was riding out of Hiroshima Castle, with cavalry escort, to inspect the parade. Prince, escort, horses and the parading soldiery were instantly vaporised. The five-storey castle was reduced to its foundations. The great stones on which it was built had been welded together centuries ago with molten lead. The lead remelted and ran out into the street in red-hot rivulets.

The heat at the centre of the blast was said to be 6,000°C. Nothing could survive it. A man and his horse-drawn cart were incinerated as they crossed the Sakai bridge not far from the museum. Man, horse and cart left a shadow on the seared bridgework showing the man's arm raised in the act of beating his horse. Burned on to the side of a bank was the outline of a man painting on a ladder. He was dipping his brush into the paint. Some 600 metres further away the heat had reduced a crowded tramcar to a tangle of buckled steel and welded its wheels to the track. Those travelling in it were never seen again. The metal stair lipping in one of the few buildings still standing, 1,200 yards from the centre, had melted and fused again. The concrete walls of this building withstood the heat although the interior was gutted. Once busy offices were blackened shells. The lifts were jammed. It was a long climb up to the roof but the view was awesome.

(Long shot, slow pan across Hiroshima; Mid-shot, American GIs, who'd followed us up, taking photographs.)

The extent of the destruction was far wider than we had imagined on the ground. The greyish rubble, coloured by layers of demolished rooftiles, stretched three miles south from where we stood to the shoreline of the Inland Sea. Four miles to the north, fog was drifting in across the flattened remains of the once-affluent suburb of Koi.

There were signs of life. The worst wreckage had been cleared, the streets swept and cleaned. People were drifting back, building small shanties of wood and fibre-board on the sites of their former homes. Others passed on news of themselves to vanished friends and relations. Signs sprouted from the rubble: 'the Kobyashis have moved to such-and-such address in the countryside'. Some were more plaintive: 'Sister where are you? Contact uncle's place at Iwakuni'. A type of barracks hut was being prefabricated by the municipal authorities, aided and advised by a young American lieutenant. The American occupation that would remake Japan was having its first beneficial effects. The prefabs sold for seven thousand yen – about seven pounds in those days.

A group of German Jesuits had replaced their ruined mission with three of these prefabs. The untreated pinewood glowed a cheerful yellow in the early sunshine. 'A great improvement,' said Father Kleinsorge. 'For months we've been living in a tent.'

The priest was a tall gaunt man with large hands and still larger feet. He talked easily of his miraculous survival. Interviewed by every foreign journalist who came to Hiroshima, he must have been the best-known priest in Japan. Now he was suffering from radiation sickness and would soon be sent to Tokyo for treatment. The good news, scientists assured us, was that the Fat Boy bomb was relatively 'clean'. Its effects had worn off over the past eight months, enabling visitors to come to the city and a limited number of inhabitants to make a cautious return. But survivors were finding their exposure to the initial radiation was still taking its toll.

'I get very tired,' the Father told us. 'A lot of people are like that. I was fortunate. People nearer the blast – the ones, that is, who weren't burned to death on the spot – were much more exposed to radiation. It's said that forty per cent of them have already died. They aren't the last, I fear.'

As a priest, what did he think of the use of the bomb against a largely civilian population? Father Kleinsorge grimaced nervously. Germans were still regarded suspiciously by the US authorities. 'I think it was unfortunate,' he said carefully. 'I'm afraid history may consider this bombing a crime.'

The pimp still dogged our heels. He dragged us towards the huddle of canvas-covered stalls that passed for the shopping area. There were more of the shrunken skulls and tiny bottles said to have melted down by the heat. A *sake* shop displaying a faded *noren* (curtain) produced a drunk in threadbare army uniform. For a moment I thought he was going to attack us. Instead he blew a raspberry in Frank's face and staggered off down the street. Girls beckoned from a contraption that might have been a king-sized campers' caravan.

'All beautiful,' the pimp urged. 'All clean. I sell you no-sweat pills.'

Children clustered round us begging for gum. Our last candy bars did not go far. The children faded away, muttering bitterly. The wind picked up again. The noodle and chestnut sellers crept closer to their braziers. A woman offered us a puppy. 'Good, good,' she said. 'Dog good, no sick.' She coughed repeatedly into her gauze face mask.

'Maybe she'll eat the thing,' laughed a passing GI. His many medals suggested acquaintance with combat. We weren't yet used to the word but Americans referred to men like that as 'veterans'. The GI said something sharply to the woman with the puppy. She gave us one hard look and slunk away. 'It's no use pitying them,' the GI said. 'The Japs asked for everything they got. Before the bomb we reckoned on another two years' fighting. That might have meant my neck. Don't tell me about the bomb. Brother, I love it.'

Frank and I went walkabout through occupied Japan. As I suspected, his over-hasty 'Aye, aye', to accommodate Commander Todd's order about the midget submarines, *was* significant. Frank's scheme was that we should work like crazy stockpiling every possible picture story on the Indian forces' activity in Japan, then have the footage shipped back at spaced intervals. We disappeared from authority, as usual, but coverage from us continued to arrive at Public Relations headquarters, Delhi. We appeared to be busily at work while nipping around Nippon on a self-awarded holiday. We picked up American girls in the ancient capital of Kyoto. Together we went to see the world's biggest Buddha in the *Daibatsu-den* in Nara. Something happened to shed new light on the US occupation. We were boarding a two-car light rail train back to Kyoto. The platform was crowded with Japanese who rushed to board the leading car. One of our girlfriends let out a cry of dismay.

'I'm not travelling,' she whined, 'among a bunch of gooks.'

The girls ordered the stationmaster to clear the leading car of Japanese. Politely he complied. We might have been back among the memsahibs. The four of us travelled alone while the car behind bulged with those who would otherwise have been our fellow passengers. There were so many of them that heads and bodies protruded from the open windows. The Japanese didn't say anything. Their faces were perfectly impassive. But the look in their eyes bothers me to this day. Surely they must have wanted to get back at us? I put this years later to a commander in the Japanese Maritime Self Defence Force. The *de facto* navy was given this extraordinary title because the post-war constitution dreamed up by General MacArthur, forbade Japan to have armed forces.

'I was on the quayside when they towed away the *Nagato*,' the commander told me. The *Nagato* was the last surviving battleship of the Imperial Navy. The Americans moored her among the targets at the Bikini Atoll tests. 'I was eight at the time,' the commander said. '*Nagato* was a pitiful sight. Her main guns had been cut off close to the turrets. My father was a former officer in the Imperial Navy. He wept as *Nagato* was towed out of Yokusaka. So did I.'

'Don't you feel any bitterness?' I asked.

'It's all long past,' he shrugged. 'Japan has recovered its self-respect.'

I hope so. But I am occasionally haunted by visions of embittered Japanese revanchists marshalling their new-found economic strength to even up the score. Maybe some are actually doing so. I prefer to think the Japanese harbour no such thoughts ... though of course, you never can be certain.

The Tokyo Press Club had been established in what the journalists dubbed Shimbun Alley. We were granted temporary membership. The corps of talented correspondents assembled for the Japanese surrender had by now dispersed but there were plenty of colourful characters left leaning on the bar. Some had made shrewd deals in real estate which turned them into dollar millionaires. Most if not all were making whoopee with the women. Wives were not yet allowed into Japan. When I imported my own wife seven years later during the Korean war an Australian colleague exclaimed: 'Christ! The bloody Nips ought to charge you corkage!'

The club maintained several dormitory floors. They seemed permanently occupied by correspondents and a rolling choice of the eager prostitutes who clustered outside in the alley. 'You've only to whistle,' said the man from the *Christian Science Monitor*. He went out and did exactly that. There was uproar when someone found he had picked up a transvestite. The club had the air of a duty-free brothel. A British correspondent described it as 'a monastery in urgent need of reformation'.

Correspondents regarded the Japanese with amused contempt. It was entirely different from the wartime *Banzai* image. A representative of one of the American wire services boasted how he 'fixed' Japanese drivers. There were not that many around. They drove tinny little cars called Toyopets, desperately underpowered. The Americans drove powerful sedans fresh from Detroit. This particular man described how he would slow down, invite a Toyopet to overtake, then speed up until the wretched

Japanese slammed on the brakes or, better still, smashed into a traffic island. 'Talk about cars!' the correspondent would chortle. 'These bastards couldn't even make wind.'

Well, that's how the foreign press felt in '46. Their more serious-minded representatives lamented the state of the Japanese economy. Much of the nation's industry had been destroyed. The train from Yokohama to Tokyo ran past nothing but ruined factories. Reconstruction seemed impossible. 'They don't have the organising ability to rebuild,' groaned one financial journalist. 'They'll be dependent on our aid until well into the next century.'

It was the general view. 'We are liable to be stuck,' wrote the experienced Australian correspondent, Richard Hughes, 'with a race of beaming limpets.'

I concurred. Visiting some of the bombed-out factories on the Tokyo outskirts I found nothing but workmen picking listlessly through the wreckage. The managers I spoke to appeared to be thinking small. I wasn't to know the best of them were in temporary hibernation planning for the future.

Frank and I joined the crowd waiting outside the Dai Ichi Insurance building. People had come to watch General MacArthur's arrival at his imposing headquarters. The building faced the Imperial Palace. The Japanese undoubtedly adored the general. It was as if they'd switched their loyalties, like Pavlovian dogs, to this newly-appointed *Shogun*. Already it was apparent that the wide-reaching reforms introduced by his régime were changing the face of the country. The most successful, land reform, was little short of revolutionary.

The great man arrived each morning promptly at ten. He sprang from his car with a vigour negating his advancing years and swiftly strode the ten or so yards into the building. This was a pro-consul as powerful as any Britain has produced. Wrapped about him was an aura of arrogant inviolability verging positively on the eccentric. There was, for instance, his manner of dress. Everyone else in the US army wore regulation uniform. Its differing shades of brown – tie, shirts, pants – were graded officially by numbers. MacArthur flouted the regulations by wearing a plum-coloured tie and the battered old cap he'd designed himself as commander of the pre-war Philippine armed forces. The Japanese did not care. When the general was fishing around a few years later for a shot at the US Presidency, a Japanese admirer with limited, phonetic knowledge of English put up the sign: WE PLAY FOR MACARTHUR'S ERECTION.

Our time, alas, was running out. Britain was no longer cushioned by Lend Lease. The Americans had cut off their largesse without warning, revealing Britain's true bankruptcy. British ships, unable to pay the Panama Canal tolls, were having to sail around Cape Horn. Food rationing in Britain was as tight as wartime. And freeloaders like Frank and me could hardly expect to continue our self-indulgent peregrinations through dollar-backed territory.

But Frank had one last nefarious plan. He was keen to make personal contact with the great Scottish film maker John Grierson ('the Daddy of documentary') then working in western Canada. Word reached Colonel Jenkins that we had bribed an American pilot to fly us unofficially on a US Air Force plane across to Seattle on the American side of the border. A fair number of aircraft on this shuttle had been lost in the wastes of the wide Pacific. We felt Jenkins privately admired our gall, and was by now used to our disappearances, but he was not prepared to suffer the permanent disappearance of the Heavenly Twins on an unauthorised jaunt. We were 'captured' and despatched back to India before we got ourselves into more trouble under his command.

Frank was disappointed at being unable to contact Grierson. He was not to know then that the time would come when the great man would contact *him*. A few years later Grierson and Sir Michael Balcon saw Frank's first feature movie, *Ha' penny Breeze*, which he directed and co-wrote. They wanted him to write and direct Grierson's first full-length feature production.

By the time we got back to Delhi the old command structure was disappearing. Brigadier Desmond Young had gone. My photographic outfit was closed. Peering in through the windows of the huts close to the *Purana Qila*, I saw nothing but trash cans filled with film and paper. Most of my best pictures were there with them.

On a blazing hot day in July I boarded a troop ship in Bombay. I'd had enough; I wanted to go home. The same dock I had arrived at four years before tinkled with money as the men who had done so much to defend India – the oft-despised British Other Ranks or BORs – threw their last annas and pice at the beggars below. A shower of sun helmets followed. The BORs struck up the song we so often used to sing about 'a troop ship was leaving Bombay ... bound for old Blighty shore, heavily laden with time-expired men bound for the land they adore'.

I joined in the singing. 'The East, you can keep it,' I told myself as we eased away from the wharf. Oh yes, I really believed it. I couldn't have been more wrong. But that, as they say, is another story.